The Fox
That Got
Away

Also by Stephen M. Silverman

PUBLIC SPECTACLES

The Fox That Got Away

The Last Days of the Zanuck Dynasty at Twentieth Century-Fox

by Stephen M. Silverman

Lyle Stuart Inc.   Secaucus, New Jersey

Published by Lyle Stuart Inc.
120 Enterprise Ave., Secaucus, N.J. 07094
In Canada: Musson Book Company
A division of General Publishing Co. Limited
Don Mills, Ontario

Queries regarding rights and permissions should be
addressed to: Lyle Stuart, 120 Enterprise Avenue,
Secaucus, N.J. 07094

Manufactured in the United States of America

Library of Congress Cataloging-in-Publication Data

Silverman, Stephen M.
    The Fox that got away.

    Bibliography: p.
    1. Zanuck, Darryl Francis, 1902-   . 2. Zanuck
family. 3. Twentieth Century-Fox Film Corporation--
History. 4. Motion picture producers and directors--
United States--Biography. I. Title.
PN1998.3.Z36S55   1988   791.43'0232'0924   88-29470
ISBN 0-8184-0485-X

To "R," a married woman. She knows who she is.

A prince being thus obliged to know well how to act as a beast must imitate the fox and the lion, for the lion cannot protect himself from traps, and the fox cannot defend himself from wolves.

One must therefore be a fox to recognize traps, and a lion to frighten wolves.

—Machiavelli

PROLOGUE

I

When the board of directors of the Twentieth Century-Fox Film Corporation convened in New York on August 29, 1969, the meeting was one month overdue. The only advance word on the delay received by the individual members of the board had been a terse memorandum signed by Fox president Darryl F. Zanuck, the hard-driven founder of the studio and still a very active voice when it concerned the fortunes of the company.

What the grand old man promised was that what would eventually be presented at the meeting would prove such a radical departure for Twentieth Century-Fox that additional time was required to collect and assess multiple layers of difficult information. That, at least, was what was promised in the memo.

"It was a laconic message, and it worked for the time being," said David Brown, the Fox vice president who actually drafted the memo and much of the far-reaching program to follow.

Brown worked closely with Richard Darryl Zanuck, known to everyone as Dick. Dick was Darryl's son and the studio's head of production.

To gather the data for the board to hear, the younger Zanuck and Brown decided to hire a team of outside business consultants. According to Brown, this was simply for reasons of backing up the ideas he and Dick had been hashing over in the first place. "Any decision to implement the suggestions," said Brown, "would remain ours." By that Brown meant his and Dick Zanuck's.

The outside agency they contacted was the Stanford Research Institute.

15

II

For the Fox board members themselves, there was little reason to believe that the news at their meeting, whenever it would be held, need be anything but positive. Postponements in the dead of summer were far from alarming, but more assuring was that from all outward signs the studio appeared to be continuing its unprecedented four-year winning streak under the tightly-knit Zanuck team.

The driving force was a phenomenal single motion picture put into production by Richard, a wholesome, tear-jerking musical about Austria's Trapp Family singers, entitled *The Sound of Music*. Opening March 3, 1965, it featured well-scrubbed children, singing nuns, menacing Nazis—who, in the climax, are foiled by the nuns—and an ebullient young British actress named Julie Andrews.

Despite dreadful critical notices, *The Sound of Music* generated such positive word of mouth and so caught on with a devoted public internationally—except, ironically, in Austria and Germany, and by sophisticates who, like its male lead Christopher Plummer, dubbed it *The Sound of Mucous*—that it outgrossed the previous box-office champion of all time, 1939's Civil War epic *Gone With the Wind*. The musical earned the industry nickname *The Sound of Money*. Its fortunes also allowed Dick Zanuck to escape at last from under the shadow of his father. Darryl Zanuck called it "our miracle picture."

For the studio, *The Sound of Music* generated one of the most dramatic turnarounds in American economic history. Only two years earlier, Fox looked to be going under.

The problems stemmed from the triple whammy of a $48.5 million loss for the years 1959, 1960, and 1961; another $3 million debt incurred over a never-finished production with Marilyn Monroe entitled *Something's Got to Give*; and, most shattering of all, the unpardonable waste that went into a period-costume picture set in ancient Egypt.

Originally it was to have been brought in for $2 million and to

16

have starred second-string actress Joan Collins; instead it wound up costing $36 million and headlining a full-fledged star, Elizabeth Taylor. Its name was *Cleopatra*.

These costly disasters of the early '60s drove out the reigning Fox regime, headed by the "Greek contingent" of chairman (since 1942) Spyros Skouras and president Peter Levathes, and returned to power the studio's founder, Darryl F. Zanuck. By this time more of a legendary playboy than a creative and business leader still to be taken seriously, the 60-year old Zanuck, Napoleonic, cigar-chomping, a crusty old son-of-a-bitch, surprisingly proved ever-knowledgeable and forceful.

One of the conditions of his returning to the company he had begun in 1933—as Twentieth Century Pictures, which two years later merged with Fox Film Corporation—was that Darryl bring in his own new head of production. To Zanuck, the choice was obvious. To others, it was a joke.

In 1962, Darryl Zanuck named to the post his high-strung son Richard, barely 27 but physically and mentally a chip off the old block.

The critics reveled, except that in less than a year the father-son team showed a profit of $9 million, thanks in large part to a pet project launched by the old man, an all-star re-enactment of the Allies' landing in Normandy, *The Longest Day*. Then Dick Zanuck gave the green light to *The Sound of Music*; once that picture struck, the Zanucks' production strategem served to influence every other major studio in Hollywood.

"We're going all out for the big, family-type show that I suppose you could call pure entertainment," Richard Zanuck told *The National Observer*. "I'm very much aware that what we do here is seen by millions of people around the world. My first responsibility is to the company I work for, but I also have a responsibility as a person and as a filmmaker to put on things of which I can be proud. I don't intend to jeopardize that responsibility."

By 1967, Fox hit an earnings peak, producing a net profit of $154.4 million. As financial matters maintained their equilib-

17

rium, so did the relationship between father and son. Each man was content sharing the responsibilities of the company and existing as Number One and Number Two Man, respectively— even though, geographically at least, a noticeable gap was separating them. Darryl ran the business from his hotel suites in New York and Europe, while Richard, with David Brown, oversaw the studio operation.

Only, more and more, the important decisions were being made by Richard.

In 1968, an interviewer put the obvious question before the son: did he, as did the rest of Hollywood since the success of his *The Sound of Music*, see himself as Darryl's heir apparent as company president?

"I don't know," the 33-year-old answered. "I'm not looking to that. I'm very happy doing what I'm doing. I don't like New York and the Wall Street atmosphere a president has to get involved in. I would think many, many long hours if it ever came to that."

III

One month before Fox's crucial summer of 1969 board meeting was to have taken place, Darryl Zanuck paid a rare visit to California. Under terms of a marriage separation agreement drawn up in 1956, when Zanuck fled Hollywood and his family to pursue independent production and a bevy of mistresses in Europe, the company chief could not set foot in the state unless the visit was formally approved by his estranged wife Virginia. At least that was the story that made the rounds among the executives at the studio, some of whom still remembered the rambunctious movie chief from his glory era—an era that had changed drastically since the days Zanuck ruled over a little company town.

Television and divestiture of movie-theater chains had left

their mark on the filmmaking capital. Twentieth Century-Fox and Columbia Pictures were now the last remaining independently run companies, although, looking to expand its operation, Columbia as of 1968 had totally restructured its organization, to offset the ever-mounting expenses of movie production.

Throughout the decade, industrial giants swallowed up movie companies like a movie-goer gulps popcorn; Adolph Zukor's Paramount went to the Gulf & Western Oil Company; Louis B. Mayer's M-G-M to Seagram's; Carl Laemmle's Universal to MCA, a former talent agency; Jack L. Warner's Warner Bros. to Kinney National Service, Inc. (which owned mortuaries and parking lots in New York, though Californians tended to confuse its corporate identity with the Kinney Shoe Company); and United Artists, founded in 1919 by silent-screen groundbreakers Douglas Fairbanks, Mary Pickford, Charlie Chaplin, and director D. W. Griffith, to the Transamerica Corporation, an insurance behemoth.

These seminal and highly publicized megadeals left Darryl Zanuck the sole surviving Hollywood tycoon, a label he relished and played to the hilt.

"Darryl F. Zanuck wore his usual working outfit," wrote the *International Herald Tribune* correspondent Mary Blume in 1968, "a gray silk dressing gown, monogrammed over the heart, a copper bracelet on his right wrist, and a huge cigar apparently hooked between the famous jack-o-lantern front teeth. His small legs were bare and on his feet were soft leather slippers. His toes wiggled as he talked, and often he made the demure but useless gesture of pulling his dressing gown down over his knees."

Less charmed, however, was a *Newsweek* writer, who profiling the mogul at the same time, considered Zanuck "something of an anachronism—his chauffered Jaguar and dark glasses and glossy aura are the trappings of a cultural dinosaur dragging his legend like some long, spiky tail."

Darryl landed in Los Angeles to meet his son after the

14-hour journey, having flown in from the South of France via Paris. Age and the journey showed on the old man, as did his years of drinking, despite his current girl friend's boasting that she had turned him away from alcohol and over to Coca-Cola and near beer.

By contrast, Dick Zanuck, though given to looks of mental preoccupation, was the picture of health, a California golden boy. His taut body was as much the result of living on nerves as of being young and athletic, and he boasted the good looks of both his parents—his father's strong jaw, blue eyes, and muscular albeit diminutive physique, and his mother's graceful facial features.

"Short and intense," *Time* magazine said of Richard, "he was once described by a tennis partner as the sort of player 'who gives you the feeling that he'd like nothing better than to smash the ball between your eyes.' "

Dick Zanuck referred to his father as "D.Z." in public, and "Dad" to his face. The latter salutation could also be found in company memos, even when the notes expressed heated disagreement, such as those Dick and Darryl had just been exchanging between California and the South of France.

It was on the Côte d'Azur that Darryl Zanuck was supervising his latest production—he already had made more than six hundred—something he conceived as a frothy romantic comedy entitled *Hello-Goodbye* and to spotlight his latest protégée, Genevieve Gilles. It was not "the big, family-type show" young Richard Zanuck had spoken of, but, with its flashes of nudity and condoning of adultery, aimed instead at the sexual frankness of the younger generation, the demographic group that was rapidly and irrevocably becoming the core movie audience.

The story of *Hello-Goodbye*, penned by Zanuck under his well-worn nom de plume Mark Canfield, dealt with an elderly European baron, played by German actor Curt Jurgens, and his lonely young wife, the perky and freckled Gilles. She comes to meet someone her own age, an automobile salesman from England (Michael Crawford), whom the baron takes into his manor so the Englishman might teach mechanics to the baron's son from a previous marriage. The wife and the visitor predictably fall into bed together, with the cuckolded baron casting a sympathetic eye on the situation.

Dick Zanuck did not take kindly to Gilles, nor to the money being eaten up by his father's vanity production, which served as an embarrassment on several levels. The parallels between the movie's storyline and the actual relationship between the 66-year-old Zanuck and Gilles, believed to be 44 years his junior, were too obvious to conceal. The cruel cackles of the crew had greeted the production from the first troubled day of shooting.

By the time Darryl had received Dick's urgent summons to California, the costs on *Hello-Goodbye* were rapidly approaching $4 million, and this was only August. As would happen, the movie was not to wrap until the last week of October. In the heat of summer, the elder Zanuck was in no mood to abandon his set, to say nothing of his unescorted mistress.

Yet what Dick Zanuck needed to discuss demanded a personal confrontation between the two men, and Dick's going to France was unthinkable at a time like this. Darryl uncharacteristically but obligingly made the trip west.

"Mr. Zanuck's proudest achievement is his son Richard Darryl Zanuck," the *Tribune* reported from Paris. "A smile flits across his face as he describes how Dick's talents and his complement each other."

There are those who said Darryl never would have turned his back on his son. Bystanders claimed, quite benignly, that the elder Zanuck's sole concern was his studio. Still others insisted that Darryl's devotion was equally divided. "When it came to Dick and the studio," recalled a longtime Darryl loyalist, "the two were really intertwined in the old man's head. He considered them both something he had built and would go on running forever."

21

Darryl Zanuck was met in Los Angeles just as he was loath to expect: by Dick and Dick's constant companion, David Brown. Brown, mustachioed, erudite, Dick's senior by 17 years, resembled an American version of the British actor Ralph Richardson. As a former boy-wonder editor of the old *Liberty* and *Cosmopolitan* magazines, Brown maintained his New York literary air even in the leisurely atmosphere of California. As such, in any environment, Brown was never at a loss for the proper word, but this was a talent that no longer impressed Darryl Zanuck. Earlier, Darryl had issued an ultimatum to his son. Aligning with Brown was not in Dick's interest, said Darryl. Dick was to choose between working with David or with his own father.

"He came to hate me," said Brown. "I was Dick's Svengali. That whole thing, I became the enemy. And I had been fond of D.Z. We were both, Dick and I, fond of him. But by this time in his life he was only good for two or three hours a day."

Richard Zanuck quickly put his cards on the table before his ather.

"We were going to have to tell the board some awful, shocking financial news about the corporation, including cutting off the dividend completely," recalled Dick. The situation was, in actual fact, worse than that. "Dad," Dick was forced to add, "we're broke."

"It was the first loss in our history," said David Brown. By "our history," he was referring to the recent period in which he and the two Zanucks were carrying the ball at the studio.

The board of directors meeting was scheduled for the next day.

"D.Z. was so shocked and stunned—he had just flown in from Paris," remembered his son. "David and I met with him and decided we'd better do some pretty big thinking before his marching into the board meeting the next day. We decided to call off the meeting altogether and hold it the following month. So D.Z. had his secretary get on the phone and call the whole board to tell them not to come to New York. And he left David and me to figure out a way to get out of this mess."

22

IV

His over-budget movie with his unchaperoned girl friend meeting God only knew what sort of fate a continent away, his son, his studio, and, by implication, himself left hanging in the balance, Darryl Francis Zanuck, the last remaining tycoon in Hollywood, exercised a normal reflex. He rolled the cigar around in his mouth, and then flicked a mountainous ash into the ashtray.

Addressing his son Richard Zanuck and Dick's colleague David Brown, two men who in only thirty days had to solve a newly revealed emergency, Darryl Zanuck posited a simple query.

"Now," he asked, "what the fuck will that plan be?"

PART ONE

I

Darryl F. Zanuck's first investiture as lord over his own studio took place six years after the screen started to talk. By that time, the profane "little giant," as he was known, had been an eleven-year veteran of a phenomenon called the movies, a seemingly illiterate artform that relied on a mechanical process perfected in 1899 by two Americans, inventor Thomas Edison and former banker turned industrialist, George Eastman, by which a frame-lined celluloid strip set a series of still pictures into motion.

The makers of movies, primarily, in the early days, East Coast practitioners, learned to tell a story, and although their labors were quick to take the world by storm, movies were not to be taken seriously on Wall Street until March 3, 1915. The occasion was the opening at the Liberty Theatre in New York of D.W. Griffith's *The Birth of a Nation*, a controversial yet brilliant epic about the American Civil War containing an underlying racist view of Reconstruction.

Griffith and his screenwriter, Thomas Dixon, Southerners both, portrayed the aftermath of the war as an assault on the dignity of the South and a violation of its women by liberal North-erners and retaliatory blacks—whose roles in the 2½-hour film were played by white actors in blackface.

The picture proved a sensation, if for no other reason than for the money it generated at the box office. In an era when one thin dime bought any thrill-seeker a movie ticket, admission to *Birth of a Nation* stood at an unprecedented two dollars.

On a societal level, *Birth of a Nation* was also revolutionary. For the first time in history, the press took to covering movies; in this case on both the news and editorial pages. In addition, the White House opened its doors to the still-fledgling medium. Woodrow Wilson, after screening the Griffith work, declared: "It is like writing history with lightning."

Movies, from the start an obvious vital cultural force, were now an important business.

By the mid-1920s, the makers of movies had flocked en masse to Hollywood, a former lemon grove in the frostless foothills of Los Angeles. To succeed in the business, the producers and studio heads turned out their product with an assembly-line-like precision mirroring that of Detroit's. Production was standardized, and company presidents looked for sure-fire sale values, finding them in the creation of stars, the repetition of a certain style or story formula, and the abundant use of advertising and publicity. Thus it was that the top three companies out west, Metro-Goldwyn-Mayer, The Fox Film Corporation, and Paramount were, respectively, the General Motors, Ford, and Chrysler of the film industry.

As with any corporation, an on-site front office was required to call the daily shots and to maintain a proper relationship between management and labor. Supervisors reported to a head of production on all facets of a movie, from formation of script, to selection of cast and crew, to the final edit and release. Top-echelon decisions, particularly those of finance, were routinely referred to headquarters. These more often than not remained in New York.

Southern California began to attract filmmakers to its outdoor sets and makeshift shooting stages as early as 1908, when former Chicago showman "Colonel" William Selig built the first studio in Edendale. The primary lures of the west were its cheap land and labor, to say nothing of the distance from the East Coast—where a film trust formed by Edison as a way to quash independent film production held an iron grip on the fledgling industry.

Originally, the wizard of West Orange, New Jersey, displayed little interest in the future profits of his moving picture invention. This situation reversed itself once he saw the enormous amounts of money being made by other producers. Edison attempted to sue his competitors for violating his basic patents on the film equipment, but in each case, the interloper was one step ahead of Edison and cleverly claimed a patent of his own.

Uncertain of the outcome or the length of his proposed litigation, Edison formed a company by aligning himself with the strongest arms in the business. This move would allow each party to validate the legal claims of the others. The nine other leading studios of the day—Vitagraph, Selig, Essanay, Kalem, Biograph, Lubin, and Kleine,· as well as the two leading French concerns, Pathé and Méliès—joined Edison in January 1909 as the Motion Picture Patents Company.

The purpose of their partnership was to declare that they and they alone held the right to photograph, develop, and print motion pictures, and as such were protected by laws of the United States, Great Britain, France, Germany, and Italy. The Patents Company decreed that no license to produce motion pictures would ever be issued to anyone else, and to insure further that no bootleg film ever be distributed, the group formed the General Film Company. Thus was complete control exerted over the wholesaling and retailing of motion pictures in the greater part of the northern hemisphere.

Though it would take him until 1917, the man instrumental in busting the trust was another movie pioneer, a portly mogul considered to have the wildest ambition. From a distance he would also play a major role in advancing the career of Darryl Zanuck, but only after his own professional life would be laid to waste. His name was William Fox.

II

William Fox, the eldest of thirteen children (of which only six survived an impoverished childhood), was born in 1879 in Tulcheva, Hungary, to Orthodox German-Jewish parents, Anna Fried and Michael Fuchs. In the old country, Fuchs was a distinguished citizen who pulled teeth. In the immigrant ghetto of

New York's Lower East Side, the patriarch was reduced to manufacturing kitchen stove polish in the main room of his waterless family tenement apartment on Stanton Street. The Fuchs children, by now renamed Fox, attended the Sheriff Street public school; their father insisted the boys also attend Hebrew school.

By age nine, Will Fox was peddling his father's homemade product for a nickel a can off a cart that also carried candy, newspapers, and umbrellas. At eleven he dropped out of school to become the family's main provider, working twelve hours a day in the garment center sweatshop, S. Cohen and Son. Fox rose, eventually, to the rank of foreman over a dozen men cutting and sewing linings into coats. Salary: $25 a week.

On the morning of his thirteenth birthday, Fox, who had been operating under the false claim that he was really sixteen, feigned illness to his boss so he could attend his own Bar Mitzvah. As a testament to his hard work and drive, within a few years Fox was able to open his own garment firm, the Knickerbocker Cloth Examining and Shrinking Company. He turned it into a modest success, showing a profit, in the second year, of $10,000.

Fox's initiation into the movie business came in 1904, when he purchased from J. Stuart Blackton* of the Vitagraph Company the Brooklyn nickelodeon (which, given the five-cent admission fee, was then the generic name for movie theatres). The location was 200 Broadway, and the price: $1,600. This was an inauspicious beginning, for, indeed, Fox had been swindled.

Prior to the sale, Blackton hired customers to fill the 146-seat house. Once the deal was closed and Fox's name appeared on the lease, the day's admissions totaled two. Faced with immedi-

---

*Blackton (1875-1941) is a long-forgotten movie pioneer. As a journalist, he so impressed Edison during an interview that the inventor filmed a series of Blackton's drawings, and came up with a cartoon documentary. Vitagraph was started by Blackton and two partners in 1897; their studio was a rooftop in downtown Manhattan. They soon expanded to a facility in Brooklyn. Among Blackton's several distinctions, he pioneered series comedies, single-frame animation, the adaptation of stage works to the screen, and the creation of the studio system, by which one production supervisor oversaw the jobs of several lower-echelon directors, and talent was contracted to exclusive service.

ate bankruptcy, Fox hired a magician in top hat and tails to perform tricks outside 200 Broadway—and invite customers inside
for free.

After the week of complimentary shows, Fox had created a
loyal clientele, and soon the Brooklyn was turning a profit. Fox
bought a second theatre, and then another. In short order he lay
claim to twenty-five such houses in Brooklyn and Manhattan,
each with under 299 seats so as not to be hindered by the fire
regulations required of more substantial theatres.

Fox booked his movies from his office at 24 Union Square, and
soon started acquiring larger theatres. This required partners:
Tammany politicians "Big Tim" and "Little Tim" Sullivan. Not
surprisingly, they cleared the need for proper permits with the
fire commissioner.

Fox's specialty was catering to the family trade, discovering to
his surprise—and to that of social reformers—that once a theatre
opened in a neighborhood, it lured so large a crowd that the fre-
quent result was a shuttering of the local watering hole. As
crowds grew larger and grander, so did the theatres. The local
bijou with its wooden seats and stretched sheet for a screen gave
way to movie palaces fit for royalty.

But such was not always the case; first there needed to be a
family trade to attract. Several exhibitors, such as Marcus Loew
and Adolph Zukor,* specialized in presenting peep shows.

In 1905, Loew, a first-generation American, joined forces
with the Hungarian-born Zukor, who had made his money in
America as a furrier. Together, they purchased penny arcades in
Manhattan and Cincinnati, and within two years they owned 40
such emporiums all over the country. Not choosy about what
they showed, they exhibited programming that others judged to

---

*Both men were to spin off their companies into separate entertainment gi-
ants. Loew (1870-1927), by 1912, owned 400 theatres and in 1920 launched a
production entity that was to become Metro-Goldwyn-Mayer; Zukor
(1873-1976), in 1912, formed his own production company, "Famous Players in
Famous Plays," which when it merged in 1916 with Jesse L. Lasky's Feature
Play Company, absorbed a small distribution company that gave the company
its new name, Paramount.

be of low moral standards. The upshot was the sudden raid of all nickelodeons in New York City on midnight, Christmas Eve, 1908. Before the sites could reopen, the exhibitors had to convince New York Mayor George B. McClellan they would offer no smut, and formed an alliance to guarantee their claim.

The man they elected as their upstanding, moral leader was William Fox.

III

William Fox stood convinced that an audience's attention span could be stretched to an hour, and thus lead to higher admissions, and so he pleaded with the leading film producers—Kalem, Selig, Vitagraph, and the seven others of the Motion Pictures Patents Company—for longer features. He was duly told not to rock the boat and to remain happy with the short subjects this trust provided.

Fox fired the first shot in 1908 by suing to break the patents trust. Four years of litigation followed. Then came the appeal. As part of the Patents Company's hold on the business, it was dictated that the price of film rental for the existing one- and two-reelers be set at twelve cents a foot. Additionally, in producing a film, a price ceiling was placed on stories, and it was further decreed, under threat of legal action, that no actor, director, or writer could be mentioned in the film's advertising.

The Patents Company's marketing aim, the General Film Company, had by 1912 acquired control of the 67 primary film exchanges supplying the pictures to the 12,869 theatres in America. Exchanges were just that; places where exhibitors met to barter for prints they had just used in exchange for others that their customers had not seen. The first had been set up in 1902 in San Francisco, by movie exhibitor Harry Miles.

The one important film exchange that General Film Company did not own was the Greater New York Rental Company, belonging to William Fox. He waved a red flag before the monopo-

lists by advertising for *any* available feature-length motion picture. General Film, represented by a professional ruffian named
Jeremiah J. Kennedy, made Fox an offer it thought the trouble-
maker could not refuse: to buy him out. Fine, responded Fox.
His asking price was $750,000.

Kennedy told Fox to go to hell.

The next day in the mail Fox received a formal cancellation of
his film exhibitor's license from General Film. Fox turned the
notice over to his attorney, Gustavus A. Rogers, whose younger
brother Saul E. Rogers would later serve as general counsel to
the Fox Film Corporation for two decades.

Gustavus Rogers, acting under the Sherman Anti-Trust Laws,
urged the Department of Justice to break up the patents trust.

Suit was brought in New York Supreme Court against General Film Company, asking for an injunction and award of triple
damages. By the time the case reached appeals court, Kennedy
offered a settlement. Should Fox agree to drop all charges, the
disbanded General Film Company would pay him $350,000.
William Fox, by now all of thirty-three years old, agreed to the
deal.

Total judgments against General Film eventually reached $25
million. Of the ten companies that once comprised the trust,
only one survived after the lawsuit, Vitagraph. And the president of that company was J. Stuart Blackton, the man who had
gotten William Fox into the movie business in the first place, by
swindling him.

IV

Darryl Francis Zanuck was born September 5, 1902, in Wahoo, Nebraska, a farming town as backwater as its almost-
Swiftian name implied. He was the second son—the first had
died in a horse accident shortly after Darryl's birth—of Iowa
farmboy Frank Zanuck and the former Louise Torpin. Frank
Zanuck believed he was working his way to California when he

settled in Nebraska and took up the job of underwear salesman in a mail order house. His and Louise's had been a shotgun wedding.

Family loyalty ranked a low priority in the Zanuck household. In Wahoo, Frank was known as a drinker, a gambler, and a shirker of familial responsibilities. Professionally, he had never risen above the position of night clerk at the hotel owned by his well-to-do father-in-law Henry Torpin, a source of embarrassment that Darryl carried with him the remainder of his life.

"I didn't just love my father," Darryl said. "I wanted to admire and look up to him, too. And that was difficult, because my father was a failure, and, as I came to realize later, not particularly ashamed of it, either. For instance, anyone who puts down his occupation as 'hotel night clerk' is admitting that he has no ambition for a start. And that's how my father described himself, as a night clerk."

That his father contentedly accepted his own fate carried no weight with the son. Darryl said of being a night clerk, "It's like admitting you're a mouse, and only dare to come out after dark and snuffle around for cheese."

Salesmen stopping at Wahoo's Le Grande Hotel, where Frank performed nightly sentry, would with no great difficulty involve him in a friendly game of poker. According to Zanuck biographer Leonard Mosely, once Frank was suitably soused, the strangers one at a time would hie themselves over to have their way with a willing Louise Zanuck.

This situation continued until the child Darryl innocently reported a scene of indiscretion to Louise's stern father Henry. She was summarily dispatched to Arizona to live with an aunt.*

Darryl subsequently was taken in by his grandparents and only allowed to visit his father once a week, until such time as news arrived that Louise had divorced Frank and married Joseph Norton, an accountant whose own father had been a fire-and-brimstone preacher. The Norton home was Glendale, California, a low-lying suburb to the northeast of Hollywood.

---

*Louise was also an asthmatic. The desert air was deemed therapeutic.

When word of the second marriage reached Wahoo, Henry Torpin immediately and without guilt fired Frank Zanuck from his job at Le Grande Hotel.

V

Darryl Zanuck was sent to Glendale, only to discover that his new stepfather, Joseph Norton, despite having a respectable profession, was a carbon copy of Louise's first husband—except, in his favor, Frank Zanuck was not a mean drunk. Joseph Norton was. In such a state, the accountant regularly beat his wife, and, after one particularly brutal incident, Darryl suggested that he and his mother return to Nebraska and live with the Torpins. Instead, Louise sent Darryl to the Page Military Academy in Los Angeles. He was eight years old.

Louise did not visit Darryl at Page, nor was the boy permitted to visit the Norton home on holidays. Such abandonment was to color Darryl's opinion of women the rest of his life. He was also to retain a low opinion of accountants.

While enrolled at Page, Darryl made a regular habit of skipping school and wandering the streets of Southern California. Once he managed to collect a veritable fortune, a silver dollar, by stumbling upon a unit of the Kalem movie company. Donning an Indian squaw's costume and wig, Darryl Zanuck entered the ranks of movie production as an extra. His employment lasted five days.

Amazingly, on another of these wanderings, he stumbled upon his father, who at last had found himself in California. Nor had Frank Zanuck lost sight of his destiny. He was gainfully employed in downtown Los Angeles, as a hotel night clerk.

The two Zanucks were able to strike up a relationship, and Frank convinced his son to return to school, the proviso being that they would both see one another twice a week. This they did with regularity, and their encounters proved friendly and invariably ended with the two of them hopping in to see a movie, a way of sitting in the dark and being transported to another world as the larger-than-life pictures on the wall flickered before their eyes.

This period of pleasant calm was not to last. Both Frank and the boy slipped back into the old habits. Frank was dismissed from his job for gambling during working hours, and Darryl once again ditched school—sadly, to search for his father, who was never to return.

After one week of combing his and Frank's new haunts, Darryl was apprehended by the police and returned to the mother and stepfather who did not want him. Soon after he was shipped back to the Torpins in Nebraska. Darryl was twelve.

As opposed to Frank Zanuck, who, like Darryl and Darryl's son Richard, never grew taller than five-foot-six, Henry Torpin was a strapping six-footer. The Midwestern patriarch was steeped in the history of the Old West, having fought off Apaches while under the employ of Union Pacific, and provided the perfect role model for the fascinated adolescent Darryl.

It was Henry who molded the slightly built boy into a wiry athlete, and who lectured him on what the old man deemed the proper treatment of women. Two reasons why Louise was a failure as a human being, her own father decreed, were because she was a female and because she had married a man like Frank Zanuck, a milquetoast who did not whip her.

Set to prove himself, Darryl at age fifteen enlisted in the army. To make the grade, he ripped the wire braces off his teeth and lied about his age. He survived the fib, and the service, but would be left forever with jack-o-lantern front teeth.

Darryl saw military action on World War I battlefields in Europe, although to his boyish regret he himself never killed a man. He did put to paper several impressions of the war, some of which were printed in the armed services newspaper *Stars and Stripes*. Others he forwarded to his grandfather, who exercised his influence to have them published stateside.

After the armistice, on the brink of his turning seventeen, Darryl returned to Nebraska and his grandparents, to announce that he was moving to California—to live with his mother and stepfather. Darryl's grandmother knew the better of the story, and staked him with money for the train ticket and another hundred dollars for emergency, and Darryl Zanuck boarded the train west, to pursue his desired career, that of a writer.

In Los Angeles, Darryl took a room in a boarding house near his father's former place of employment, and made do by accepting hard-labor jobs, including one in the Long Beach shipyards. In his spare time he applied a florid writing style to a number of highly moralistic adventure stories intended for pulp magazines. The formula did not come easily. Darryl could have kept warm at night by setting fire to his pile of rejection slips.

"I was never much of a writer," Darryl admitted late in life. "Every man is a captive of his own nature, his own talents."

The turnaround arrived in 1921. Publisher Bernarr Macfadden bought for his *Physical Culture* magazine a story by Darryl Francis Zanuck (as he called himself*) entitled "Mad Desire," told in the incongruous voice of a virtuous young heroine named Loma. Loma's mad desire was for a ne'er-do-well named Malcolm Dale. Malcolm's mad desire was dope and women of easy virtue.

Near suicide, his life and body laid to ruins, Malcolm is nursed back to health by a regime of healthy exercise and the love of his devoted Loma. Luckily, for Loma, the no-account snaps to. "Yes, Loma dear," Malcolm confides at the finish, "it was happiness and you—or grief and dope. I chose the first."

Darryl's life snapped to as well. He decided "Mad Desire" would make a perfect movie scenario, and with his usual cockiness, went about getting the manuscript into the hands of John Gilbert, a popular matinee idol who had entered the industry through family connections and finally made his mark once he starred opposite Mary Pickford in the 1919 *Heart o' the Hills*. Gilbert took Zanuck's script and mislaid it.

---

*His formal name was shortened to the use of his middle initial only the moment that the full "Darryl Francis Zanuck" elicited audience giggles when his first screen credit appeared.

To entrench himself in movie circles, Darryl decided to take up residence at the highly exclusive Los Angeles Athletic Club, and relied on grandfather Torpin's social connections for sponsorship.

Torpin wired money to express his pleasure over his grandson's course of action, but somehow the membership committee of the restricted club mistook Zanuck for being Jewish and the young comer was blackballed. Grandpa Torpin intervened, successfully, and Zanuck, Wahoo forever behind him, found himself mingling with the Hollywood elite.

"At the Los Angeles Athletic Club," Charlie Chaplin's press officer once explained, was where the beloved tramp of the movie screen was "domiciled during his stay in Los Angeles. Until time to dine, Chaplin lounges about the corridors, talking with friends or reading the afternoon papers. Dinner over, Chaplin goes immediately to his room, where he dons his 'gym' suit, and repairs to the club's gymnasium. Here he spends an hour each evening boxing, wrestling, tussling with the weight machines, and bag punching, followed by a plunge in the pool. Following this, unless he has an engagement to spend the evening with friends, at a theatre, Chaplin remains in his suite, answering the mass of correspondence that reaches him every day from admirers in every section of the universe."

Darryl landed a job with Chaplin, but later claimed that the genius begrudged Zanuck his youth and the very idea that Chaplin's own movie art should require writers. Zanuck was soon sacked. "And," said a longtime associate of Zanuck's, "Darryl never thought Charlie Chaplin was the least bit funny. But a lot of that might have had to do with Darryl being the all-time champ at holding a grudge."

Other Zanuck acquaintances at the club were Chaplin's older brother and manager Sidney, a well-seasoned skirtchaser under whose personal adage, "fucking is the best revenge," Zanuck would undertake a lifelong devotion to womanizing; Fatty Arbuckle, whose own "cockmanship," a favorite Zanuck euphemism, would lead to his trial for the rape and murder of starlet

Virginia Rappe during a wild party over Labor Day weekend 1921 in San Francisco, an incident that would subsequently instigate moral reforms both on and off the screen;* and two producers whose lives would intertwine with Zanuck's.

The first was Mack Sennett, a one-time plumber's helper and then, later, an actor turned director turned producer. In 1912, Sennett formed his own company, Keystone, devoted to slapstick comedy. Zanuck worked for Keystone, again as part of the pool of gag writers. He described Sennett as a slave driver, but it was while under his employ—at $150 a week—that Darryl learned to keep a script's action moving.

The other producer with whom Zanuck rubbed shoulders at the club was Winfield Sheehan, production chief to the maverick head of the Fox Film Company, William Fox.

VI

On February 1, 1915, William Fox formally incorporated the Fox Film Corporation in New York. The next year he bought the Selig Studio in Edendale (Selig had moved to east Los Angeles), and in 1917 Fox opened his own studio on Sunset and Western Boulevards in Hollywood. By 1919, he was able to settle into his own world headquarters, a cathedral-like fourth-floor office with stained glass windows located atop a red-brick fortress at 850 Tenth Avenue in Manhattan.

On March 7, 1919, Fox and his production chief Winfield Sheehan** set sail for a two-month trip to Europe, where they established foreign offices for the Fox Film Corporation in Paris, Rome, Berlin, London, and Dublin. These long-distance outposts, each governed by a Fox-appointed manager, would en-

---

*Arbuckle was acquitted, but because of the trial's publicity and the public's outrage over the incident, his career abruptly ended.
**A one-time crime reporter, Sheehan (1883-1945) met Fox while working as a secretary of the police commissioner; Sheehan actually protected Fox when the latter was threatened with bodily harm as a result of taking on the Motion Picture Patents Company.

sure that Fox pictures would be booked into foreign theatres at the maximum going rate, and serve as home offices for Fox talent scouts to comb Europe in search of prospective movie talent and stage shows for possible adaptation to the screen.

During his travel period, William Fox put on the payroll his two brothers-in-law, Jack and Joe Leo, to mind the store back home. Jack was in charge of distribution; Joe, the Fox theatres. Strangely, William Fox did not trust his own two brothers as he did those of his wife Eve (who used to read books for her husband in search of suitable movie scenarios), but he nevertheless took his two siblings into the fold. Thus was the Fox Film Corporation firmly established as a family business.

Maurice Fox, the youngest brother, with a sweet disposition, went to work as a clerk in the studio printing department. Middle brother Aaron, considered the pretentious Fox, was named treasurer of the corporation, though he clearly had no knowledge of the business.

Under the Leo brothers, Fox Film Corporation expanded, with Jack second in command as executive vice president, and Joe overseeing the expansion of the theatre division, whose holdings would grow to include the $5 million cathedral of the motion picture, the 6,200-seat rococo Roxy in New York.

At the Hollywood Studio, the Fox stable included stars such as the cowboy Tom Mix, whom William Fox met one morning in 1916 outside the Sunset Boulevard gate.

Another Fox discovery was one of the screen's first sex symbols, Theodosia Goodman, the daughter of a Cincinnati tailor, hired in January, 1916, for $75 a week. She was thrown into exotic dress and re-christened Theda Bara, which the Fox publicists, who spoke of her mystical powers, soberly insisted was an anagram for "Arab Death."* At her peak, she earned $4,000 a week.

Claiming to be the lovechild of a French artist and an Egyptian mistress, Bara provided reams of newspaper copy by arriv-

*In court papers it was later shown that Theda was an abbreviation of her first name, while her surname was taken from her maternal grandfather, a Swiss named Francis Bara de Coppet.

ing at press conferences in a white limousine tended by Nubian footmen, and granting interviews in dimly lit hotel rooms as pungent incense burned. Her first role was the lead in *A Fool There Was*, based on the Rudyard Kipling poem, The Vampire. It made her famous overnight, chiefly for the dialogue title that was quoted nationwide, "Kiss me, my fool."

Of her forty motion pictures during her short-lived, three-year career, the one that best fixed her in the public's memory was produced in 1917. It delivered her wearing a flower-blossom brassiere, and told the tale of the queen of ancient Egypt. Its name was *Cleopatra*.

VII

Lecturing the Harvard Business School on his role in breaking up the Motion Picture Patents Company, William Fox painted an unvarnished portrait of the omnipotent trust.

"They regulated the wages paid in every branch of the industry," he said. "In their judgment, no man who wrote a story and gave his brains to create material for motion pictures was entitled to more than $25 for the finest story that he could write. For those men who were known as directors of motion pictures they established a salary of $50 a week. The highest salary they agreed to pay a performer was $60 a week."

By killing the trust, Fox explained, he "opened the door to the world to enter the motion picture field. That dissolution invited great brains to write for the screen. The price is no longer measured by its length but by the greatness of it and, instead of $25 for a story, as high as $250,000 was being paid to reproduce a great story in motion pictures. Instead of paying the men who direct motion pictures a uniform scale, the men who direct motion pictures earn all they are capable of earning, depending entirely on their ability, and their salaries range from $100 a week to half a million dollars a year. Men in all walks of life have applied and asked to be of help and aid in the motion picture."

Starting in 1923, Darryl Zanuck enjoyed entrée to sell his

fiction to the movies at the Fox Film Studio, thanks to two fellow members of the Los Angeles Athletic Club, Fox production head Winfield Sheehan and the studio's cowboy star William Russell. Russell, was a former professional athlete, had chucked the boxing ring for vaudeville before making movies, and, protective of his image, rejected "Mad Desire" as too downbeat. Still, he did champion Zanuck's writing.

Sheehan agreed to let Russell purchase another Zanuck effort, "The Scarlet Ladder," and turn it into a movie. The plot concerned the kidnapping of a young man who falls in love with the daughter of a ship captain. As luck would have it, the captain was actually the scoundrel who had first shanghied the young man. The captain's daughter's name was Loma.

The sale yielded Darryl $500. Yet the buzz to be heard in the club's halls was that a writer of a screenplay was usually paid more by the studios than the man who had created the original material, so Zanuck set about selling himself as a screenwriter who was also an accomplished author. Slapping together four sections of hodgepodge, he paid a vanity publisher to set it between two hard covers. The volume, entitled *Habit: A Thrilling Yarn That Starts Where Fiction Ends and Life Begins*, contained two rejected scenarios, one original story, and a testimonial for Yuccatone Hair Restorer—a genuine medicine-show product derived from an old Indian recipe and hawked, thanks to Zanuck's hucksterism, on the theory that no one ever saw a bald Indian.

Zanuck sold all four chapters to the movies, earned $11,000, and witnessed three of his works, including, remarkably, a drama about an Indian hair restorer, turned into silent pictures.

Darryl Zanuck's reputation as a Hollywood writer was assured.

VIII

The woman who was to become Mrs. Darryl F. Zanuck, until death did them part, was born in Wheeling, West Virginia, at the turn of the century.* Her name was Virginia Fox—no relation to William—and her father was a prosperous import-export dealer who also owned a coal mine. The family fortune allowed the girl to attend a proper finishing school in Sarasota, Florida.

The Foxes spent their summers in Santa Barbara, California, a highly restricted beach resort about 100 miles above Los Angeles. One summer weekend, Virginia and a girl friend who knew Mack Sennett drove south and paid a visit to the Keystone Studio. Once inside, Virginia was spotted by Sennett, who ordered her to return for a screen test the next day—in a bathing suit. Part of Sennett's company were his Bathing Beauties, so-called because they spiced up his comedies in scenes showing them frolicking at the shore, coquettishly tossing beachballs and ogling the camera with a come-hither glance.

As instructed, the next day Virginia returned in a swimsuit. She got the job. Her parents were outraged, yet obviously were in no position to control their adventurous daughter.

Virginia debuted as a Sennett Bathing Beauty before soon graduating to leading lady roles opposite one of the great comic geniuses of the screen, Buster Keaton, a former vaudevillian from Kansas whose deadpan reaction to absurdist situations made him the rival, both commercially and artistically, of Charlie Chaplin. Virginia's gift was not for comedy, nor, by her own admission, for acting of any kind. Her specialty was following a director's orders, faithfully.

"If I was hanging from an elk's head and they said, 'Hold it,' I held it—even if they went to lunch. I did whatever I was told," Virginia told writer Mel Gussow, who painted a firsthand portrait of Zanuck in the 1971 authorized biography *Don't Say Yes Until I Finish Talking*. Gussow utilized the quote again, to underscore Virginia's disciplined obedience, in the 1982 obituary he wrote for her in *The New York Times*.

"She was the most charming girl, happy, funny, and always willing to go along with the most outlandish suggestion," remembered Mrs. Jean Negulesco,** the former model Dusty

---

*This made her a couple of years older than Darryl.
**Film director Jean Negulesco was to join Twentieth Century-Fox in the late 1940s, and he became a longtime trusted associate of Darryl Zanuck's.

Anderson. "Virginia was absolutely the sweetest thing, with the most beautiful fair skin."

Virginia met Darryl on a blind date arranged by the director and fellow member of the Los Angeles Athletic Club, Mal St. Clair. Darryl did not make much of an impression on the slender brunette, a factor he interpreted as her playing hard to get. The next day she received a dozen roses and a copy of *Habit*. The gesture was appreciated, but not overwhelming. Virginia was practically a movie star. Zanuck was an unknown screenwriter.

The shipment of flowers was to continue. By Virginia's account, the more she resisted the more he persisted. After six months Virginia found Darryl's undaunted efforts endearing. They were married by a Justice of the Peace on January 24, 1924. The only family present were her father and brother. There were no Zanucks.

After a honeymoon in San Diego, Darryl and Virginia settled into a bungalow in Beverly Hills that was part of a small residence court owned by Darryl's mother. Louise had purchased it with money left her by her late father. Louise's wedding present to her only son and his bride was six months' free rent. Virginia's father awarded the newlyweds with an automobile.

The latter gift came in especially handy. Several times during the early months of the marriage, Virginia threatened to go home to her parents.

IX

Darryl Zanuck's rise to prominence in the industry he had embraced was tied to the fortunes of four brothers who, like the others running the smaller film concerns during the early 1920s, generously benefitted from the trust-busting efforts of William Fox. Their name was Warner. Individually they were Harry (born 1881, in Kraznashiltz, Poland), Albert (1884, Baltimore), Samuel (1888, Baltimore), and Jack (1892, London, Ontario, Canada).

Their father was a Polish immigrant, a cobbler who also plied the trades of butcher and bicycle salesman. His responsibilities were heavy: the Warners had 12 children. The youngsters, the four boys in particular, were required to assist with earning a living. The same year William Fox entered the movie business, 1904, so did the Warners, when they acquired a nickelodeon in Newcastle, Pennsylvania. During intermission, young brother Jack entertained the audiences by singing.

In 1905, the Warners attempted to enter the field of film distribution, only to be stymied by the Patents trust. Following their retreat, Jack and Sam Warner, yearned to enter film production, but calmer instincts prevailed, and the family stuck to motion picture exhibition. That is, until 1912, when the Warners produced some short features. They were not successful.

Came the Great War, the Warners produced some anti-German propaganda dramas. These proved very profitable indeed. Their earnings allowed them to buy a studio in Hollywood, at 5842 Bronson, near Sunset Boulevard. There, in 1923, they formed Warner Bros. Pictures, Incorporated. By April of 1925, they expanded, purchasing, at the corner of Talmadge and Prospect in Hollywood, the 14-year-old Vitagraph studio, started by J. Stuart Blackton and his partner Albert E. Smith, and where Virginia Fox had made her movies with Buster Keaton.

The Warners changed the name to Vitaphone Studios, portending what they hoped would be the coming of sound to motion pictures. With the Vitagraph purchase came that company's network of film exchanges as well as its theatre chain, First National.

The brothers divided the powers of their company, although none was ever eager to give an inch to the other, and they were widely known to argue ferociously among themselves. Harry, the eldest and shrewdest, served as president and held court in New York, where the tight-fisted Albert, as company treasurer, also was stationed. The loudest and brashest of the quartet, Jack, ruled the studio as vice president in charge of production, enjoying overall responsibility of running the facility and seeing that the films were released.

To Sam, the humane brother, fell the role of referee, being

frequently called upon to make the five-day train journey from New York to Los Angeles in order to clean up the bad blood between the brothers Warner.

X

Mal St. Clair,* who introduced Darryl Zanuck to Virginia Fox in 1923, that same year also introduced Zanuck to Jack and Harry Warner, who were impressed with Zanuck's enthusiasm. St. Clair worked on the lot directing the minor company's one major star, a German Shepherd named Rin-Tin-Tin.

Born in 1916 and named for the finger-length doll that French soldiers carried with them into battle during the Great War, "Rinty" was discovered as a half-starved puppy in 1918 by American corporal Lee Duncan in an abandoned German war-dog station. A captured German sergeant fluent in English instructed Duncan in the dog's training, and by the time Duncan brought the animal home at war's end, Rinty could perform tricks. A high-jump of his performed at a California dog show was captured by a movie cameraman, and, when spliced with added shots of some dog trials, provided complete footage for a short feature. A sequel followed, this time showing Rinty leaping off a 30-foot cliff. Rinty's take from the two movies was $850, and inspired Duncan to escort his breadwinner, on a leash, on a round of the Hollywood studios. The Warners bit, and Rinty returned the favor by becoming their chief source of revenue.

Once Zanuck was brought on board to create scripts for the

*St. Clair (1897-1952), a Los Angeles native, had been a newspaper cartoonist before going to work for Mack Sennett when he was 18, as a comedy writer and screen extra. By 1919, he was directing shorts at the studio, then he turned freelance director for Buster Keaton before adapting to feature work in 1923. During the movie's silent days his comedies were compared by the critics to the stylish romps of Ernst Lubitsch, yet St. Clair's career plummeted with the advent of talkies. Darryl Zanuck, once in a position to, kept St. Clair employed the remainder of his life. Among his final films for Twentieth Century-Fox were some tepid Laurel and Hardy comedies.

star, he would act out Rinty's part during story conferences. When Rinty's movies went on location, the Zanucks, Mr. and Mrs., went along. To Darryl's taste, the more rugged the setting, the better.

A lumber camp in Oregon proved a particular delight. While Virginia dressed for a dinner party to be thrown by St. Clair to mark the end of a shooting, Darryl hightailed it to a lumber camp to roll logs with the lumbermen. Returning to his wife, who decided it was time for him to dress for dinner, Darryl announced he had no such intention.

The evening ended in a violent argument, with Virginia leaving Darryl as he stood naked screaming at her. When she returned after dinner, she discovered that her husband had ripped her entire wardrobe to shreds.

XI

Zanuck parlayed his screenwriting position at Warners into one of the highest paying jobs in Hollywood. Dropping the purple prose of his early work, Zanuck's experienced style read slick, speedy, and economical. He relied on action, humor (not necessarily wit), and romantic interest. Logic was not a high priority.

Zanuck proved so prolific that in 1925, under different pseudonyms—he used three: Melville Crossman, Gregory Rogers, Mark Canfield—he penned nineteen scripts. The price for this, as Zanuck sat at the typewriter all night, was paid at home. The Zanucks had only been married one year.

"I was always going back to Mother," said Virginia, who made one last film with Keaton after marrying Zanuck. She then retired from acting forever. "I didn't understand him. He used to pull tantrums. One day I said to Mother, 'I can't stand this.' She said, 'He's a genius.' I said, 'A genius, heck!' "

Virginia did not leave.

With his understanding of the basic construction of a movie

and the administrative politics of the studio, Zanuck graduated to the role of producer. His career rise was relatively meteoric. Only twenty-five, he was boosted to the position of head of production. Equally impressive was his salary: $5,000 per week. Jack Warner's only advice to his young colleague was that he needed to look older.

Darryl F. Zanuck grew a mustache. And he started smoking a cigar.

With his new affluence, the Zanucks traveled. Darryl indulged his love of the game of polo, and began accumulating a stable of ponies from Argentina. In Hollywood, the sport was so closely identified with Zanuck and his fellow players, the actor Spencer Tracy and the humorist Will Rogers, that their watering hole at the Beverly Hills Hotel on Sunset Boulevard was renamed the Polo Lounge.

On the lot, Zanuck, sporting leather boots that provided added height, attended production meetings in full polo garb, swinging his mallet in threatening gestures when he needed to stress a point. The point for which Zanuck was best recognized, first in a perfunctory albeit good-natured manner, later in a way that bordered on the psychotic, was his penis.

"Darryl was a sensualist, so they say," recalled writer-director Elia Kazan, who was to direct *Pinky* and *Gentleman's Agreement* for Zanuck. "Maybe so. A small city boy out of mid-America often has his ego attached to his fucking."

Continued Kazan, "When it came to judging a new actor's sex appeal, Darryl Zanuck would call in his wife, Virginia; he thought highly of her judgment and candor. Or he'd gather secretaries who were sure of their jobs and would speak their 'truth.' He might also be interested by what was known as the actor's 'track record.' But when it came to actresses, not Darryl, not [Columbia's] Harry Cohn, not Louis Mayer, not Sam Goldwyn needed consultation. They went by a simple rule and a useful one: Do I want to fuck her?"

Though Kazan chose not to wager on what went on behind Zanuck's closed office door, he did acknowledge the story that Zanuck required a minimum of daily afternoon sexual service by actresses wanting better roles at the studio. Zanuck's role model was Sidney Chaplin, Charlie's brother, for whom Zanuck had written comedy scripts.

"Sidney Chaplin was the greatest cocksman that ever lived," Zanuck told biographer Mel Gussow. "I never saw anyone as ruthless and successful, and bold. He used to stand across the street from Hollywood High School and watch the kids come out and he'd approach them—using his real name. Ruthless! At Yosemite once I saw the guy get a married woman on her honeymoon!"

Marcella Rabwin, in those days a candidate to become Zanuck's secretary, recalled over 50 years later being "nearly paralyzed with fright by Zanuck's sexual demands during the interview. When I refused he started screaming," said Rabwin, who had the presence of mind to leave Zanuck's office, although not before he had chased her around his desk—twice, she said—and threatened that unless she gave into him, she would never work anywhere in Hollywood.*

Myrna Loy, a Montana-born movie actress with an illustrious career, which inexplicably began with her playing exotic vamps, Asian mostly, in Warner costume pictures for Zanuck, said of Zanuck: "I always had trouble with him, which puzzled me."

Her entire life, Loy said, she received Darryl's cold shoulder. "I never could figure it out. I opened the wrong door at the studio once, and caught a sort of half-star at Warners sitting on his lap.

"I quickly closed the door, but maybe he never forgave me for that. I used to tease him about it, which didn't help matters. He had enough trouble on that score. His wife, Virginia, used to invade his office wielding a pistol."

XII

In 1926, one year after Zanuck had assumed his title as head of production and two after he and Virginia had married, the writ-

---

*Soon after, Rabwin found employment as executive assistant to producer David O. Selznick, whom she said, by contrast to Zanuck, "was a gentleman and a talent."

ing was on the wall. Warners was going to be squeezed out of business by the other studios, in a type of replay of the battle against the old Edison trust.

The deciding factor this time was who would own a sufficient number of first-run movie theatres in the newly lucrative small towns and suburbs so as to guarantee that their products be played. Warners, possessing large downtown theatres, was losing the race.

Rather than scramble to acquire additional screens, Warners sank all available resources into a new process developed by the Bell Telephone system called Vitaphone, by which the moving image on the screen was synchronized to a sound accompaniment on a record-like disc. Vitaphone, believed Zanuck and the Warners (Sam, not Harry, who portended to his brothers: "Who the hell wants to hear actors talk?"), could prove to be as revolutionary and profitable as *The Birth of a Nation*.

In truth, sound was not a new idea. As early as 1911, while still at Yale, inventor Theodore W. Case experimented with lights in order to photograph sound on film. Case's partner, Earl I. Sponable, said later that it was during World War I that he and Case "invented a secret system whereby infra-red light rays could be used for the transmission of signals between ships."

Finally, the two men perfected an AEO light so sensitive to light vibrations that tiny lines of sound could be photographed onto movie film—and they demonstrated their discovery by showing a close-up of a canary bird singing, complete with sound.

Their brief clip premiered in Parlor B of the William Fox newsreel studio at 54th Street and Tenth Avenue. Credit for securing the first look was due Fox's brother-in-law Jack Leo, who for $10,000 had the screening room secretly equipped to handle the sound demonstration while William Fox was in California.

After the unveiling, William Fox announced that he was convinced it had been a trick of ventriloquism. Told otherwise, he ordered his private screening rooms at home and the office immediately equipped with sound, even though the best any of the men at the meeting could foresee for the sound moving picture was demonstrations on the Atlantic City boardwalk.

Possibly, someone suggested, the invention might also be used outside theatres to attract audiences inside, to see silent pictures.

Still, Fox was now in possession of a sound process, which he dubbed Movietone. Instead of rushing it before the public, a costly maneuver requiring the investment of new theatre equipment, he instead requested that further tests be made, to improve sound quality. Among the handful of stage stars who submitted to the Fox cameras and microphones were Raquel Meller, Harry Lauder, and the former British music hall performer, now the Broadway actress, Gertrude Lawrence.

XIII

As the Movietone tests gathered momentum and talk of them circulated within the industry, Adolph Zukor of Paramount requested a demonstration. His reply to Fox afterward: "I told you that you couldn't do it."

Warners, on the other hand, desperately wanted to do it. They needed to rush a sound picture in front of the public before its own silent pictures were forced off the screen for good. The studio was considered washed up simply for pinning its hopes on and borrowing to its teeth for a gimmick that the major companies already had witnessed and rejected.

Initially, it appeared that the worst was true. The first official tryout of Vitaphone took place on August 6, 1926, at the Manhattan Opera House in New York. John Barrymore starred in the Warners' production of *Don Juan*, an ordinary silent costume drama with one difference: the musical soundtrack was recorded on Vitaphone instead of performed by a live orchestra. The experiment was applauded, but rival theatre owners did not rush to install the costly Vitaphone equipment. The future looked dim.

Warner's next step was to experiment with some dialogue se-

quences in their movie adaptation of the Samson Raphaelson
New York stage play *The Jazz Singer*. Harry Warner had purchased the property for $50,000. The idea was for the voice of
the leading man—George Jessel, star of the Broadway
version—to be heard, synchronized to the moving picture.

It was considered lunacy.

Equally uncommercial was the overly sentimental storyline of
The Jazz Singer. It would have seemed only to be of interest to
the American Jewish population, and come to think of it, not
even to them. A young man disobeys his orthodox rabbi father
and enters show business. As it so happens, on Yom Kippur, the
holiest day of the year, the father is dying, and the son must answer to the dilemma of giving up his debut in the big time or
singing "Kol Nidre" in the synagogue.

As production drew near, Jessel experienced cold feet. He
boosted his asking price from $30,000 to $50,000. Warners was
not prepared to pay. Eddie Cantor was next approached. He
passed. Zanuck considered the third possibility, Al Jolson, himself the son of a cantor, as nothing more than a professional
"mammy singer." Nevertheless, Jolson was the one to get the
role. *The Jazz Singer* rolled.

Relying on his own troubled paternal relationship, Zanuck
contributed a major scene to the screenplay, that of the dramatic
confrontation between father and son. Of the actual filming,
"We used to have to work at night, because Warner Bros. was
right on Sunset Boulevard when the traffic was awful all day
long," recalled actress May McAvoy. She played the jazz
singer's gentile girl friend. "So we waited until night time, when
the traffic died down.

"One time, Mother and Father Warner came over to the studio. They wanted to see how sound was being done. They were
put into a couple of rocking chairs on the set where they
wouldn't be too much in the way. Right in the middle of a very
important scene, dear little Mrs. Warner started rocking back
and forth, and the chair began squeaking." The take was ruined.

Not all of McAvoy's anecdotes were so jocular. "I was having difficulty with one of the bosses," she said. "With Zanuck. I had a great deal of trouble with him, as many people did. I was very unhappy there for that reason. I didn't want to get into a scandal of any nature, which could have happened because his wife thought I was trying to get him or something, when all I was trying to do was fight him off all the time."

XIV

The Jazz Singer premiered at New York's Warner Theatre October 6, 1927. In one of the strangest ironies in all movie history, Sam Warner was seized by a heart attack the day before the premiere, and died. The strain of the new venture was blamed. Life imitating art, his brothers had to face the dilemma of attending the premiere or singing "Kol Nidre" for their sibling. As occurred in *The Jazz Singer*, faith and family came first.*

Darryl Zanuck represented the studio at the unveiling. Virginia Zanuck cried** when she saw *The Jazz Singer*. Twenty-two days after its premiere, William Fox presented the first all-sound Movietone newsreel at the Roxy Theatre. It depicted the sights and sounds of Niagara Falls, the steam engine, the Army-Navy game, and a rodeo.

Sound was now fully launched.

Solidifying Warner Brothers' position in the industry, as well as Zanuck's position within the studio, *The Jazz Singer* led the company to such commercial smashes and artistic and technical embarrassments (the public was too starry-eared to care) as the all-talking melodrama *The Lights of New York*. Zanuck thought it garbage; it paid his salary. Jolson's second feature, the slap-dash *The Singing Fool*, worse garbage, topped all box-office rec-

*Harry Warner died in 1958, while Jack was vacationing in the South of France. When the news reached Jack, he continued his holiday.
**This reaction from his wife would prove to be Darryl's preferred gauge in assessing his movies.

ords of its day. The mammy singer turned movie star looked to do no wrong.

Born in St. Petersburg, Russia, in 1886, as Asa Yoelson, Jolson had joined the circus before finding his niche singing in blackface. In vaudeville he was considered the entertainer's entertainer. The movies made him an international household name, and nearly single-handedly he inspired an entire movement within the industry to produce musicals.

Beginning in 1929, Hollywood went music crazy. Ukelele players, tap dancers from Broadway, practically anyone who could hum descended upon the movie capital. For the first time since the music industry inaugurated west coast headquarters, vocal coaching became a legitimate profession.

Desperate to feed the public's hunger for this type of entertainment, studios forced many of their non-singing performers into musical roles, and indiscriminately shined up musty old operettas and restaged them for the camera and microphone.

Then, as suddenly as it had begun, the fad died. Within two years, audiences were satiated with Jolson.

Everyone was fed up with the sound of music. Critics loathed the genre: "Here is a reminder of the dear dead days that we thought beyond recall," one wrote of a late effort. "For this musical extravaganza . . . must have been long delayed in release, for all its much-touted principals have now gone back to the obscurity from whence they came."

XV

The Warners' Vitaphone proved unreliable. Sound and picture frequently fell out of sync. William Fox picked up the slack with his Movietone sound-on-film system.* That became the industry standard.

Fox, despite ownership of in excess of 1,000 theatres and con-

*Popularized by his western hit, *In Old Arizona* (1929), which was also the first talkie to contain scenes filmed outdoors.

trol of the voice of the movies, was not satisfied with his position. He chose to expand and dominate the industry. Holding
the patent on sound films, he borrowed $15 million from the
American Telephone Company and the New York banking
house of Halsey, Stuart, and Company. Then William Fox went
on a buying spree.

His biggest purchase was the crown jewel of the movies,
Metro-Goldwyn-Mayer, which became available following the
death of Marcus Loew in 1927. Fox sought the controlling block
of the parent company stock, including those shares owned by
the impresario family of Broadway, the Shuberts, as well as the
Loews themselves, Loew's vice president Nicholas Schenck,
and company treasurer David Bernstein. In all, 400,000 Loew's
shares—53 percent of the company—were to go to Fox for $50
million.

The transaction took place in the Hotel Ambassador, 299 Park
Avenue. Fox and Winfield Sheehan pulled checks from their
wallets and handed them to a Loew's lawyer. Funny, but $20
million was missing. Treasurer Bernstein shot a glance at Nick
Schenck, as if to say he knew the whole thing was a bluff.

Fox frisked himself, emptied and explored his trousers, then
finally discovered the dog-eared certified check for the missing
amount in his watch pocket.

The deal was done.

In deference to the M-G-M studio logo, the roaring Leo the
Lion, industry wags referred to the maneuver as "The Fox Swal-
lows the Lion."

In actual fact, William Fox got mauled, chewed up, and spat
out.

Simultaneous to the Metro deal, Fox purchased for $20 mil-
lion New England's Poli theatre chain and half-controlling interest in British-Gaumont, an Anglo-French movie concern.

Yet it was the Fox-Goldwyn-Mayer deal that rankled Hollywood, in particular M-G-M head of production Louis B. Mayer.

Mayer, a staunch Republican, played footsie with the newly
elected President Herbert Hoover. Shortly after the controversial merger, William Fox paid a visit to the chief executive. Fox

spoke of his own generous contribution to the recent Hoover campaign, and of the enormous influence of his Movietone newsreels. Hoover turned a deaf ear. Mayer was already pulling strings within the administration.

"You must have known that I have moved heaven and earth to prevent this consolidation," Mayer told Fox. "Surely you felt that someone used his influence to have the government change its opinion with reference to these shares. I was responsible."

November 27, 1929, nearly a month after the stock market crashed, the United States attorney general filed suit against Fox Film Corporation. The charge: restraint of trade.

On July 31, 1931, U.S. District Court Judge John C. Knox ruled that Fox must divest his Loew's stock.

The domino principle took over. Halsey, Stuart, and Company, representing the Chase Manhattan Bank, contacted Fox stockholders to request support in rejecting William Fox's proposed financing plan with Lehman Brothers and Dillon Read and Company. The Telephone Company began exercising its patents on the Movietone sound system. A pretender to Fox's throne, Harley Clarke of the General Theatres Equipment Corporation, began his move to assume control of the Fox theatres. Clarke was successful.

In 1930, William Fox lost the company he had founded, when $100 million in loans to his studio became due.

XVI

In 1930, Zanuck announced that films produced at Warners would be based on spot news. This phase saw the evolution of the popular gangster film, whose script seemed to have been taken from the day's headlines, to the studio's specialty, what was called the topical film.

Topics of current interest were meshed with a modicum of moral homily. One example was Edward G. Robinson in *Little Caesar*, which gave birth to the gangster cycle. The other was

James Cagney in *The Public Enemy*, the drama that earmarked the tough guy for stardom. It was Zanuck who invented that film's most famous scene, wherein Cagney shoves a grapefruit into Mae Clarke's face at the breakfast table.

Another Zanuck discovery was Bette Davis. Despite her battles with Jack Warner, she would come to reign as the queen of the Warner lot. In 1930, the Warners took over the First National Studio in Burbank, where its facilities were to remain ever after. Burbank was located to the northeast of Hollywood, in the San Fernando Valley.

Zanuck's socially conscious production, *I Am a Fugitive from a Chain Gang*, starring Paul Muni, shed light on the criminal-labor situation in the United States and forced major reforms in the penal system.

Zanuck was also capable of blunders. A terrific error was his personally produced Biblical spectacle *Noah's Ark*. It was an attempt to duplicate the epic popularized at Paramount by Cecil B. DeMille and the grand scale of D.W. Griffith's successor to *Birth of a Nation*, entitled *Intolerance*. *Intolerance*, a lengthy treatise on hypocrisy through the ages, was intended as a *mea culpa* to the charges of racism in *Birth of a Nation*. No one was interested. *Intolerance* died an instant but noticeable death at the box-office. *Noah's Ark* died with far less dignity.

Zanuck's script juxtaposed life in ancient Babylon with that of modern society. Parallels were drawn between God's wrathful obstacles faced by Noah and his sons Shem, Ham, and Japheth (as told in *Genesis 5:8-9-29*) with the ravages of World War I.

Contract player Dolores Costello,* with whom Zanuck openly carried on an affair, played two roles: Miriam, a servant girl, and Marlene, a Viennese *mädchen*. George O'Brien played Japheth and an American doughboy. Noah Beery played King Nephilim and a godless soldier named Nicholoff. Hired to direct was Michael Curtiz, who, still at Warners two decades later, made the wartime romance *Casablanca*, with Humphrey Bogart and

---

*Her father, the actor Maurice Costello, tracked down Virginia Zanuck and personally pleaded that she stop her husband from seducing his daughter.

Ingrid Bergman, and the Joan Crawford drama of a mother's sacrifices, *Mildred Pierce*.

Seventy-five hundred screen extras were required for *Noah's Ark*. They had to be blanketed head-to-toe in dark pancake makeup because of their skimpy costumes. The cover in turn needed to be water-proofed to survive the 15,000 tons of rainstorm. The water supposedly buried several non-swimming screen extras, although Warners held firm to its statement that no one was injured let alone killed during filming.

Then came the second major casting call, taken directly from the source material for the screenplay: "every living thing of all flesh, two of every *sort* . . . of fowls and their kind, and of cattle after their kind, of every creeping thing of the earth after his kind, two of every *sort*."

There was not a zoo or animal sanctuary within a 750-mile radius of Southern California that was not depleted. The stench was enormous.

Of the final result, *The New York Times* declared it "a great test of patience. A cumbersome production [that] frequently borders on the ridiculous." The newly launched *The New Yorker* dismissed it as "an idiotic super-spectacle."

For the 27-year-old Zanuck, *Noah's Ark* represented a crushing defeat. Price of his folly: $2 million (in terms of 1988 purchasing power, approximately $60 million). His salvation was that these were such fat times for the studio that Warners easily absorbed the loss.

XVII

Zanuck mounted one last attempt to revive the musical. He was successful. He put into production *Forty-Second Street*, a backstage story about the life-and-death struggle of putting on a Broadway show. Warner Baxter, Ruby Keeler, and Dick Powell appeared, and the film featured a pervasive sense of irony, unusual for such escapist entertainment.

Perhaps a greater irony was that Zanuck had voluntarily departed Warner Bros. by the time the musical was released.

As a delayed but direct result of the Depression, Hollywood in 1933 sustained a financial reversal. Austerity cuts of 30 percent on every paycheck were instituted at each of the studios for a period of eight weeks. The accounting firm of Price Waterhouse and the Motion Picture Academy determined when full salaries would be reinstated, and Harry Warner, who opposed outside intervention, entered into open battle over the issue. Jack Warner tried to mediate in the dispute, but the problem remained; Warners extended the slashed paychecks an additional two weeks and, staging his own protest, Zanuck bolted.

Another factor, a large one, was that no matter how close and important he may have been to the Warners, Darryl Zanuck would never be a blood relation. Besides, he wanted his own studio.

A breakfast meeting at Romanoff's restaurant, April 17, 1933, forty-eight hours after walking off the Warners lot, set Zanuck's destiny into motion. United Artists president Joseph Schenck,* whose younger brother Nicholas headed Loew's Corporation, sat across the table and handed Zanuck a check from Louis B. Mayer for $100,000.

The arrangement called for Zanuck to hire William Goetz, Mayer's son-in-law, who was at the time, to his father-in-law's mind, working beneath his position. Goetz was an assistant director at RKO but now was to become Zanuck's executive assistant at Zanuck's new company, Twentieth Century Pictures. The name came, it was said, from Darryl's manner of playing polo. He did not play the game as if this were the nineteenth century, but, rather, the twentieth.

*Born in Russia (Joseph in 1878, Nicholas in 1881), the Schencks emigrated to the U.S. and opened an upstate New York amusement park and Palisades Park in Fort Lee, New Jersey. In the latter venture, their partner was Marcus Loew, with whom they entered motion-picture exhibition and became top executives in M-G-M. Nicholas stayed with Loew, while Joseph spun off into independent production in 1917.

The deal was sweetened by Zanuck's receiving access to Metro's stars via loan-outs. This talent pool included Clark Gable, whom Zanuck once passed on as a contract player at Warners because he felt the actor's ears were too large. Offices were set up at United Artists and Twentieth made its first film, *The Bowery*, with Wallace Beery, George Raft, Fay Wray, and Jackie Cooper. Raoul Walsh directed.

Beery played an orphan who grows up in the bowery, becomes a professional boxer, and enters an upper social circle. Fay Wray, who the same year fell into the clutches of the giant ape King Kong, was the socialite with whom Beery falls hopelessly in love. As luck would have it, George Raft already has his sights set on her, and the two men go to great lengths to woo her. For sentimental good measure, Beery adopts little Cooper.

The public bought it all.

In the next two years, Zanuck's Twentieth Century turned out twenty films, only two of them clunkers. The profitmakers included such long-familiar titles as *The House of Rothschild* with George Arliss and Boris Karloff, and, as an innovative twist, four final minutes (Nathan Rothschild's audience with Queen Victoria) in highly experimental Technicolor; *The Mighty Barnum* with Wallace Beery as the great showman and humbug artist; *Clive of India* with Ronald Colman and Loretta Young; and literary adaptations such as Victor Hugo's *Les Miserables* with Fredric March and Charles Laughton, and Jack London's *Call of the Wild* with Loretta Young and Metro's Clark Gable.

In 1935, as Zanuck's Twentieth was prospering, the Fox Film Corporation under new president Sidney R. Kent* was faltering. Prospects for turnaround seemed unlikely, especially given what was to happen in August of that year.

The studio's main attraction, Will Rogers, was killed in a plane crash that seemed to leave the entire country in mourning.

---

*Formerly in marketing, Kent rose from salesman to general manager at Paramount, before moving to Fox, where he replaced William Fox's immediate successor, Harley Clarke, one of those who had ousted the company's founder from his berth.

XVIII

The only requirement deemed necessary to save the Fox Film Corporation was a strong new head of production. The company did not lack for physical assets, claiming a Hollywood studio at Sunset and Western, and another, called Fox Movietone Film Studios (Movietone City, for short) and built exclusively as a sound facility in 1928, located in the Westwood section of Beverly Hills. Fox offices were to be found at headquarters in New York and in branches throughout Europe. There was also the chain of Fox theatres, although with a downturn in movie attendance during the early 1930s, that once-profitable arm of the company was being eroded.

This last turn of events, involving the theatres, brought into play at Fox the Greek-born Skouras family, owners of the Skouras Theatre chain in St. Louis. Charles Skouras, eldest brother of business partners George and Spyros Skouras, had been appointed receiver of the Fox West Coast Theatres in February, 1933, during a film-business slump. A month later, the Fox Midwest Theatre chain also entered receivership. Business turned so sour in Kansas City that 40 Fox theatres closed their doors.

Given such dire circumstances, by 1935 it was believed that the Fox Film Corporation could swallow Twentieth Century and bring in Darryl Zanuck to supervise production. This was not to be.

Zanuck had become disgruntled with his distribution arrangement with United Artists. Having contributed so many box-office successes to UA, he resented being treated as merely an employee—without stock, profit-sharing, and voting privileges. Demanding to be made a full partner with Charlie Chaplin, Mary Pickford, and Douglas Fairbanks (the company's fourth founder, D.W. Griffith, had sold his entire share in 1932 to stave off personal bankruptcy), Zanuck was rebuffed.

This was interpreted as a danger sign to UA president Joseph Schenck, who decided to align himself with the forward-thinking Zanuck.

When Twentieth Century was approached for takeover, Zanuck and Schenck blocked the buy-out. Instead, a merger was arranged. Schenck would resign the presidency of United Artists and for $130,000 annual salary become chairman of the newly formed Twentieth Century-Fox. Sidney Kent, president of the Fox Film Corporation, would continue in that position, for $180,000 a year. He would receive another $25,000 as president of a Fox affiliate, National Theatres Corporation. Winfield Sheehan, the last hold-out from William Fox's founding days, negotiated a contract buy-out of $420,000. He left the studio and became an independent producer.

Darryl F. Zanuck swung the best deal of all. As vice president in charge of production, his annual pay was $260,000, dollar for dollar his salary at Twentieth. On top of that, he would take ten percent of the company's box-office gross. In accepting the merger of the two companies, Darryl Zanuck would also hold enough stock to guarantee earnings of an additional $500,000 a year.

PART TWO

I

"There was never a more devoted father than Darryl," said a member of the Zanuck inner circle, one of Darryl's contemporaries, film director Jean Negulesco. "He was wonderful to his children. The money he would spend. They had to be the most beautiful, the most brilliant. There was nothing he wouldn't do for Dick, from the time Dick was a young, strong guy and Darryl had to get him out of jail for beating up Mexicans."

Palm Springs police once hauled Richard into the station when he was caught brandishing a knife during a fight in that desert oasis.

"He was such a wild boy," interjected Mrs. Negulesco, the former model, Dusty Anderson. "Poor Virginia. Remember what she had to go through?"

"Yes, my darling," Negulesco said to his wife, "but Dick came out a mogul."

After the Dolores Costello affair, Virginia Zanuck presented her husband with an ultimatum. She had by then exhausted conversation on the subject with her own parents and resigned herself to his extramarital affairs; her modest request to Darryl on the matter was that he maintain discretion. Thereafter, Virginia, in deference to her genteel Southern upbringing, could enjoy her social position in the community where, understandably, she was a studio widow.

"We were married in January, 1924," she told Zanuck's biographer Mel Gussow in the late 1960s. By then she and Darryl had been estranged for more than a decade, and yet the public face still existed. So did communication between the two of them. Darryl had arranged her interview with Gussow. "We had 33 wonderful years," she said. "There was so much love. So much harmony."

There were three children. The first was Darrylin, born August 28, 1931, and the second, Susan, born August 30, 1933. Richard arrived December 13, 1934. Darryl was on hand, poised with a movie camera inside the delivery room: "I wanted to be there rather than waiting for an answer," he told Gussow. "I especially wanted to be there when the boy came."

For all that, Darryl was a neglectful father. The children were frequently entrusted to nannies while their parents traveled. (Before the children's arrival, Virginia developed into a seasoned big-game hunter in Africa. The escapes were less elaborate once the Zanucks became parents, due in part to the cooling of the relationship between the two principals.) Darryl's day was devoted to his studio. He communicated with his children via scribbled notes left at home, signed, "Love, Z. See you later."

"So far as I was concerned, he was an absentee father and a distant figure during my childhood years," said Richard. "He was never there when I needed him. It was hard for me to go to him and have a father-son conversation on the most basic levels because his working habits were so strange. Weeks would go by where I would never see him, even though we lived in the same house. I would go to school in the mornings and come back and he would still be sleeping because he had been out late the night before. On weekends he'd leave on Friday night right from the studio and go down to the house at Palm Springs, and we would be left on our own for the weekend."

Still, the streets Dick Zanuck roamed as a child were a far cry from those of the *shtetls* of Eastern Europe or the Lower East Side of New York, let alone Wahoo, Nebraska. The Zanucks lived their summers in a rented beach cottage on Ocean Front, along Santa Monica's Gold Coast. This they later purchased and replaced in 1937 by a three-story, 30-room beach house designed by architect Wallace Neff. The rest of the year was spent at home in Beverly Hills.

On weekends, Virginia and Darryl retreated to their Palm Springs estate, Ric-Su-Dar, named for their three children. Zanuck had purchased the luxurious house and grounds from Joseph Schenck in the early '40s, when Schenck needed to raise money after being convicted for tax evasion.*

Ric-Su-Dar was known as the croquet-playing capital of the West after Zanuck had traded in his polo mallet for a croquet stick after being struck in the head by a ball while atop a horse. "Even if Darryl was mad at you, you could be on suspension from the studio, he would invite you to Palm Springs—if you were a good player and he needed you on his team," remembered Jean Negulesco.

Childhood playmates of Darrylin and Susie Zanuck describe the household on the beach in Santa Monica as a permissive one. "The only rule," said one, "was that when we were shown movies in Darryl's den, we weren't allowed to touch the cigars in his humidor."

The Zanuck girls were described as boy-crazy. "They knew," said the old pal, "that they could have any guy in Los Angeles they wanted. That seemed to be the only thing they talked about with their best friend, Diane Disney, Walt's daughter. The number-one requirement, for some strange reason, was that Darryl and Virginia pushed for them to marry blond boys."

This prerequisite sent one suitor directly toward a bottle of peroxide.

And Richard Zanuck? "Poor Dick," said the former playmate. "His sisters totally ignored him, or teased him a lot. Darryl and Virginia were not what you would call attentive parents. Dick was a hellion as a kid, probably just so his parents would sit up and notice him, and so he could compete with his sisters."

Richard Zanuck conceded he was hard to handle. "My parents

---

*Schenck had actually been framed. He had acted on behalf of the major studios in dealing with labor racketeers Willie Bioff and George E. Browne, passing to them more than $1 million. When word of this leaked to an investigative committee, Schenck was found guilty of claiming $89,000 in expenses to earn his 1937 salary of $117,000. Included in those charges were $130 to fly his personal masseuse across country, $209 for a girl friend's car insurance, $40,000 for operation of his yacht (which he rented back to the studio for $25,000), and $53 for a mattress for his sister-in-law, Mrs. Nicholas Schenck. He served four months and five days in federal prison in Danbury, Connecticut, but was later granted a full pardon by President Truman.

tried to hide me from guests because I might punch somebody in the stomach or butt him with my head," he said.

The Sunday evenings he returned from Ric-Su-Dar, Darryl held regularly scheduled wrestling matches on the living room sofa with his son. The routine called for Darryl to land Dick in a tight headlock until the youngster would shout "Give!"

"He loved to win," noted the son. This competition started when Dick was eight.

"Then came this fateful night I'll never forget," Dick said. "I guess I was now fourteen and partly because of my father's inspiration, and because I was so eager to emulate him, I'd become a pretty good athlete. I'd also started playing around with girls, and I guess my father must have seen me doing—well, you know what randy kids get up to when they have a pretty chick around."

As this particular bout progressed, remembered Richard, "I could just feel, for the first time, that perhaps I was as strong as he was. Well, suddenly, I got him in a perfect headlock. And I began to squeeze. I played it just as he did, and I showed him no mercy.

"His face became all red, and his eyes were almost bulging out of their sockets, and I thought: 'Hey, this guy is going to die if he doesn't give up!' But I just kept squeezing, and I could hear a voice saying over and over what he had asked me to do over all these years. And it wasn't until he finally blurted out 'Give!' that I realized it had been my voice which had been giving him the ultimatum—and my God, I had beaten him! It gave me no pleasure at all, the moment I saw his face. This was my father, for Christ's sake, the invulnerable man! I just wished it had never happened.

"It was just the way he looked at me. It wasn't nice at all. I still loved my father, but suddenly, everything was different—and maybe I didn't admire him so much anymore."

Three days after his sixteenth birthday, Dick smashed his present from his parents, a brand new automobile, and nearly killed the occupants of the oncoming vehicle. Darryl's only disciplinary action in the matter was to ask Dick if he brushed his teeth properly.

Susan Zanuck's driving record was little better: when she was 18, she was sued for $25,000 by a man, Emerson A. Auld, who said he suffered permanent injuries when her car ran into his while she was riding with a girl friend. The case was settled out of court. Darryl frequently saw to it that his children were absolved of their shenanigans.

"For a while," Dick admitted later, "I was the wildest kid in the West—rough, rowdy, an all-American brat. Maybe I had a Napoleonic complex, but I kind of settled down when I was 21."

Academically, Richard Zanuck was an undistinguished student, though he did attend good schools: Harvard Military Academy in Los Angeles, considered several notches above Catholic school in the discipline department, and Stanford University in Menlo Park. Summers he worked at the studio, in the story department. For a time he envisioned becoming a writer and traveling the world from beach to beach with a pen and pad of paper. Dad would not have it, even though he himself had entered his profession behind a typewriter.

The son of Darryl F. Zanuck had to start higher. Once Darryl formed his independent company, DFZ Productions in 1956, he left Robert Jacks in charge of its small office at the studio. Jacks was Darryl's son-in-law, married to Darrylin. Richard, fresh out of Stanford, served as office assistant.

Three years later, Jacks was on location with DFZ when a quick decision had to be made at the home office regarding a property, so at the age of 23, Dick was tapped by his father to produce the film adaptation of the Meyer Levin novel *Compulsion*, a modern-day version of the 1924 Leopold and Loeb case about two handsome, spoiled, upper-crust kids (played by Bradford Dillman and Dean Stockwell), homosexual pals, who kill for kicks. Onscreen, their lawyer Jonathan Wilkes (played by Orson Welles) stole the show.

Offscreen, producer Richard Zanuck was sporting a DFZ-style mustache.

II

In 1935, Darryl Zanuck earned $650,000. It was estimated on Wall Street that for his company he earned 12 times that. Much of the fortune could be laid at the tap-dancing feet of a moppet star Darryl inherited from the Fox regime, the daughter of a Santa Monica bank teller, Shirley Temple.

By the time she turned four she had starred in a one-reel comedy in which she parodied popular movie stars of the day. Within a year after that appearance, she *was* the most popular star of the day. She also served as a playmate for Darrylin and Susan Zanuck.

Her curly-top look was imitated by little girls around the world, and her face adorned the commissary wall at the studio. The mural had been commissioned by Darryl; the painter was Alberto Varga, best known for sketching scantily clad cuties for the men's magazine *Esquire*. Having Varga render America's innocent sweetheart*—fully dressed, in mid-curtsey—was something of a joke. Darryl loved jokes.

The studio grew. To the original 150 acres of Fox Movietone lot there were added, commencing in 1940 and continuing through World War II, 280 acres. The purchases encompassed land originally belonging to the Westwood Hills Golf Course and used by Twentieth Century-Fox, in one of several incarnations, to serve as the French country town of Lourdes for the Easter perennial starring Jennifer Jones, *The Song of Bernadette*, about a young girl's visions of the Virgin Mary.

Zanuck's filmography included productions steeped in Americana: the biographical *Brigham Young, The Story of Alexander Graham Bell*, and *Wilson*; message pictures: *Pinky*, about black relations, *The Snake Pit*, about treatment of the institutionalized mentally ill (instigating legislation governing such treatment, as

*At a May 1988 press conference, an adult Shirley Temple revealed that while a child star she had been propositioned by a movie producer who exposed himself to her. (He did nothing else.) She would not name the culprit.

had Darryl's *I Am a Fugitive From a Chain Gang*), and *Gentleman's Agreement*, about anti-Semitism (inspired, it was said, by Darryl's own experience at the Los Angeles Athletic Club).

"To be where he was and to run the studio," said Negulesco, who made 22 films for Zanuck at Fox during the '40s and '50s, "he had to believe he was the best—and he was. No one ran a studio like he did. And to do that, he had to have an enormous conviction in himself. That he had, too.

"Whenever he gave me a script I didn't believe in, I wouldn't say, 'Darryl, I don't want to make it.' I'd say, 'It shouldn't be made.' He'd say that was his decision. Like every director, I have the conceit to say what would make a great picture. Well, I wish I did know. I tried not to be a 'yes-man' to him. I'd try to be logical. Most of the time, that worked.

"If you made a great picture, he was grateful, and happy for your luck. But if you didn't make a good picture and you tried to apologize for it, he'd say, 'What are you trying to do, be a hero? *I* made all the decisions. Believe me, if a picture's great, I'll take the credit. But if it's not, then let's try not to make the same mistakes next time.'

"What else impressed me," said Negulesco, who spoke in his London Mayfair flat and clearly missed the days of Darryl Zanuck, "was how much he cared for the studio. After a day's work, after dinner, he'd look at the pictures of the small studios, like Republic, to compare them to what we were making. He'd ask one of us, one of his boys, to see it with him. Why? He'd say, 'It's making money. Let's find out what people like.' He wanted to make pictures that would keep his studio on top.

"There was no greater studio head than Darryl. Louis B. Mayer had a great legend attached to him, but to me he was a sentimental genius. He never considered you a partner, as Darryl would, but as a child. After you'd have a few successes at Metro, you were taken care of the rest of your life. Fox got into that sort of arrangement too late. Twentieth was a family of workers. There was dignity to working there."

71

III

Fox did not have a Clark Gable, but it did have Tyrone Power, the only actor Zanuck would allow to share his office steam room.

Fox did not have a Jean Harlow, but it did have its blondes. The first was Alice Faye. Then came Betty Grable.

"During World War II, she became the GI's pinup girl," said Darryl in 1970. "But the amazing thing is that she kept on going—14 years at the top of the exhibitors' popularity poll. No one else has reigned, I would say, even half that time. Fourteen years—and then she dropped off totally. She had a great run for her money.

"We put her in a good role in one of our not top pictures. I don't remember what it was. And here the press did her—and us, as it turned out—a great favor. At that time, Alice Faye was under contract to me, a big star. These two were generally the same type, except that Betty was smaller, thinner and younger. One of the gossip columnists got what I think was a clever line, although it caused me a lot of trouble. She said that Alice, who was also very pale and very blonde—they were not look-alikes, but not un-look-alikes either—that Alice was fading and Zanuck was grooming Grable to take over her roles. Fading! Christ, all hell broke loose.

"Alice was a little bit hurt by it. It looked like we were putting her on the shelf. But she was a very nice girl. In time, she and Betty became quite friendly, and I used them together in a picture, the name of which—God, I can't remember."*

In the 1950s arrived one last Fox blonde, Marilyn Monroe.

"One day, a great friend of mine, Joseph M. Schenck, brought over to my home in Palm Springs this very beautiful girl who was also on the plump side," Zanuck recalled. "I didn't jump up and say, 'Oh, this is a great star,' or anything like that. Later on, Joe said, 'If you can work her in some role or something, some,

*Tin Pan Alley, 1940, distinguished only by the dancing of the Nicholas Brothers.

72

you know, supporting role, do so.' I did, but I didn't think that I had found any gold mine.

"Then came the calendar, with pictures of her nude. When it turned up, everybody said, 'Oh my God, how can we suppress it?' But one man, Harry Brand, who was in charge of publicity, said, 'This isn't going to kill her. It's going to make her. I'd like to get a piece of this business.' She ended up on ashtrays and on everything else, and we never got a penny of kickback on any of it. John Huston gave her a hell of a good role in *The Asphalt Jungle*. Jesus, she was good in it. I thought it must have been the magic of Huston, because I didn't think she had all that in her. But then I put her in *All About Eve* as George Sanders' aspiring-actress protégé, and she was an overnight sensation."

IV

Perhaps the most notable director to work under the Zanuck banner was John Ford, whose films unquestionably provided Zanuck's studio with its greatest prestige in its first decade. Two examples perfectly characterize Ford's populist style in dealing with everyday existences, as well as show off Twentieth's ability to produce realistic films within the realm of Hollywood drama. They were the 1940 *The Grapes of Wrath*, based on Steinbeck's monumental saga about drought-plagued Oklahoma farmers and their mass migration to California, and the 1941 *How Green Was My Valley*, an affectionate rendering of the Richard Llewellyn novel, linking several episodes about a Welsh coal-mining family by a single first-person narrator.

The latter won for Darryl the Oscar for Best Picture of the Year, and the statuette was to remain in his studio office for many years after his departure from the studio.

Came the Second World War, Zanuck treated it like another production. Before leaving the studio, he left his twenty Argentine polo ponies to West Point, and his three children to the care of Virginia. In his final weeks on the lot, Zanuck showed he was keenly aware of the taste of the times and ordered a slew of patriotic pictures with such titles as *Cadet Girls, A Yank in the RAF, Berlin Correspondent, To the Shores of Tripoli, Crash Dive,* and *Tonight We Raid Calais.* Even Zanuck's comics, the team that had once worked for Sennett, Stan Laurel and Oliver Hardy, donned uniforms, for *Great Guns*; as might be expected, the basic training adventures of these slapstick artists (the formula has been used over the following four decades) proved futile but funny.

Connections in Washington provided Zanuck with the commission of colonel in the Army Signal Corps before he left the studio in the command of his vice president and executive assistant, William Goetz. Goetz's tenure at the studio since being taken in nine years earlier in exchange for his father-in-law Louis B. Mayer's investment in the new company had proved unremarkable. Left to stand in the indelible shadow of Zanuck, Goetz nevertheless had been responsible for discovering two of the studio's greatest assets, Alice Faye and Betty Grable.

Zanuck's departure to serve his country at last paved the way for Goetz to join the board and be named production chief.

Darryl rendered some use to the war effort, and his influence was far-reaching. Shortly after Pearl Harbor, 37-year-old actor Henry Fonda, the star of *The Grapes of Wrath*, had enlisted as a sailor and reached boot camp in San Diego when, without explanation, he was collected by shore patrol and returned, post haste, to Los Angeles. The reason, Fonda eventually found out, was, he said, "because Darryl F. Fuck-it-all Zanuck had pull in Washington and demanded, 'I want Henry Fonda for a picture I'm planning. It's for the war effort and I need him.' And he had enough weight to swing it."

Holed up in a lavish suite at Claridge's in London to oversee production of training films, Colonel Zanuck did join a group of British commandos raiding Calais. In North Africa to do a documentary, Zanuck carried heavy artillery: a .45 automatic and a tommy gun. He took a pot shot when a German plane flew overhead, but did not think he made a hit.

When he returned to the studio after the war, on the other

hand, Zanuck took aim at Goetz and hit a bull's-eye. Goetz's offenses were substantial; while Darryl was at war, Goetz had redone Darryl's swimming pool, steam room, and barber shop, and had the Zanuck office repainted from the shade of Zanuck green (inspired, it was said, by the nail polish color of Darryl's mother, Louise Torpin Zanuck Norton) to Goetz blue. In addition, Goetz decorated the walls with pictures of baseball players, and bricked up the backdoor entrance that the starlets used for the four o'clock sex rituals.

Perhaps most unsettling to Zanuck was the fact that Goetz, in Darryl's absence, had at last distinguished himself. Under his leadership, the studio had turned out hits like the musical *Hello, Frisco, Hello,* in which Alice Faye sang what was to become her theme song, "You'll Never Know," a definitive war film, *Guadalcanal Diary,* and *The Song of Bernadette,* although Darryl was to claim that it was his editing savvy which saved that once-lugubrious inspirational drama from oblivion.

Darryl immediately ordered the walls returned to Zanuck green but, strangely, left the backdoor blocked. He also pronounced Goetz's upcoming productions "crap" that "make me vomit—and will make the public vomit too if we make the mistake of showing them."

In Darryl's eyes, Goetz had usurped too much power. In Goetz's own eyes, he was merely carrying out the duties of his office.

"When Darryl went to war," said Jean Negulesco, "Bill Goetz came in as head of the studio, and the studio ran beautifully. All the creative people liked Goetz, who was a gentleman, and they wrote to the New York office to see about having Goetz remain. Of course, those people who signed the letter, when Zanuck came back, were fired."

The difference was resolved. Goetz left the studio to form International Pictures on the Universal lot, bankrolled, as had been the case when Goetz came to Twentieth, by his father-in-law Louis B. Mayer.

Darryl's studio was again unquestionably his own.

V

Like Vitaphone for *The Jazz Singer* and the experimental Technicolor finale to *The House of Rothschild*, the new, the gimmicky held an attraction for Zanuck. He convinced Hollywood in the 1950s to fight the small-screen demon at home by offering the awkward but awesome CinemaScope, a photographic process that widened the size of the 35 mm movie picture which had remained fairly constant since Edison set the standard ratio to a width and height of 1.33:1 (4.3). CinemaScope shot the picture through a lens that squeezed the image, then reversed to project the image and unsqueeze it.

The process was not entirely new. William Fox had dabbled in similar showmanship as early as 1930, and called it Grandeur. The system, utilizing 70 mm film, projected the early John Wayne western *The Big Trail*, directed by Raoul Walsh, onto the screen of New York's Roxy Theatre. The public, still taken with talkies, was not much interested in the experiment to support another production in the technique, yet the precedent for widescreen had been set.

In 1951, Earl Sponible, who played a crucial role in converting the movies to sound, was serving as vice president of Twentieth's research division. At the studio lab in New York, Sponible experimented with expanding the size and scope of the cinematic image. Though he was to fail at this, Sponible did learn of some experiments in France by a Professor Henri Chretien and Chretien's subsequent development of an anamorphic lens that filmed and then projected, undistorted, an image wider than standard ratio. Twentieth took an option on the system—and its new ratio, 2.35:1—and dubbed it CinemaScope. It premiered at the Roxy September 16, 1953, turning a mundane Biblical movie, *The Robe*, into a spectacular event.

Still, the novelties had worn off. Very quickly, after overseeing his final production, *The Man in the Gray Flannel Suit*, a

drama starring Gregory Peck as a man caught in the conflict between a career and a personal life, Darryl Zanuck announced his
retirement from the Los Angeles movie colony, leaving behind
his studio and his wife.

"He felt he had been doing the same thing for 20 years. He
was bored," said his son Richard. "Though he would sometimes
take off for four weeks to ski or go hunting in Alaska or Africa, he
really felt he was a slave to his position and to his studio. He
needed a change."

The California life for Darryl ended in 1956.

VI

"My separation and break-up from Mrs. Zanuck came at the
same time as my divorce or break-up with Hollywood," said
Darryl Zanuck. "Both came to a head together. My mood was to
escape, to get away from the scene, the social scene, and everything connected with it."

The 54-year old Zanuck, still athletic (and on one drunken occasion publicly stripping to his waist and chinning himself at
Ciro's nightclub to prove it*), complained that in the 1956 New
Hollywood the shots were being called by agents and actors,
who had suddenly become independent producers. Worse, his
own salary was being eaten up by the I.R.S.

His solution was to take his mistress Bella Darvi, the first foreign beauty he would unsuccessfully attempt to make a star, and
move to Europe, where he formed his own production company. His link to his old studio, other than an annual $150,000
consultant's fee to be collected out of the Paris office, was that
his pictures would be distributed internationally by Fox. He

---

*A photograph and a legend both live because of the incident, though Zanuck
in the sobering morning-after sought to censor the story and the snapshot. The
gathering, which included Jimmy Durante, Jean Simmons, Mitzi Gaynor,
Linda Christian, and Ed Wynn, was to welcome home actress Terry Moore
and Susan Zanuck, after they had entertained GIs over Christmas. Susan was
attempting to launch a song-and-dance career.

would also need approval from the Fox board should any of his movies exceed a budget of $5 million.

"Darryl was a genius as a producer," said Jean Negulesco, "but in his personal life I think he was a naïve man, a little boy, really. For that reason, any time he transferred his attention from his professional life to his personal one, he got into trouble. With Bella Darvi and Juliette Greco and all that, he was no longer D.F.Z. He was nothing but a little naïve boy."

"He was faithful to these girls he picked up," said one member of Zanuck's Paris office staff. "There was certainly no professional courtesy extended on their part. But can you really blame these girls for carrying on behind the back of this aging Lothario?"

"There isn't one starlet that I ever had an affair with," Zanuck said in 1972. "Any indiscretions were with *people*, not actresses." Throughout his life, Zanuck insisted he was a model of rectitude, especially on the Fox lot. Curiously, he never removed the wedding band Virginia placed on his left hand in 1924.

In her 1983 autobiography *Has Corinne Been a Good Girl?* actress Corinne Calvet recounted one afternoon in Darryl Zanuck's office. "Dramatically, he turned on his heels and stood a few feet away from me with his erect penis standing out of his unzipped pants."

Calvet insists she remained a good girl and left Zanuck standing there, content with his exposure.

"My wife and I never commented on Darryl's women," said Jean Negulesco, recalling this period. "That was his business. It is still something we do not talk about."

"Oh, that Bella Darvi," chimed in Mrs. Negulesco.

"*La* Bella Darvi," said Negulesco. "The Polish girl."

"Poor Virginia," said Mrs. Negulesco.

"She was something," Negulesco had to concede.

"They both loved her," said Mrs. Negulesco, her head shaking.

Mrs. Negulesco was in no way speaking out of school. Nor was her observation meant in any way as a *double entendre*. The Negulescos, too, clearly loved Darryl and Virginia Zanuck. Yet so many others who worked on and off the Fox lot, affiliated with the Zanucks during this particular period, spoke of Bella Darvi serving as the sexual plaything of *both* Darryl and Virginia that it is difficult to dismiss the story as merely idle rumor. A similar circumstance surrounded a certain pretty boy Fox contract player in the early 1950s, who was later to become the handsome leading man on a couple of popular American television series in the 1960s and '70s. He was also said, by several inside sources, to have played bedmate to both the Zanucks. The actor was eventually to rise to such stature in the Hollywood community that questions addressed him on the matter would be unthinkable.

"She was a nice girl," Jean Negulesco said of Bella Darvi as he shrugged his shoulders. "Hmmmm."

"Oh, poor Virginia."

"She didn't want to be a star," insisted Negulesco. "Darryl and Virginia forced her. All she wanted was to have a small car. A little Cadillac. A convertible. Darryl kept saying, 'Her mouth. Her mouth. She'll be bigger than Garbo.' He adored her mouth."

HOLLYWOOD—A newly arrived French doll by the name of Bella Darvi, who has a voice like Marlene Dietrich, eyes like Simone Simon, and the allure of Corinne Calvet, is hitting Hollywood with the impact of TNT.

Discovered in Paris last year by the Darryl Zanucks, she was invited by the producer and his wife to pay them an American visit, then was handed a contract and a starring role in her first movie.

—Hearst wire service,
July 11, 1953

Bella Darvi (the studio-created surname was a joining of the monickers Darryl and Virginia, which gave rise to all sorts of evil speculation) was born Bayla Wegier in Sosnowiec, Poland, October 28, 1928. As an infant she was taken to Paris, and at age twelve was placed in a concentration camp. Released when Paris was liberated, she remained in the capital city where she made the acquaintance of prominent businessman Alban Cavalade. They were married in 1950 and participated in a highly active social life which revolved around automobile fashion shows in Cannes, Deauville, and Enghien.

By then the green-eyed beauty with the attractive mouth had gained the reputation as a playgirl, which did no good to the marriage. Through actor Alex D'Arcy, Bella Wegier, as she was then calling herself, was introduced to Virginia Zanuck at a Paris fashion show. Virginia in turn introduced Bella to Darryl. The affair began instantly, and resumed the following year in the Zanucks' Santa Monica beach house. Bella's trip to America had been at Virginia Zanuck's invitation.

"In January 1953, Darryl F. Zanuck suggested to Bella Darvi a film test, in CinemaScope," declared studio release #112753SRjl. The Fox publicity machine at her disposal, Bella was going to be made a star, or, as the release predicted, "the Cinderella of CinemaScope."

Her first film for Darryl's studio was director Samuel Fuller's undersea war adventure *Hell and High Water*, with Richard Widmark. She followed with the pre-Christian historical drama *The Egyptian*, as the Babylonian courtesan Nefer. Her eye-catching costumes were bare at the hips. There were also holes in the script. Marlon Brando was to have co-starred with her, only at the last minute his agent informed Zanuck that the brooding method actor could not stand Bella. Zanuck vowed Brando would never work for Fox, and studio contract player Edmund Purdom replaced him. The movie bombed. In 1955, Darvi made her last film in Hollywood, *The Racers*, with Kirk Douglas.

As her 1971 Associated Press obituary stated, "The reviews for her performances ranged from 'unconvincing,' through 'without magnetism or charm,' to 'contributing very little.' "

While still in Hollywood, Bella continued to live with the

Zanucks, and slept in the same bedroom as daughter Susan. It was Susan who forthrightly discussed her father's affair with Virginia, and pleaded that Bella be evicted. Susan's warnings were to no avail. When at last Virginia threw Darryl and Bella out of the house, simultaneous to D.Z.'s resignation from the studio, the illicit lovers moved to Europe. It was not to be an idyllic existence.

Bella, addicted to the charms of baccarat, racked up heavy losses at casinos all over the continent. "She is so sensationally unlucky that [in Monte Carlo] the Casino's hardened croupiers and dealers have begun to feel sorry for her," went one "What Ever Happened To. . . ?" news feature account. Always Bella would rely on Darryl to bail her out. When he could not save her, or would refuse to, she would pawn his gifts. On one occasion her losses were so great Darryl was forced to rely on his old acquaintance, industrialist Howard Hughes, to make good on Bella's $50,000 I.O.U. Darryl and Bella parted company in 1957, though aides insist Darryl, showing some loyalty, kept tabs on her.

Remaining an incurable gambler, Darvi by the early 1960s had sold off her jewels, furs, clothes, and furniture to cover herself financially. She went so far as to sell her two French poodles, and then began a series of suicide attempts: in Monaco in August 1962, at Roquebrune-Cap-Martin in April 1966, and in a Monte Carlo hotel in June 1968. September 17, 1971, in her Monte Carlo apartment, she opened the gas taps on her cooking stove for the last time.

The newspaper reports of her death took note of her gambling, made small mention of her movies, and led with the description, "a longtime friend of the film producer Darryl F. Zanuck."

VII

Juliette Greco, a brunette chanteuse with a fiery voice and matching temper, became Darryl's protégée after Bella Darvi.

81

Her story had been that of a Parisian street sparrow, arrested at age 14 for protesting the Gestapo's removal of her older sister for working on behalf of the Resistance. Released a penniless orphan at war's end, Greco moved to the Left Bank, became part of the local color for her habit of wearing men's outfits, and attached herself to a group of Existentialists who congregated in a coffee bar of their own, called Bar Vert. It was there that she sang, and came to the attention of the married couple, the actors Audrey Hepburn and Mel Ferrer. Ferrer was one of the stars of Darryl's independent production, an adaptation of Ernest Hemingway's *The Sun Also Rises*,* and the Ferrers both recommended Greco for a part while shooting took place in Mexico City. Darryl took to her immediately upon their introduction, though Juliette played it cool, as she continued to do for the remainder of the relationship. Zanuck remained absolutely besotted over her.

Once *The Sun Also Rises* was in the can, Darryl decided Juliette should have a starring role in one of his pictures. "But first, he thought she'd better have some acting experience," said a member of the crew. "He sent her to Germany, and had her star in some little picture there. God knows whatever became of that."

The starring role that Zanuck selected for her was in the adaptation of the Romain Gary novel, *The Roots of Heaven*, directed by John Huston and again starring Flynn, with Trevor Howard as an idealist attempting to prevent extinction of elephants in Equatorial Africa. Juliette insisted the filming take place in

---

*Directed by Henry King, *The Sun Also Rises* also starred Tyrone Power, Ava Gardner, and aging Errol Flynn, and a fresh-faced 27-year-old actor named Robert Evans, a former garment-industry executive (it was a family-owned business) who was to join Paramount in 1966 as vice president in charge of production, rising to executive vice president three years later. Recalling working for Zanuck exactly 30 years after the event, Evans said: "I was the first actor ever put under exclusive contract to him. No one on the movie wanted to give me an inch, and they all wanted me fired. Then, one day on the set, Darryl picked up a megaphone and announced: 'The kid stays on the picture. And anybody who doesn't like it can get the hell out.' " Evans added that, when the time came, he intended to call his autobiography *The Kid Stays in the Picture*.

Chad; it was a French protectorate. "It was the armpit of the earth," said a crew member.

"Darryl had made no secret of his infatuation with Juliette Greco," remembered John Huston, "but I realized fairly soon that it was a one-sided affair. She was openly rude to him and spoke slightingly of him behind his back."

Her third film for Zanuck was the nondescript successor to *Compulsion, Crack in the Mirror.* Set in a courtroom, the action shifted back and forth to detail the murder of a business associate who kills his older partner. Greco played the mistress of the old man.

During the making of *The Roots of Heaven*, Greco was the subject of a five-part series in *Paris Match*. "One of the installments, the second, I believe, was about Darryl," said Fred Hift, Twentieth Century-Fox European publicity director. A scholarly gentleman, Austrian born, Hift was keenly aware of the terrain, having luckily managed to stay one step ahead of Hitler as the 1930s darkened over Europe.

"Among the stories she told was that on some specific occasion Darryl'd been a great bore," said Hift. "Then she went on to talk about how he'd go to bed at ten after she'd gone to bed at nine, and how quiet he'd be. He'd tiptoe all around in his nightgown and look utterly ridiculous."

Hift added as an aside, "She did go to bed at nine, but not because she had to be on the set early the next morning. She'd go to bed at nine because he'd go to bed at ten. Then she'd wake up and stay out until three."

When the article was published, Hift recalled, Zanuck was furious. His anger was directed at Greco's singular comment about his sleeping costume.

"That bitch!" Darryl ranted. "She didn't understand. This was the latest fashion from Paris."

Hift recalled that Greco used to tell stories about the sexual favors she would perform for Zanuck. Once he made her undress in front of him and remove everything except for a strand of pearls.

"If she would do this and that to him," Hift said, "she could keep the pearls. She did them, and then when someone asked her why on earth, she answered, 'Well, they were nice pearls.' "

Darryl's sexual reputation around the Fox Paris office was that of a voyeur. "He liked to arrange things so he could watch," said a former employee.

What kinds of things? "You name it. Wild. With groups."

Greco and Zanuck quarreled publicly, which made for good newspaper copy. The mistress once let the master have it for having her followed.

"How dare she accuse me of that!" an enraged Zanuck told Fred Hift. "All I did was put a private detective on her for a few days."

After a final, particularly rancorous argument—her nickname for Darryl was "Mr. Fuck Machine"—Juliette walked out on Zanuck and began writing *Je Suis Comme Je Suis* (*I Am What I Am*), her autobiography. Zanuck's subsequent defamation of character suit prevented the book from seeing the light of day.

Through it all, Darryl remained love drunk. "He was a very busy man," said Jean Negulesco. "He had to go around carrying the dogs of Juliette Greco."

He also took to the bottle.

VIII

Irina Demich followed. "She was the nicest lady you could imagine," said Anne Head, who worked as a production assistant out of the Fox Paris office. "All she ever wanted to be was a housewife."

As Head remembered, "Darryl was very nice to each and every one of these women. They were all able to buy apartments or houses, even Juliette Greco. It wasn't a bad setup."

"The day Darryl called to say he was sending over Irina to the publicity office," said Fred Hift, "he called her the most exciting woman he'd met in his entire life."

The explanation had as much to do with Zanuck's love of the movies as with his appreciation of women.

"The search had been long to find an actress to play the one large female role in *The Longest Day*," said Hift, who described Demich as "not very pretty but extremely self-assured. There was nothing shy about Irina. Her background was Russian, very hearty."

The daughter of Russian émigrés, Irina—her professional name was changed to Demick—was an advertising model in Paris when she was introduced to Zanuck by Edward Leggewie, formerly Darryl's French teacher, promoted afterward to "handy man" in the Paris office of Twentieth Century-Fox. Viewed in the movies she made for Zanuck, Demick comes off stunningly attractive, yet lacking any star magic.

Hift kicked off the Demick publicity campaign by arranging an interview with *Paris Match*. "To be honest, Darryl set it up. Irina didn't want me at the interview, even though it was the first time she had ever met a member of the press one-on-one. She felt there wasn't that much she could be telling the fellow, and having me around would probably just make her nervous."

It was Hift who grew anxious: "About a week later, someone called my office to say there was a big spread on Irina in *Paris Match*, but had I by any chance read the story?"

A copy was brought to Hift. "It contained the most godawful, embarrassing things," he said. "The reporter would ask, 'Miss Demick, of all the men that you must meet, how did you come to end up with the most important motion-picture producer in the world?' And she said something like, 'I went to this cocktail party and this creepy old man started asking me out on dates, and I said, "O.K., I'll go out with you," and then he said, "I've got this picture I'm making called *The Longest Day*, and you'd be perfect for it," and I said, "Oh, yeah. Sure. I've heard this before." He was so ugly and obnoxious, but he did offer me a part in the movie, so I thought, "What the hell, I've nothing to lose." ' "

Hift waited for Zanuck to ring. "Darryl was a Francophile and very sensitive to his image in France," said Hift. As expected, the call came through.

"Isn't it fantastic?" said Zanuck. "Look at the space they gave her."

"Darryl couldn't speak French very well," said Hift, "but he could read the language. Still, he insisted the write-up was wonderful. 'She's so clever,' he kept saying. He was so blinded by love."

Irina played a Resistance fighter in *The Longest Day*, and to raise her profile, Darryl dispatched her on an international publicity tour on behalf of the film. "It was my job," said a veteran New York publicist, "to see to it that whatever Darryl Zanuck wanted, I got him. Concerning *The Longest Day*, it was my special assignment to make Irina Demick the Pia Zadora of her day."

As a lover, Zanuck was, not unexpectedly, possessive. "I was told by Darryl to get to Rome because there was about to be filmed the movie scene to end all scenes," said Fred Hift. The picture was *The Visit*, in which the vastly wealthy Ingrid Bergman returns to the small town where as a youth she had been seduced and driven into prostitution. Anthony Quinn played the villain.

"Irina was to do a nude swimming scene in the picture," said Hift, "in which she was to come out of the pool and walk by some bushes that were going to hide her. To Zanuck this was the event of a lifetime, and I was summoned from Paris to bear witness to this spectacle. He'd ordered everyone unnecessary to the shot off the set, except for a photographer. Then he hired hundreds of police to keep away any intruders."

When the scene was completed, Zanuck commandeered the roll of film and handed it to Hift. "He was hysterical," Hift recalled, "absolutely irrational."

"You are to put this in a vault," Zanuck instructed. "And if any of this ever comes out, I will hold you personally responsible."

Hift returned to Paris, found a temperature-controlled locker in the photography lab of the Fox office, then nonchalantly forgot the film roll and the incident.

Two months later, Seymour Poe in Fox's New York headquarters contacted Hift with a kindly warning. "Look," said Poe, "you are about to receive a phone call from Rome. It'll be Zanuck. Whatever you do, don't provoke him or he'll probably fire you. Just listen to what he has to say and more than likely it will blow over."

"I never loved Darryl Zanuck," Hift thought as he envisioned his head on the chopping block. Zanuck put through the call.

"You've betrayed me!" screamed Zanuck, who proceeded to call Hift every name in the book. "How much did you make off of this!?"

As best Hift could decipher from Zanuck's stream of obscenities, there was a newspaper in Grenoble, Switzerland, which had been seen by a friend of Irina's mother, who told the mother, who told Irina's sister, who told Irina, who told Zanuck. The paper had allegedly printed a nude photograph of Irina.

"That's impossible," Hift told Zanuck.

"You're lying," was Zanuck's retort.

Hift dutifully rang the editor of *The Grenoble Post*. "The man was very annoyed," said Hift. He told me, 'We do not print nude pictures.' "

There *had* been a photograph printed of Irina, the editor volunteered. She was pictured sunbathing, with a towel covering her up to the neck. At most one could see the outline of her body.

"A Fox man was sent to Grenoble just to pick up a copy," said Hift, who was then ordered by Zanuck to fly it and the developed roll of film to Rome personally.

"I met Darryl in his hotel room, where he greeted me in his robe. I could already read the expression on his face. He hugged me and said, 'That stupid woman.' All was forgiven. Then he asked for the envelope and said, 'Now, let me see what still you have.' "

Hift produced the contact sheet with the 36 shots. "The most you could see, out of all of them, was one breast hanging out. Darryl took the whole thing over to the window so he could get a better look. He held it up to the light, rolled the cigar around in his mouth, and declared, 'These are terrific. Which do you like?' "

Hift had a look, then told Zanuck, "This one is nice, Darryl," and Zanuck inspected it closely.

"Yeah," said Zanuck approvingly. "Can you get it on the front page of *France Soir?*"

IX

RICHARD ZANUCK TO WED STARLET

HOLLYWOOD, Nov. 21.—It was a very sentimental evening last night, when Mrs. Darryl Zanuck announced the coming marriage of her only son, Richard, to beautiful Lili Gentle, young screen star from Alabama.

Lili came here from Alabama a year ago and was immediately called star material by Twentieth Century-Fox. She just finished the lead opposite Tommy Sands in *Sing, Boy, Sing*. She also played the lead in *Young and Dangerous* and an ingenue role with Jayne Mansfield in *Will Success Spoil Rock Hunter?*

Lili is 18 and Dick is 24 and an independent film producer with his father. Darryl himself was unable to be here because of a location trip he is making with *Roots of Heaven*, his next picture.

—Louella O. Parsons,
November 21, 1957

There's one thing that young people like Richard Zanuck (who's 24) are experts on. That's young people.

Sitting at lunch at "21" his 19-year old bride who's expecting in September, behind a small mustache very much like his father, Darryl Zanuck's, he spoke glibly of Hollywood croquet games, and of private planes, and when he mentioned a figure like "one" or "two," he meant $1,000,000 or $2,000,000.

"One thing Hollywood can do is present the younger generation more mature subjects," Dick Zanuck said. "If the only pictures we make are about werewolves, the teen-agers will go but they want something better."

—Earl Wilson,
March 10, 1959

At the time *Compulsion* was announced, a press conference was held on the Twentieth Century-Fox lot in Westwood. The questions stayed polite, to the point of being obsequious.

Publicist Fred Hift, who assisted in coordinating the morning event, had dealt with Darryl Zanuck's brand of bluntness firsthand, and felt perfectly comfortable stepping forward with an obvious—yet, given the egos, uncomfortable—question of his own.

"Richard," Hift asked the young star of the hour in front of the assemblage, "don't you find it difficult to operate in the shadow of your father?"

An audible gasp spread through both the press corps and the executives of the studio. To his credit, thought Hift, Dick Zanuck answered quickly.

"Yes, of course," said Richard. "I'm constantly measured against Dad. And in such a situation it's hard to find an identity of my own."

X

"In the early 1960s, Darryl was concerned while he was in Europe making what he knew was going to be the most important picture of his career, *The Longest Day*," said Fred Hift. Hift served as unit publicist on Darryl's all-star recreation of the D-Day invasion of Normandy, based on the book by Cornelius Ryan. The title came from German Field Marshal Rommel, who ordered six-million mines and abstingers on every beach, in every gulley, and along every cliff of that portion of the English Channel.

"Not a single Englander or American shall reach the shore, not a single Englander or American shall set foot on the beaches," said Rommel. "The first 24 hours of the invasion will be decisive. For the allies as well as Germany, it will be the longest day."

Across the ocean, Fox executives in New York were determined *The Longest Day* would not successfully invade American movie theatres.

"The New York office did not believe in the film. Period," said Fred Hift. "It was in black and white, for starters, and then they thought, 'Who cares about World War II at this late date?'"

Richard Zanuck, poised at the studio as his father's representative, warned D.Z. that his career was being viewed as on the skids. Stories had circulated about Zanuck's down-and-out condition following the departure of Juliette Greco, and his bouts with the bottle. The low opinion of Zanuck was also coupled with the necessity for a scapegoat; Fox had by this juncture embarked on a picture called *Cleopatra* that was already afloat in a sea of red ink.

Zanuck instructed Hift to fly from the Fox Paris office to New York and to speak to Charles Einfeld, vice president in charge of advertising, publicity, and exploitation. Hift's sole mission was to find out what the advertising campaign would be for *The Longest Day*.

"When I got to New York, Charles said, 'Come back tomorrow, and I'll show you the campaign then,'" Hift recalled. The next day, Hift showed up as planned and was taken to a conference room with the entire advertising staff. At the front of the room stood an easel covered with a cloth, which Einfeld removed when he entered.

Underneath was a poster on which were drawn several wavy lines to denote the English Channel, and between them, someone had added little toy boats. "Lots of them," said Hift, "the sort a child would draw of ships in a bathtub. This was to be the campaign? I didn't say anything, mostly because I couldn't believe what I saw, although I waited until everyone on the staff had left the room. That's when I said, 'Charlie, there's no way I can take that back to Darryl.' "

Einfeld became enraged. "You're just the goddam errand boy," he shouted.

"Fine," Hift replied. "It's your funeral."

Hift took the poster from the easel and transported it overseas to the Studio Boulogne in France, where Darryl was working. The mogul was eagerly awaiting what New York had prepared.

"He was walking around his desk, puffing his cigar, rolling it around his mouth as he always did," said Hift.

"You've got the campaign?" Zanuck asked.

"I do," said Hift.

"Is it any good?"

Hift placed the poster in the window ledge, so Darryl could see it properly in the sunlight. "This," he told his boss, "is to be your campaign for *The Longest Day*."

Now it was Zanuck's turn to turn silent. He rolled the cigar around his mouth for several moments, then smacked his upper lip with his tongue. The words came out of his mouth calmly and precisely.

"Fred, remind me, when I become President of Fox, the first person I fire is Charlie Einfeld."*

XI

Joseph L. Mankiewicz, the sturdiest hand to stir the *Cleopatra* stew, said that the Egyptian epic "was conceived in a state of emergency, and wound up in a blind panic." In retrospect, he called it, "The three toughest pictures I ever made."

At a 1986 Columbia University salute to Mankiewicz, the filmmaker's nephew, Washington journalist Frank Mankiewicz, provided the final and most accurate assessment of what was once the most publicized, talked about, and gossiped-about pro-

*He did.

duction in the history of Hollywood. Confidentially, Frank said to the critic Judith Crist, "I call *Cleopatra* the Eisenhower movie. The more years that go by, the better it begins to look."

In 1958, producer Walter Wanger originally pitched the project of adapting Italian novelist Carlo Mario Franzero's *The Life and Times of Cleopatra* to Fox president Buddy Adler, Darryl's personal choice as successor. The proposal called for a script from Nigel Bachin, a budget of $2 million, and Joan Collins in the lead. The casting seems amusing only in light of the actress's later success as the bitch-goddess in the late 1970s television soap *Dynasty*.

"In Hollywood, no one was interested in Joan after 1957," said her former husband, Anthony Newley, in 1985. "It was like, 'Thank you very much, but go away,' " he said. "She was a joke."

Fox's casting department submitted the name of Dana Wynter, although by this time Wanger had elicited the services of director Rouben Mamoulian, and Mamoulian had set his sights on someone else altogether, Elizabeth Taylor. The decision could not have come at a worse moment; the raven-haired, violet-eyed beauty, who had been an M-G-M star since the age of 11, was something of a pariah for having broken up the perfect Hollywood marriage of singer Eddie Fisher and actress Debbie Reynolds. Fisher became Taylor's fourth husband,* and the scarlet-woman reputation, the studio feared, could keep American women from the box-office. Mamoulian stood firm. He was convinced Taylor would prove a boon to the movie.

"I didn't care for the script," said Mamoulian. "I was interested only in the principle. I didn't want another movie of battles, armies, and a naked dame on a couch."

The first hitch arrived, thanks to Taylor's agent, Kurt Frings, who told Fox that his client would require $1 million for services to be rendered. As the salary would have gobbled half the picture's budget, Fox replied No Deal.

*The previous three had been hotelier Nick Hilton, actor Michael Wilding, and showman Mike Todd (1907-1958).

"I called Elizabeth and she started to cry," said Wanger, informing the actress that the studio did not think she was worth seven figures. Between tears she obviously was willing to barter. How about if she did *Cleopatra* for $750,000, against a percentage of seven-and-a-half of the box-office gross?

Buddy Adler would go no higher than $600,000. Wanger was too embarrassed to tell her, so in the end Taylor got the $750,000 plus the percentage, plus a guarantee of $50,000 per week should the picture go into overtime. Another major chunk of money would arrive in the form of a royalty as *Cleopatra* was to be shot in Todd-AO, a patented widescreen process several steps more advanced than CinemaScope, developed by American Optical and Taylor's late husband, producer Mike Todd. His ownership of Todd-AO had been left to Taylor in the Todd will.

Wanger and Mamoulian hired Stephen Boyd as Marc Antony and Peter Finch as Julius Caesar, and the director flew to Rome and ordered sets. Once they were built, the studio claimed dissatisfaction with the results and summoned the production back to Hollywood. The edict was short-lived.

Phase Two called for *Cleopatra* to film interiors in London and exteriors in Rome. The reason for the relocation: Elizabeth Taylor's tax situation. By shooting abroad, her Swiss corporation, MCL Films, S.A., could skirt certain American taxes.

Mamoulian, who was having less to say in these matters, opposed London, warning that Fox "would be taking a chance with the lousy English climate and Miss Taylor's health. She was always catching cold."

She caught pneumonia. It developed out of an abscessed tooth, which a dentist yanked, though not until the infection had spread to the protective membrane shielding Elizabeth Taylor's brain. A bout with influenza graduated into staphylococcus pneumonia, inflaming both lungs. Elizabeth Taylor's health, and her teetering on the brink of death, made headlines.

Mamoulian and company attempted to shoot around her, only to realize her presence was required in nearly every scene. "We just sat around the studio twiddling our thumbs and around four o'clock . . . end up at the bar," said Peter Finch. "It was a very sad business."

Fortunately there was a happy ending to this chapter. The star had regained her health in time to make a triumphant acceptance of an Academy Award for her role as the call girl in the stilted M-G-M adaptation of the John O'Hara novel *Butterfield 8*. The win, and the conquest of the illness, erased the blight on the Taylor name in the public's mind.

It also hiked her movie salary.

XII

By the time *Cleopatra* entered her sixteenth month of production, $7 million had been spent and not so much as one reel of usable footage had been created.

Rouben Mamoulian and the picture parted company January 3, 1961. Among replacement directors to be sought was Alfred Hitchcock, who informed producer Wanger that he was busy, and intended to film a suspense story based on a work by Daphne du Maurier entitled *The Birds*.

Spyros Skouras* contacted Joseph L. Mankiewicz while the Oscar-winning screenwriter and director of *A Letter to Three Wives* and *All About Eve* was vacationing in the Florida Keys. The studio head assured Mankiewicz that completing *Cleo* would require only 15 weeks, and agreed that Fox would pay Figaro, a production entity owned jointly by Mankiewicz and NBC, $3 million in order to spring the director from an existing exclusive contract.

Mankiewicz tossed out Mamoulian's sets and script and started from scratch, and Elizabeth Taylor renegotiated her contract. She would now receive $1 million against 10 percent of the gross and a new proviso: that the picture shoot in Hollywood.

*President of Fox since 1942, when he replaced the imprisoned Joe Schenck.

The star now decided she wanted to buy a home in California and play housewife to Eddie Fisher.

She lost on that second point.

Mankiewicz, a robust scholar, wanted Italy, for authenticity, and Fox wanted Italy, for savings. Italian labor was cheaper, although as Skouras realized too late: "We didn't make an Italian picture. We made an American picture in Italy. Ninety technicians we sent by jet, with hotel accommodations and living expenses for all of them."

Another wrinkle in the per-diem costs was the price of the catering on the picture. As was discovered during later investigations, Skouras's own catering company was supplying the *Cleo* crew with its food, then double-billing the expenses back to Twentieth Century-Fox.

Stephen Boyd and Peter Finch were handed exit visas. Scriptwriters were hired and their work ignored. Mankiewicz requested Lawrence Durrell and he got him, only to discover that the novelist who had turned out exquisite prose for his *The Alexandria Quartet* was a neophyte when it came to screenwriting. Sidney Buchman next outlined a plot for *Cleopatra* (Mankiewicz's strong literary background came to the fore; the unwieldy finished product still reflects heavy reliance on Shaw and Shakespeare). Ronald MacDougal then fleshed out the story, to 350 pages. Producer Wanger and Mankiewicz trimmed the MacDougal draft to 220. One page of script usually adds up to one minute of screen time. *Cleo*'s eventual running time was a seat-straining 243 minutes.

Casting Richard Burton as Antony was Mankiewicz's idea. At the time the Welshman was starring as King Arthur on Broadway opposite Julie Andrews' Queen Guenevere in *Camelot*. Fox spent $50,000 to break his stage contract, and at his farewell party, a drunken Burton vowed to his Broadway male cronies, "Within 48 hours I am going to bring Cleopatra to my knees."

Rex Harrison was cast as Julius Caesar after Laurence Olivier passed on the offer. Then the rains came—two months' worth.

Darryl Zanuck borrowed Burton for *The Longest Day*, and learned from the actor of the troubles on *Cleopatra*. Fox was losing $40,000 to $75,000 a day in Rome on account of bad weather. Delaying production would have increased the expenditures further. Asking Elizabeth Taylor to postpone her role until the sun came out the following spring was not a cheap proposition. Her price would have been another million. The movie marched ahead.

"Skouras," said Fox head of production Peter Levathes, "shot the works. He gave Mankiewicz and Wanger carte blanche. All he told them was to make the greatest picture that has ever been made. Mankiewicz is a creative man and he had no restraints on him, but he is no financial genius. I remember, he wanted to go to Egypt for a confrontation scene, where the two armies would just look at each other. He said it would cost only $100,000. It would cost you that just to assemble the cast and serve coffee!"

Mankiewicz rewrote MacDougal's script by night and shot by day. He went from a six- to a five-day week, in order to turn out script pages on weekends. So he wouldn't bite his nails, he wrote in longhand.

Because of the haphazardness of the ordeal, *Cleopatra* could not be shot in sequence. "None of the savings that motion-picture logistics permit were available to him," noted an observer. "That was the biggest single reason for the expense."*

In the heat of *Cleopatra's* post-production, following exposure of 700,000 feet—120 miles—of film, Mankiewicz blamed the crux of the project's difficulties on an edict issued in Rome during shooting: "The girl's on salary—let's get something on film."

"If they had first let me finish the script," said Mankiewicz, "it wouldn't have cost nearly as much. Whose fault was it? I can't

---

*"I told Skouras I wasn't going to be the fall guy," Mankiewicz said at his Bedford Hills New York home in 1981, a few days after *Time* magazine published a story on the costly movie disaster *Heaven's Gate*. By its own calculations—old dollars vs. new—the newsmagazine figured that *Cleopatra* still remained the most expensive movie ever made. In 1980 dollars, *Cleopatra* cost $110.6 million.

name any one person, or any group. It was the absence of knowledge edgeable motion picture administration."

XIII

At the three-hour May 1962 stockholders' meeting of Twentieth Century-Fox, the biggest round of applause came when Fox Chief Executive Officer Spyros Skouras uttered the line, "By next week, the scenes with Elizabeth Taylor will be taken."

The studio's revenues the previous year were $117,428,059, off slightly from 1960's $118,356,457. But in 1961, Fox suffered an operating loss of $22,532,084, as opposed to a $2,868,113 writeoff the preceding 12 months.

And so, another head to roll as a result of *Cleopatra* was that of Spyros Skouras, who in one of several last-ditch attempts to save the studio and his job clandestinely had contacted Howard Hughes about buying into the company. Hughes arrived in a beat-up pickup truck and met Skouras at midnight on the Fox lot. The studio chief emerged from the shadows and scared off Hughes, who in the first place could not make head or tail out of the nervous Greek-born Skouras's heavy accent. No deal was consummated.

Skouras's stockholders by this point had experienced their fill of stories about *Cleopatra*, especially of its escalating costs and of the romance between Elizabeth Taylor and Richard Burton, which made daily headlines around the world. What they had not experienced was a look at the movie. There was still no movie to show. Some wiseacre at the meeting placed Elizabeth Taylor's name in nomination to the Board of Directors.

Darryl Zanuck, meanwhile, contemplated buying back *The Longest Day*, as the current Fox administration refused to see it as a reserved-seat, roadshow production, and wanted instead to force it into saturation bookings to earn fast money. Darryl contacted Jack Warner as a backup distributor. The two moguls maintained a friendly rivalry over the years; in 1961 when Richard Zanuck's production of *The Chapman Report*, a drama based on the Kinsey Report's findings about suburban sex, was canceled by Fox, Darryl moved it over to Warners in a maneuver so swift it impressed Richard.

"I thought, Jesus, he'll go absolutely berserk," said Richard when Skouras and Peter Levathes put the red light to the movie.

"But he was very calm," said Richard. "Absolutely ice cold. I've never heard him like that. . . . It was like he was saying, 'They'll never know what hit them.'"

XIV

With his mistreatment over *The Longest Day* and *Cleopatra's* plundering of Fox's resources, Darryl Zanuck in spring of 1962 was concerned over his personal fortunes. At stake was not only his considerable pride but, as majority stockholder, his 280,000 shares in the Twentieth Century-Fox Film Corporation.

Hollywood for some months had been rife with rumors of Skouras's imminent forced retirement, or else a shutting down of Twentieth Century-Fox altogether.

"[Board member] John Loeb wanted to liquidate the company right then and there," recalled Charles M. Lewis, a Manhattan-based film industry analyst and stockbroker who was also to play a key role in the fortunes of Fox in the early 1970s.

Lewis, then related by marriage to theatre-chain owner Harry Brandt, remembered in 1962 Spyros Skouras's approaching Brandt—a major Fox stockholder—with the plea to keep him in power. Brandt feared that if the company went under, so would he, given the overabundance of shares he held. Brandt turned a deaf ear to Skouras.

"It was then decided," said Lewis, "that the one man qualified to bring the company back to where it was, was the same man who had founded the company. So we contacted Darryl, and we presented a deal: There were to be no girlfriends involved. Just get the company back to functioning properly, and there would also be a place for Dickie in the corporation."

Zanuck responded with a memo dictated June 6, 1962.

In part, it said:

"If and when Spyros decided that he wanted to step out of the presidency, I would present the following concrete recommendations based on the industry as it exists today. Whether or not I become the President is actually immaterial. . . . I would close down the studio and only complete the films that are either already in production or committed for. . . . I would sell the studio to the Fox Realty Company or a third party.

"During the transition period, the President of Fox, who should also be in my opinion, the Chief Producer, would take four or even six months to not only complete and edit the films already in production, but to weed out the misfits and to study story properties and make future constructive production plans. . . . I firmly do not believe that our world grosses will suffer radically even if we do not start another picture in the next six or eight months. . . ."

Thus the stage was set for Richard Zanuck's eventual shutdown of the studio, and Darryl moved closer to his seat of power. His lawyer in New York, Arnold Grant, alerted Zanuck in Paris that Skouras would be out as soon as the next board meeting, to be temporarily replaced by the Chairman of the Fox board, Judge Samuel Rosenman. Zanuck flew to New York a few days later and met with board member Robert Lehman and Rosenman, only to discover they had no idea or intention of returning him to the president's chair, or even one on the board of directors.

Zanuck came home to Paris and fired off a cable to the board, first running it past his attorney. Grant suggested Darryl delete his original opening line, "I do not seek the Presidency of Twentieth Century-Fox."

The full text was published in newspapers, which served to alert Skouras and the board that Zanuck might be considering a proxy fight. To bolster its flanks, the Zanuck side also enlisted heavyweight attorney Louis Nizer; the maneuver also prevented Skouras from hiring Nizer. As it so happened, the battle would be less difficult than Zanuck had imagined.

The former president was put through his paces by a selection committee. They interrogated Zanuck on his publicized drinking bouts after the departure of Irina Demick, as well as his mistresses in general, specifically what they had cost the company. The line of questioning may have seemed overly personal, but it was done merely as a sop to satisfy a small faction of anti-Zanuck soldiers.

Days later, after a protracted debate, Zanuck passed muster. His first order was to call Richard in California and demand that he close the studio.

Richard obediently followed orders.

PART THREE

I

"Fox pictures were like Darryl F. Zanuck: clean and sharply focused," said David Brown, looking back. "They weren't like Metro pictures. Those were fuzzy and lush."

Brown had been with Fox since 1952, when Darryl Zanuck personally hired him on the East Coast to serve as Fox story editor.

"At the time," said Brown, "Fox had 28 producers under contract, almost as many directors, a full roster of stars, contract players, a full symphony orchestra under Alfred Newman, who composed the Fox logo theme, which is hardly heard anymore, and writers who were guaranteed 40 weeks work and 12 weeks vacation."

The 1950s, Brown suggested, marked the last hurrah for the major studios, which had been swiftly losing ground since a 1948 Sherman Anti-Trust decision forced movie companies to sell off their theatre chains. Fox, like the others, was deeply affected by the law. It had owned 30 first-run houses in major cities, guaranteeing Fox movies and only Fox movies would play such venues. As such, Fox and the studios had formed an illegal trust. (Fox owned one more theatre than RKO and six more than M-G-M, but five fewer than both Paramount and Warner Bros.)

Then there was television. By 1951, 3,000 of the nation's movie theatres closed. The world built by men like William Fox was hanging on by a thread.

"When I arrived in Hollywood," said Brown, "the heads of the studios were D.F.Z. at Fox, Jack Warner, Thalberg was gone and Dore Schary, who had been at RKO, was at M-G-M, D.H. Duran was at Paramount, and Universal was not yet owned by M.C.A. and run by William Goetz. These men were there for the rest of their working lives. There was no such thing then as a three-year contract."

Brown's job was "to negotiate for acquisition of literary properties, usually sending a memo to Zanuck saying if you really want, say, [the William Inge stage drama] *Picnic*, it will cost you $250,000 plus ten percent of the gross after breakeven, and he'd either say go ahead or not. Then I'd make the deal, with an agent, Irving Lazar, whomever. Today all that is handled by a business affairs person, who is usually very skilled in knowing the going rates of properties but probably isn't qualified to assess the true value of something."

When Darryl Zanuck left for Europe in 1956 and Richard Zanuck remained in California as the West Coast contact for the family's independent producing company, David Brown sat at the studio in a liaison position between the Zanucks and the new President of Fox. The first man to serve that office after Darryl was Buddy Adler, a producer whose string of prestige films included the Oscar-winning Columbia picture *From Here to Eternity*, based on the novel by James Jones. For Fox he had spun gold out of *Bus Stop*, *Anastasia*, and the film adaptation of Rogers and Hammerstein's stage landmark *South Pacific*, an egregious movie musical that nevertheless generated immense profits and paved the way for the stage authors to sell the studio *The Sound of Music*.

Adler was considered more of an artisan than administrator, and the pressures of the job buried him. He died of cancer July 12, 1960. "A date I remember as well as I remember Pearl Harbor," said David Brown. It was Adler who ratified the remake of *Cleopatra*, an idea that also had passed through the story department of David Brown.

"Meanwhile, the studio went through some dizzying changes," said Brown. Robert Goldstein, head of the studio's European operations, was appointed President.

"He resigned, as I recall," said David Brown.

"He was *fired*," said Richard Zanuck.

The next choice was Peter Lavathes, former head of the Fox television division. Like Fox Chairman of the Board Spyros Skouras, Levathes was Greek; their background was reflected in their film slate, which included such titles as *It Happened in Athens* and *The 300 Spartans*. It was Levathes who was sitting at the helm in 1962 when Darryl Zanuck was presented his advertising campaign for *The Longest Day*. The list of possibilities to replace the doomed Levathes included television executive James Aubrey and producers Mike Frankovich and Otto Preminger.

"Utterly idiotic recommendations," fumed Darryl Zanuck. "I frankly wanted to vomit."

"Frankly, *I* thought I should have been made head of the studio myself," said David Brown, "considering the competition at that time." The jockeying for top position landed Brown in a lame-duck situation. "I found it very difficult to get any projects going. They weren't particularly welcome."

Richard Zanuck, himself stuck in limbo, was sitting on the West Coast, an inopportune location considering that the power had shifted to the East. Brown requested and received a transfer out of the story department. Professionally, he preferred to sit out his contract in a producer's post; socially, he and Richard Zanuck remained on excellent terms.

"Dick used to read my scripts and give me what moral backing he could," said Brown.

Before D.F.Z.'s return to the company in 1962, [Dick and I] used to have lunch in the [San Fernando] Valley together, so they wouldn't think we were allies against management. We were."

Brown divulged this secret to Spyros Skouras, "And in his lovable way he made my opinion known to the executives. I was supposed to produce *Something's Got to Give* which was to star Marilyn Monroe. Instead, they gave the picture to Henry Weinstein, who was a friend of Marilyn's analyst."

Then D.F.Z. returned to Fox. The first order, carried out by Richard, was to shut down the studio and concentrate on saving

Cleopatra. By this time *The Longest Day* was on its way to becoming the highest-grossing black-and-white film in history, a record it retains. Despite that, at the time of its original release its box-office looked to be swallowed up by the Elizabeth Taylor-Richard Burton history lesson about Egypt and Rome.

Richard Zanuck's installation as head of production was so swift and sudden that the studio publicity department did not have a formal photographic portrait of him to accompany announcement of his position.

"So you know what Richard gave them?" recalled an old–time Fox publicist. "His high school senior photo."

Richard Zanuck recalled the period as "unpleasant."

"The only thing that was shooting was *Cleopatra*, and there was nothing. No television. Nothing," he told journalist Anthony Haden-Guest. "And there was a big studio. Thousands of employees. And we came to the conclusion that the only thing to do under these circustances—and this was after reading about 70 screenplays that had been prepared—was to shut the studio down. And fire everybody."

Included on the hit list was David Brown, who made tracks back to the literary world in New York. He established the hardcover division of the New American Library, which published Ian Fleming's British novels about secret-intelligence agent James Bond for the first time in the United States, and he saw his third wife Helen Gurley Brown through two great successes. Her first was the saucy handbook for young women, *Sex and the Single Girl*; the other, her editorship of the newly revamped *Cosmopolitan*, a slick monthly magazine aimed at her reading audience.

HELEN'S BOOK WAS A SHOCK TO HER MOTHER

Mrs. Brown, a chic, young-looking 40, waited 36 years for the right man. Her husband, David, 46, is a 20th Century-Fox producer who was twice divorced.

"It's still a love affair between us," said Mrs. Brown in a soft, cultured voice, "but a very mature love affair.

"David put me up to writing the book, so to speak. I was out of town visiting my sister, and he came across carbon copies of letters I had written to other men. (Isn't that egotistical—I saved my letters to them, but I didn't save their letters to me?)

"They were letters I had written before I was married—not really love letters. Anyway, David was very pleased and when I came home, he said: 'You really write very nicely.'

"We had talked about how deprecating most articles about single women have been, and after about six months he said I ought to write about single women."

After a year of pounding a typewriter on weekends and holidays at their Mediterranean-style home over-looking the Pacific, Mrs. Brown came up with "The Unmarried Women's Guide to Men, Careers, the Apartment, Diet, Fashion, Money and Men"—or "Sex and the Single Girl."

—Art Berman in *The Los Angeles Times,*
June 24, 1962

David Brown was credited with thinking up the zippy book title. He also, every month, wrote the cover blurbs for his wife's magazine, which would be messengered back and forth from her office to his at Fox in New York, where the Browns lived permanently and enjoyed their status as a high-profile celebrity couple.

II

"The Hollywood gossip was that we would never open again," said Richard, "that what we were doing was just window dressing, and that the real plan was to close the studio down and develop the whole property. My father never came to the studio. He spent time primarily in Paris."

D.F.Z.'s European headquarters were in a penthouse suite at the Georges V. In New York, he called the Plaza Hotel home. Richard Zanuck lived at the beach in Santa Monica, though most of his hours were spent on the Westwood lot. In fact, the studio was to remain shuttered for eight months.

"I called everyone in who had served over ten years and, personally, you know, let them go," Richard recalled. "I just kept some janitors and a handful of people to develop screen-plays."

One was a property that Henry Klinger, a New York story editor since the days of Willian Fox, had purchased, *The Sound of Music*. When that opened, said Richard, "Fox was back in business." And Brown was back with Fox, after some negotiating.

Said Richard Zanuck: "I was at a party with Ernie Lehman, who scripted *The Sound of Music* and grew up with David, and I said, 'How's David?' And Ernie said, 'Fine. It looks like he's going to join Paramount.'

"And I said, 'Gee! I didn't know that!' I'd always wanted to be in a position to bring David back. So I was flying to Europe, and the first thing I did was mention it to my father. I said, 'What we need is a strong guy at the literary end, and the best guy in the business is David Brown.' And he said, 'By all means.' So I got on the phone and reached him from Paris. He was in the photo gallery of Paramount, and they were taking a picture to go along with the announcement that he had joined Paramount. I said, 'Jesus! Don't join anything 'til I get there.' "

DAVID BROWN JOINING PAR
AS N. Y. STORY DEPT EXEC

David Brown, formerly a producer at 20th-Fox, has been named by Paramount as its exec in N.Y. in charge of story material and purchases, Gotham sources reported yesterday. Brown's duties will encompass purchase of Broadway plays, novels, etc., for the studio.

—Variety,
November 27, 1964

DAVID BROWN DEAL OUT

NEW YORK—Negotiations for David Brown to join Paramount as eastern story editor have fallen through, it is reliably learned. Recent reports printed elsewhere had the deal set. It is understood a decision was made late, last week.

—The Hollywood Reporter,
December 7, 1964

DAVID BROWN RETURNS TO 20TH CENTURY-FOX
David Brown, formerly an executive and story editor of 20th-Fox, has returned to the company in the newly created position of executive in charge of story operations. He will report directly to company president, Darryl F. Zanuck, and Richard D. Zanuck, v-p in charge of production.

—*The Hollywood Reporter*,
December 8, 1964

Zanuck and Brown struck a deal in a room at the St. Regis Hotel in New York. "He was the Number Two guy," said Richard. He quickly corrected himself. "I was Number Two. D.Z. was Number One. I was Number Two. So David was Number Three."

III

In July 1962, Darryl Zanuck returned to the presidency of Fox and Spyros Skouras was kicked upstairs as Chairman of the Board. But the war to save *Cleopatra* was far from over.

"Zanuck played it very cozy," said one of the executives handed a pink slip. "If the picture doesn't go, he can say he came in on it too late. If it does go, he can take the credit for it."

Zanuck referred to his expensive inherited problem child as "one headache. I had enough headaches to handle, straightening out an organization, closing a studio, everything. I was not in the mood to accept another responsibility from left field." But accept it Zanuck did. After viewing the rough cut, he fired Joseph L. Mankiewicz.

"If any woman behaved to me like Cleopatra treated Marc Antony," posited Zanuck, "I would cut her balls off."

Mankiewicz let the comment hang for Freudian interpretation.

"On completion of the dubbing, your official services will be terminated," Zanuck wrote Mankiewicz October 21, 1962. "If you are available and willing, I will call upon you to screen the re-edited version of the film. After you have done so, I will meet with you and go over it reel by reel and debate any points of difference that may arise."

"I've been a cotton picker too long not to know that Old Marse can do with the cotton exactly what he wants," replied Mankiewicz, philosophically. "I made the first cut, but after that, it's the studio's property. They could cut it up into banjo picks if they want."

A much-publicized feud lasted from October until December. Among the shots fired, Zanuck said of Mankiewicz, "I think that after a year and a half of directing *Caesar and Cleopatra*, some of the tinsel may have rubbed off on him."

Mankiewicz countered by stating, "With things the way they are in the world today, I don't think the public gives a damn who cuts *Cleopatra*."

An armistice was agreed upon.

"I told him," Zanuck said, "that I'd work with him hand in hand, and that I would bend over backward, artistically, so that I wouldn't have to exercise [my rights as President] unless it became absolutely essential. Joe accepted that, took the scenes that I had blocked out crudely and roughly, went to work on them and wrote them."

Mankiewicz told the press he was "theoretically in accord on the handling of the additional material" for the film. With $2 million more of Fox money, Mankiewicz added a large-scale battle scene with 1,000 soldiers, and 1,500 horses, shot in Spain.

Richard Zanuck and David Brown, meantime, were dispatched to Paris to play their own roles in the drama. Lawsuits had been filed in every direction: Wanger vs. Fox for being fired, Skouras vs. Wanger for mismanagement of funds, Rex Harrison vs. Fox to demand equal billing with Taylor and Burton, Taylor vs. Fox for forcing her to shoot additional scenes, and Fox vs. Taylor and Burton, claiming their public love affair damaged the film's financial prospects.

"We went to a meeting with Elizabeth Taylor at the Plaza Athénée Hotel," David Brown recalled.

"The *purpose* of the meeting," said Dick Zanuck, "was to settle a $50-million lawsuit on *Cleopatra*, and nobody was speaking to anybody at that time. The lawyers had given up. So David and I were dispatched to try to handle this from a personal standpoint."

"We brought our wives with us," said Brown. "Elizabeth Taylor opened the meeting by saying, 'Richard, you're a brat, and you always were a brat. I'll never forget when you tied me to a—' "

"Where did you tie her?" Brown asked Zanuck long after the mission had taken place.

"Irving Thalberg, Jr., whom I grew up with, and I tied Elizabeth—who was then just starting at Metro—to a beam in his basement, with her hands behind her back," said Zanuck. "And she started screaming like mad, because she thought we were going to lock her in. And her nurse came down, and slapped Irving across the face. So then we tied the nurse to another beam, and we got into all sorts of trouble. I had completely forgotten about it, but she hadn't. So we were sitting there, kind of hat in hand, with a $50-million lawsuit staring us in the face, and she went on the offensive immediately. And then, out of the corner of my eye, I saw Burton moving in on my wife."

"Which angered Elizabeth even more," said Brown.

"Which angered Elizabeth even more," said Zanuck. "*Needless* to say, we did not settle the lawsuit during the course of that meeting."

IV

Although the press had been reporting on movies since *The Birth of a Nation*, with a few exceptions movie critics in the nation's newspapers and magazines exerted little power regarding decisions made by the ticket-buying public or the movie-producing companies. Until the 1960s, consumer reporting was unheard of for the most part in any industry, let alone show business. Then, suddenly, *Cleopatra* raised the stakes. The studio had a solitary investment to protect, and the public developed a new curiosity about how $36 million could be spent. For the press, it seemed, it was now open season on the once-sacrosanct economic domain of the movies.

A singular offshoot of this new freedom of expression began one summer afternoon in 1963, when the Era of the Critic was born. It signaled the arrival of reviewing columns in nearly every major American publication, and the insertion of showbusiness segments on television news broadcasts. Leading the pack of these opinion-makers, who in several instances became every bit as celebrated as the people they critiqued, was the critic for the New York *Herald-Tribune* and television's "Today" show. Her name was Judith Crist.

"People couldn't wait to see *Cleopatra*." Crist recalled in 1986. "The studio had arranged an afternoon screening for the working press. This was before the fancy dress screening that night.

"I remember it was held in a big Broadway house.* Here I'd been reviewing off-Broadway and, occasionally, Broadway. I was nervous and anticipatory. I mean, this was *the* movie news event of that decade if not of many a decade before. *Cleopatra* was so publicized, so talked about, so gossiped about. And that cost! To think you were going to see something that expensive. Remember, in those days $36 million was money."

There were rumblings reported within the industry that the admission to *Cleopatra* might be set at a record five dollars, or an unbelievable ten dollars.**

The preview alone was such an event, Crist said, that her hus-

*The Rivoli, demolished in 1987.
**The highest price of a movie ticket, $4.80, was established the year before by Columbia's *Lawrence of Arabia*. *Cleo* commanded a full five dollars for her roadshow engagement.

band Bill Crist took the day off from work to join her. "We smok-
ers sat upstairs," she recalled. "In those days, every theatre had
balconies, not two more theatres upstairs."

The movie, which, because of its length, ran in two parts, un-
reeled. "I sat through it stunned," said Crist. "During intermission, Bill and I said not a word. And, when it was over, finally,
my most vivid memory is of walking down Broadway and suddenly realizing [*Times* film critic] Bosley Crowther was walking
ahead of me, and then speculating with Bill on his reaction. My
guess was, he couldn't possibly have liked it, but I wondered
whether he hated it as much as I did."

Bosley Crowther turned the corner at 43rd Street and proceeded to the *Times* office. Crist continued the three–block distance to her paper, took to her desk, and began writing. Earlier
in the year, on March 25, *Newsweek* magazine devoted four full
pages to "The Fortunes of Cleopatra" ("For love of her, Caesar
gave his heart, Antony gave his life, and Twentieth Century-Fox
a corporate treasure"), and, after reporting on the disaster-
plagued production, popped a question: "Whether *Cleopatra*
will turn out to be a monumental accident or an accidental mon-
ument."

For the June 13, 1963, edition of the New York *Herald-
Tribune*, Crist's editor Dave Paley answered with the seven-
column headline he ran atop her review:

"CLEOPATRA" A MONUMENTAL MOUSE

. . . it is at best a major disappointment, at worst an exercise in
tedium.

. . . I think a bit more has been expected of this 1958-'63
Cleopatra under the aegis of Walter Wanger, with script and direction by Joseph L. Mankiewicz. We were led to expect a fresh
and sophisticated character-oriented approach. . . .

[Miss Taylor] is an entirely physical creature, no depth of emotion apparent in her kohl-laden eyes, no modulation in her voice
that too often rises to fishwife levels. Out of royal regalia, en neg-
ligee or au naturel she gives the impression that she is really carrying on in one of Miami Beach's more exotic resorts than inhab-
iting a palace in ancient Alexandria. . . .

The *Times's* Bosley Crowther found the same movie "surpassing entertainment, one of the great epics of the day." His review portended early that Crowther might have been out of touch; his 1967 pan of the pop-gangster romance *Bonnie and Clyde* is generally considered his self-written ticket to retirement.

The movie-going public, as did *Herald-Tribune* publisher John Hay Whitney, sided with Crist.

"Jealous, smart-asses like Hollis Alpert* said, 'My God, she wrote seven columns on *Cleopatra?* What would she have devoted to something she'd have liked?' " remembered Crist, who also said of her review, "It would be better if I wrote it today. It would be shorter and sharper. But I'm 20 years smarter."

As for the reaction from Twentieth Century-Fox, Crist said it was "astonishing. Remember again that we'd never had movies cost anything like that before." By the same token, few writers, especially in the show-business columns, had the temerity to bite the hand of such a generous advertising source.

"I could barely get my coat off at the office the day the review appeared when the phone started ringing. You have to think back to the temper of newspapers in the early '60s to be gutsy enough to question the quality of this great spectacle."

Fox did not yank its ads from *The Herald-Tribune*, as Warners had done when Crist took a broad swipe at that studio's Easter picture at Radio City Music Hall, *Spencer's Mountain.* But neither did Fox provide publicity materials on *Cleo* for Crist's appearance on the "Today" show.

Said Crist: "In those days we weren't using film clips in television reviewing, we were using stills, and Al Morgan, the producer of 'Today,' told me, 'They won't give us any more photographs to use on the air.' Al went all the way to Darryl Zanuck, because Al knew everybody—and he knew Darryl from 'way back—but Darryl even said, 'You think we're crazy, after what she did to us the first time?' "

*Critic for *The Saturday Review*.

There was debate as to whether Crist should raid the stills file from her newspaper, but instead she and Morgan opted to use the one still in the "Today" collection, that of Cleopatra's $250,000 procession into a heavily populated Rome atop a two-ton sphinx drawn by 300 slaves.

"I used a pencil," Crist said, her voice rising a few octaves, "and on the air pointed to a tiny little dot and said, 'See this? This is Elizabeth Taylor as Cleopatra, and if you look over here, that little speck is Rex Harrison. . . .' "

Crist's reputation was made. "I became rich, famous, and beautiful," she said. "Anything after that was anti–climactic."

There were aftershocks. The *International Herald-Tribune* reprinted her review, and Elizabeth Taylor read it in London. The star cried when she got to the "Miami Beach" reference. In a retaliatory move, Fox showed its displeasure by pulling out of a Newspaper Women's Club of New York banquet where Crist was to be honored with a Front Page Award. Traditionally, every studio purchased a table at the benefit, but Fox publicity man Jonas Rosenfield, instead of sending the $250 check, dispatched the message to club president Christina Kirk:

"We are sure you do not want us as your guests to embarrass you by our presence during the ceremonies and you must see the irony of the company that made *Cleopatra* using *Cleopatra* money to support an affair which would affront it."

Rosenfield described the Crist review as a "full-page abortive assassination" of the movie.

"The saga didn't end there," said Crist. "An anonymous benefactor sent the club the money for the table." The mystery man? Revealed Crist: "It was Joe Mankiewicz. That was pretty elegant."

Over the years, Mankiewicz, whom Crist greatly admired, became a friend, "And never once," she said, "has the name *Cleopatra* passed between us. But he did make me realize one of the great lessons of *Cleopatra*."

That was, "No one ever sets out to make a bad movie."

V

In the early 1960's, a writers' strike in Hollywood erupted over pensions and welfare funds, as well as how large a percentage writers would receive when their movies were sold to television. When the six-month disagreement ended, Fox celebrated by announcing a record deal that had for some time been brewing in the background: The studio would pay $1.25 million for the rights to the stage hit *The Sound of Music,** which had a score by Richard Rodgers and Oscar Hammerstein II and a book by playwrights Howard Lindsay and Russel Crouse, best known for their long-running period domestic comedy *Life with Father*.

Indeed, the musical, which on November 17, 1959, *Times* critic Brooks Atkinson basically liked but still found "conventional," "disappointing," and "succumbing to the clichés of operetta," was distinguished in that it married the two teams that provided Broadway with its two longest runs; *Life with Father* held the record for a straight play,** and Rodgers and Hammerstein reset the measuring stick with their 1943 wide-open-spaces musical *Oklahoma!*

The Sound of Music cost $420,000 to mount at the Lunt-Fontanne Theatre, and even before the first note was sung in New York it set a box-office advance record, with more than $2 million in the till. (The figure remained impressive decades later, as the average ticket price in 1959 was under five dollars. In 1988, when the Broadway musical *The Phantom of the Opera* opened with an advance of $17 million, ticket prices had increased more than ten-fold.)

The stage star was Mary Martin, playing an orphaned postulant named Maria who comes as a governess into the home of a widowed Austrian sea captain with seven children. Theodore

*There had been a non-musical German film version of the Trapp family story, which Paramount in the 1950s had optioned for its star Audrey Hepburn; the option lapsed and the rights were then picked up by the stage producers of what was to become *The Sound of Music*.
**And still did mid-1988.

Bikel played Captain Georg Von Trapp. The setting was the 1930s, immediately prior to Hitler's takeover of his native Austria.

The songs from *The Sound of Music* included the title number; "Do-Re-Mi," which Maria employed to teach the children to sing; "My Favorite Things," Maria's laundry list of items that cured her everyday depression; and "Climb Ev'ry Mountain," the direct-steal inspirational inspired by "You'll Never Walk Alone" from the songwriters' vastly superior score for *Carousel*, the 1956 movie version of which proved a loser for Fox. The public perceived *Carousel* as an opera and no amount of advertising could sway their opinion.

Rodgers and Hammerstein had a link, if not a tradition, with Twentieth Century-Fox. One of Zanuck's last personally supervised productions before he left the studio in 1956 was the grand adaptation of their 1951 stage vehicle for Gertrude Lawrence, *The King and I*, which in turn had been adapted from the 1946 Fox film with Rex Harrison and Irene Dunne, *Anna and the King of Siam*. The movie version of *The King and I* starred Deborah Kerr and Yul Brynner, and despite a certain staginess was arguably the most enjoyable transference of Rodgers and Hammerstein from Broadway to Hollywood.

The creative team first came to Fox soon after conquering Broadway in 1943 with *Oklahoma!* Zanuck believed appropriately, the men would be ideal to compose a score for a musical remake of Fox's 1934 *State Fair*, which had originally starred Will Rogers as the head of a household that travels to its local agricultural fair. The cast for the updated musical would be Jeanne Crain, Dana Andrews, Dick Haymes, and Vivian Blaine.

"One unusual aspect of our work for *State Fair* was that after we had completed the score, we were told that Darryl F. Zanuck, then the head of Twentieth Century-Fox, wanted to see us in Hollywood before shooting was to begin," said Richard Rodgers. "Obviously there must be important things that Zanuck wanted to discuss with us that required a face-to-face meeting.

117

"So the Hammersteins and the Rodgers got on the cross-country train and spent a week in Hollywood. The accommodations were elegant, we met friends, attended some parties and saw a few screen tests of actors who were being considered for roles in the film. It wasn't until the day before we were to return home that Oscar and I were at last summoned by Zanuck. We were ushered into his pale-green office and there he was, riding crop across his lap, sitting behind a huge desk chewing on a huge cigar. And what did we talk about? Actually, I can't recall that Oscar or I said much. For 20 minutes Zanuck held center stage as he reminisced about his recent wartime experiences in North Africa. Then, when our allotted time was over, he rose, we rose, and we were ushered out of the office. We never saw him again.

"Why was Zanuck so anxious to have us travel three thousand miles to see him after we had completed our work? Largely, I think, it was a matter of pride and muscle. He had paid us a lot of money and had acceded to our working conditions, but he wanted the satisfaction of being able to make us do as he wished. It was one more example of the kind of ego-satisfying extravagance that eventually helped contribute to the downfall of the Hollywood studio system."

In 1960, studio president Buddy Adler claimed *The Sound of Music* purchase price was the highest ever paid for Broadway material. *Guys and Dolls, Can-Can,* and *Born Yesterday* previously were each bought for $1 million, though in the years that followed, new records would be set by the $5 million pricetag on *My Fair Lady,* $5.5 million for *A Chorus Line,* and the staggering $9.5 million for *Annie.*

Agent Irving Lazar spearheaded the *Music* deal. According to the contracts, in 1972 the property would revert to the stage producers, Rodgers, Hammerstein, Leland Hayward, and Richard Halliday, who was Mary Martin's husband. A second proviso was that the movie could not be released until 1964, by which time the stage version could play out. Lazar did not think the show's producers would suffer in any event, as he managed to insert a clause that provided them with 10 percent of the movie's gross once the movie had made $12.5 million.

By his own speculation, Lazar was counting on the four producers making $2 million in toto on the entire deal. His example had been *South Pacific*, the box-office take of which had reached $18 million. Instead, as *The Sound of Music* became a phenomenon the size not even the Zanucks expected, the movie—and, subsequently, each producer—made approximately ten times what Lazar had predicted.

As part of the same 1960 deal, Rodgers and Hammerstein were to provide new songs for a remake of their 1945 movie musical, *State Fair*, this time to star Pamela Tiffin, Bobby Darin, Pat Boone, Ann-Margaret, and, as a rural mother, Alice Faye. The second musical version proved a portent of most '70s musicals—inflated and uninspired—yet that it was made at all was considered a miracle. This was at the height of the period when word at the Schwab's drugstore counter and in every agent's office was that Fox was being permanently buried by *Cleopatra*.

Irving Lazar went to Richard Zanuck and offered to buy back *The Sound of Music* for $2 million, providing the studio with a $750,000 profit on a movie yet to be made. Richard Zanuck decided to forge ahead. The director he selected was William Wyler, then 60, who had never made a musical before but who was always up for a challenge.* His recent picture *Ben-Hur*, the 1959 Biblical spectacle, had won him his third Oscar, and his other movies included *Wuthering Heights*, *The Little Foxes*, *Dodsworth*, and perhaps the most beloved movie of the 1940s, *The Best Years of Our Lives*. Ernest Lehman had written the movie script for *The Sound of Music*, and Wyler went to scout locations in Austria.

"Willie got as far as Salzburg when he realized he didn't want

---

*Wyler was also personally invited to sit on the Fox board by Darryl Zanuck once the studio reopened after its 1962 closure. Although Wyler only attended two board meetings, his position there was important, as it helped Fox gain the respect of filmmakers who had been outraged when Dick and Darryl had shut down production.

to deal with Nazis in a musical," said Aviva Slesin, documentary filmmaker who made the 1986 portrait *Directed by William Wyler*. Wyler was an Alsatian Jew who had escaped Europe long before Hitler, though Wyler had lost relatives in the holocaust. Mounting song and dance numbers around Gestapo tactics rightly seemed to him a trivialization of history. Wyler entered into a stormy dispute over the material with Richard Zanuck and he left the project.

"Willie just wouldn't deal with the Nazis," reiterated Slesin. "Robert Wise made the picture. And—Willie always said afterward—Robert Wise was the right choice. He made the better picture."

"I knew Willie and Dick Zanuck had had a disagreement over something, but I never knew what," said Robert Wise. "I certainly never discussed it with either of them. I'd come back to Fox in 1963, to start preparations on *The Sand Pebbles*, but it soon became apparent that it would take a long time to get the appropriate locations in the Pacific, so I started looking around for something else to do."

It was Richard Zanuck who recommended *The Sound of Music*, for it had been Wise who won the Oscar for directing *West Side Story*, in 1961. Wise was not excited by the prospect, however. "I thought I'd done my musical," he said. "I was looking for something else."

Wise had not seen the stage production of *Sound of Music*, but he was provided with Ernest Lehman's screenplay. Some musical numbers from the show were dropped, others had shifted their position in the story. As Wise said, "I was simply handed this package that had already been completely prepared."

A Fox executive at the time described the package further: "*The Sound of Music* had been entirely blocked out, scene by scene, by Roger Edens, who had worked with Wyler. It was Roger's idea to open the picture with the sound of the wind coming from the plane. All Robert Wise had to do was pick up the script and shoot the movie."

A casting director in the New York Fox office, whose vestibule was located directly opposite the office of Darryl Zanuck ("Darryl positioned me there because he insisted on checking out every young actress who tried out for [television's] *Peyton Place*"), recalled that Darryl's choice to play Maria was Doris Day. She had also been under consideration to play the lead in *South Pacific*, but neither role went her way. Darryl declined intruding into matters of *The Sound of Music* after that, and his next encounter with the property, according to Dick Zanuck, was when he attended the New York premiere.

"That must have been when I met the man," recalled Julie Andrews, who eventually did play Maria. "Gosh, I can remember him but I can't seem to remember the occasion. He *was* dynamic. I remember being thrilled. You could sense this legend."

And *Richard* Zanuck?

"Well, he'd been around a lot."

Richard Zanuck cast Julie Andrews in *The Sound of Music* after an agent had showed him a few scenes from Walt Disney's *Mary Poppins*, which was then in production. Andrews had been Rex Harrison's co-star on Broadway in the musical *My Fair Lady*, a 1956 stage sensation based on George Bernard Shaw's *Pygmalion*, but had lost out in the casting of Jack Warner's movie version when the studio head opted for a box-office name in Audrey Hepburn. It turned out to be one of the most serendipitous career flukes in movie history. A deluge of sympathy was showered upon Julie Andrews not only for losing the role she created on Broadway, but because Jack Warner rudely had insisted she was not photogenic. Disney cast her in *Mary Poppins*, based on the P. L. Travers stories about a magical flying nanny in Edwardian England, and the picture outgrossed *My Fair Lady*, although the latter clearly was the better production. *Mary Poppins* also won an Oscar, possibly undeserved at the time in view of her better later work, for Julie Andrews, but what was especially unusual about the large turnout for *Mary Poppins* was the makeup of the audience. The musical fantasy brought people to the movies who had not set foot inside a theatre in years, including the slowly vanishing adult audience.

Greater success was achieved with *The Sound of Music*. "It's

121

uncanny," Andrews said in 1986 of the reverence audiences still held for the picture (two decades after its theatrical release, *The Sound of Music* was again an astounding success, on the video-cassette market). "I suppose it had something to do with the way it showed the strength of the family."

VI

This last, most remunerative, and least inspired, let alone sophis-ticated, of the Rodgers and Hammerstein collaborations, is square and solid sugar. Calorie-counters, diabetics and grown-ups from eight to 80 had best beware.

. . . let me tell you that there is nothing like a super-sized screen to convert seven darling little kids in no time at all into all W.C. Fields indicated darling little kids are—which is pure loathsome.

Blown up by stereophonic sound, the pedestrian lyrics go clump, the melody pounds away out of all proportion, and a pleasant little family singing group is given all the status of the Sistine Choir.

. . . I hasten to add that in addition to God, country, and mother, I am fond of dogs.

—Judith Crist,
New York *Herald-Tribune*
March 3, 1965

"Oh, the hate mail I received for not liking *The Sound of Music*," recalled Judith Crist. "From priests and nuns."

Pauline Kael dismantled *The Sound of Music*, which she found manipulative, and found herself without a column in *McCall's* magazine. *The New Yorker* soon picked her up, a situa-tion that received no shortage of media attention. The stir caused Joseph L. Mankiewicz to comment: "The critic has now become a performer. He has an agent. He gets booked. He or she has to create a box-office name and demand."

"*The Sound of Music* got terrible reviews. Simply awful," re-membered David Brown. "It affected the box-office, at first. The picture started slow. The premiere party was like a wake.

"In those days, you used to be able to buy the bulldog editions of the papers as you left the theatre. There was Bosley Crowther and Judith Crist, and they were fulminating, as though we'd committed some crime against humanity. Reviews such as those put a terrible strain on the psyche. Invariably, a bad review seems to be the honest one."

It also, as the reviewers began zeroing in on rapidly spiraling picture budgets, helped to send up a red flag to Wall Street.

VII

The Sound of Music sent the major Hollywood studios scurrying to the orchestra pit, desperate to imitate its success, much in the same manner as in 1927 when the panic-stricken movie industry rushed into talkies in the wake of *The Jazz Singer*.

Darryl Zanuck had long exhibited a penchant for musicals, though they were said never to be to his personal taste. One of his first part-talkie screenplays, in 1928, was tailored for the vaudeville comedienne and torch singer Fanny Brice, entitled *My Man*, about a woman whose man had gone ruefully wrong. Zanuck repeated the formula with the 1939 *Rose of Washington Square*, starring Alice Faye as a thinly disguised Brice (who sued for defamation of character and was compensated out of court). Brice's own life was later done on film starring newcomer Barbra Streisand (*Funny Girl*, 1968),* with the one constant in the three versions being the musical lament, "My Man." The lyrics tell of a faithful woman who loves her man despite his wanderings. As later seem, this could have been the anthem of Virginia Zanuck.

Darryl was not to lose his commercial instinct for musicals, although he fell short in an attempt to pull off his most ambitious idea. In 1956, before Zanuck shifted from studio chief to independent producer, he instructed a factotum to contact poet Richard Wilbur, who had just completed adapting Voltaire's

---

*A Columbia roadshow that finally marked William Wyler's bow as director of a musical.

Candide with composer Leonard Bernstein and playwright Lillian Hellman.

"I was told to think about adapting *Gone With the Wind* as a movie musical," recalled Wilbur. "I thought it was a crazy notion, one of the worst I've ever heard of, and besides, I wasn't really in the musical racket. Still, I'll never forget the words of the man who called me: 'Be prepared to hear from Zanuck.' That impressed the hell out of me."

In the mid- to late 1960s, other studio executives shared Zanuck's enthusiasm for musicals, employing any cockeyed idea that seemed to enter their heads. No expense was spared, solely because *The Sound of Music* paid off so handsomely, and casting offices were never above signing the most unlikely or ill-suited star as story departments frantically raided Broadway and their own studio libraries for properties.

Warners sank $15 million into *Camelot* and another $6 million into *Finian's Rainbow*. Paramount gambled a combined $50 million on Tommy Steele in *Half a Sixpence*, Lee Marvin, Clint Eastwood, and Jean Seberg in *Paint Your Wagon*, Julie Andrews in *Darling Lili*, and Barbra Streisand in *On a Clear Day You Can see Forever*. (Trouncing competition, Paramount landed the prized rights to *Coco*, the stage musical about couturier Coco Chanel, for $1 million.) M-G-M dusted off two old chestnuts, added music and an intermission, and presented Peter O'Toole in *Goodbye, Mr. Chips* and Horst Buchholz in *The Great Waltz*. Metro also had in development an Irving Berlin biography entitled *Say It With Music* to star Julie Andrews. Universal employed Andrews for *Thoroughly Modern Millie*, and Shirley MacLaine for *Sweet Charity*, and a cast of unknowns for *Jesus Christ, Superstar*. Disney enlisted Fred MacMurray and Greer Garson for *The Happiest Millionaire*. United Artists set off *Chitty Chitty Bang Bang*, *How to Succeed in Business Without Really Trying*, *A Funny Thing Happened on the Way to the Forum*, *Fiddler on the Roof*, *Man of La Mancha*, *Promises, Promises*, and *Hair* (that is, it owned the rights; the company never found the proper director and stars for *Promises, Promises*, and took a decade to package *Hair*). Columbia secured *Oliver!*, *Funny Girl*, *1776*, and *Lost Horizon*. Independents, not to be outdone, found the millions necessary to confect *Scrooge*, *Song of Norway*, and *Cabaret*.

Of those 28 properties, 25 were actually produced. Five made money.

In the immediate wake of *The Sound of Music*, Twentieth laid down the policy of two exclusive-run roadshow pictures a year in order to enhance the company's prestige and its coffers. Oscar-winners invariably premiered as roadshow attractions, meaning they played one-theatre-per-major-city, open-ended, two-a-day screenings in high-priced, reserved-seat movie palaces.

The problem was, during this period of the 1960s, movie palaces were crumbling, as were their downtown neighborhoods. The action in exhibition, sadly to the minds of Darryl Zanuck and the producers of large, lumbering musicals, was in small-screen mini-plex cinemas springing up like McDonald's hamburger stands across the breadth of suburban America, wherein movies were meant to be a convenient amusement, not necessarily an event.

For 1967, Fox roadshowed *Doctor Dolittle*, a children's musical fantasy based on Hugh Lofting's stories of the eccentric, English country veterinarian, with Rex Harrison in the title role. In 1968, there was *Star!*, a glamorous biography of the late British stage legend Gertrude Lawrence, with an unusually crisp Julie Andrews in the lead. In 1969, the year of Woodstock, Fox pulled out all the stops with *Hello, Dolly!* an extravagant adaptation of the Broadway stage smash, set at the turn of the century. It was about a pushy New York matchmaker (Barbra Streisand) who spent two acts trapping herself a husband.

[Darryl] Zanuck rolled the cigar around in his mouth and then flicked a mountainous ash into the ashtray. "We've got $50 million tied up in these three musicals, *Doctor Dolittle*, *Star!*, and

Hello, Dolly!, and quite frankly, if we hadn't made such an enormous success with *The Sound of Music*, I'd be petrified. You're never sure of a hit in that category. You're never sure of a hit any goddamn time, but when you're talking $20 million, it's a bigger gamble. . . ."

—John Gregory Dunne,
The Studio (1968)

VIII

"That fucking *Doctor Dolittle* killed off merchandising tie-ins for the next decade," said a retired Fox promotions employee in 1986. He was referring to the line-up of, among 300 items worth $200 million retail, Dolittle clocks, watches, hats, medicine kits, and talking Rex Harrison dolls (pull the string and hear: "Hello. I'm Doctor Dolittle").

"I'll bet there are still Mattel (Toy Company) warehouses in California bursting at the seams with that crap. What a mess that was. You needed a year to tool up to make these things in the toy factories in order to capitalize on the Christmas sales, only Mattel and the other companies saw that after *Dolittle* went bust they weren't going to put any more trust into movie studios coming to them pitching their tie-ins.

"Of course, what's funny is, that all got turned around again after *Star Wars*, and that was another Fox picture."

Doctor Dolittle was one of the most ballyhooed productions in 1967; one couldn't open a magazine or listen to a popular music station without encountering it somehow. It also managed to garner some important Academy Award nominations the following year, because Fox still had enough employees on the payroll to vote in a block. Yet the *cognoscenti* knew from the start that the musical about the veterinarian who could "talk with, walk with, squawk with the animals" was a dog. It had animals and expensive locations but no cohesive storyline.

In 1963, former publicist turned producer Arthur P. Jacobs

convinced the Zanucks to commit $6 million to adapt the dozen Hugh Lofting books about Dr. John Dolittle, English country veterinarian. Rex Harrison was the casting choice for two reasons, primarily because of his strong musical-stage identification thanks to his Henry Higgins elocutioner's role in *My Fair Lady*, and, second, because at the time his Julius Caesar seemed the only unembarrassing performance in *Cleopatra*. If one were to examine Lofting's quaint illustrations in the Dolittle volumes, however, it appeared that the model for the bulbous-nosed country doctor was W.C. Fields.

As the librettist, Jacobs hired the literary musical genius Alan Jay Lerner,* author of *Brigadoon, My Fair Lady, Camelot*, and *Gigi*. But by then Lerner had entered into a period of artistic decline, and among his eccentricities was an erratic work habit. Collaborators in New York and Hollywood reported that Lerner would agree to meet for a work session, say Monday morning, and then phone long-distance Monday afternoon to announce that he had decided to go to Paris.

"Alan never had any intention of writing *Dolittle*," said a close associate. "His name was used by Fox purely as a lure to get Rex Harrison to play the lead."

Harrison snapped at the bait, and from reports snapped all through filming; Lerner never wrote a single note on paper, said his associate. Leslie Bricusse, whose fame at that time came chiefly from two shows he had written for and with Anthony Newley, *Stop the World I Want to Get Off* and *The Roar of the Greasepaint, The Smell of the Crowd*, undertook the score. It sounded nothing more than serviceable, except for the cute "Talk to the Animals" and the haunting "Beautiful Things" (overly reminiscent of "My Favorite Things"), which in the end was clumsily performed by the love interests, Anthony Newley and Samantha Eggar, and practically hacked out of the film as it was. The Lofting stories were weakly linked by the doctor's on-going global search for a giant pink sea snail, travels never as

*The composer was to be André Previn.

127

daring or as interesting as Dorothy's in *The Wizard of Oz*, a classic movie whose appeal this cumbersome musical was sadly trying to imitate.

Harrison talk-sang his numbers as he had done in *My Fair Lady*, only on this occasion the lyrics were devoid of sparkling wit, and the star put no energy into the effort. Watching him was a strain that lasted for more than two and a half hours.

"After the film opened we had field people reporting back to us," said a Fox executive onboard at the time. "They said even the kids were walking out."

"We were plagued from the start," remembered another. The bad luck was not confined simply to the goat who ate director Richard Fleischer's script or the parrot who would shout "Cut!" in the middle of intricate musical numbers, incidents which, combined with foul weather on location in the Caribbean and the English countryside, tripled the $6 million original budget.

"Black pressure groups condemned the picture because they hated the Hugh Lofting books. They said the stories had a subversive history. The doctor was an English imperialist, and in one of the tales he went into the jungle and came across a tribal king who wanted to be white. The groups were ticked off that Lofting tried to present this as humorous. But listen, it didn't matter. That picture went right into the toilet."

IX

After the *Dolittle* debacle of 1967, Fox's next Christmas turkey, for 1968, was *Star!*, which Richard Zanuck openly came to refer to as "our Edsel." And yet, even a good Edsel can appreciate in value; nearly two decades after its disastrous engagement, its director Robert Wise, its leading lady Julie Andrews, and some overzealous film buffs were saying, to quote Julie Andrews, "*Star!* wasn't that bad at all. I just think it was something the critics were gunning for after the immense success we'd had with *The Sound of Music*." Robert Wise labeled it, "The one picture of mine I'd like to try again."

Examined several years after its release, *Star!* still contained musical numbers that, though sometimes anachronistic, were spectacular. The book was something else. There simply wasn't any.

"The rags-to-riches life of Gertrude Lawrence often sounds like the script for a singularly appalling Hollywood musical," wrote Lawrence biographer Sheridan Morley in 1981, "and once indeed it did become just that—a film called *Star!* for which she was impersonated by Julie Andrews, a lady bearing about as much resemblance to her as to Mickey Rooney."

What no one could ever argue was the presence of a score, famous songs by George and Ira Gershwin, Kurt Weill, and Noel Coward. The Coward contribution was particularly important to the project, if only to lend some authenticity. Beatrice Lillie, whose stage career had been linked to that of Gertrude Lawrence, had refused permission to have her name used in the film, because the producers flatly denied her request to play herself. Coward, who first befriended Lawrence in 1913, when she was 15, and then went on to write *Private Lives* for her in 1930, was approached in July 1965 by screenwriter William Fairchild and David Stone of Fox to discuss what was tentatively entitled *The Gertrude Lawrence Story.* Coward told them, "I heartily disapprove."

Of the meeting, which took place in his London home, the droll theatrical personality reported, "They stayed forever. We argued back and forth. Julie Andrews is to play Gertie, about as suitable as casting the late Princess Royal as Dubarry. However, she's a clever girl and will at least be charming and sing well. *Why* they are doing the film I shall never know. There isn't any real story beyond the fact that she started young in the theatre, became an understudy [to Beatrice Lillie], then a star, lived with Philip Astley, Bert Taylor, etc., married Richard Aldrich, and died [in 1952]. I really do think the Hollywood mentality is worse than ever."

Timing was undeniably bad. Despite the stature of such standards as Gershwin's "Someone to Watch Over Me," Weill's "My Ship," and Coward's "Someday I'll Find You," the late '60s was a period when such songs had fallen out of favor, particularly with young audiences. If anything, taste in music served as another departure point in the split between generations.

Nevertheless, *The Gertrude Lawrence Story*, retitled *Star!*, moved forward.

"My life is an anecdote," commented veteran lyricist Sammy Cahn as he collected his memories of the film in 1987. Cahn, a soft-spoken, owlish-looking man, said, "One day the phone rings. It's Saul Chaplin, who tells me he's producing this Gertrude Lawrence biography. 'Fine,' I say. Now, how well do I know Saul? I was the one who changed his name from Sollie Kaplan. I hadn't worked with him in 20 years, but now he's calling and says he needs a title song for this movie, *Star!* 'Fine,' I say. 'Sollie, why don't we write it together?' I say. 'No, no, no,' he says."

Cahn went to work with his usual collaborator, composer Jimmy Van Heusen. Their songbook, which was closely linked to Frank Sinatra, included "High Hopes," "Call Me Irresponsible," "All My Tomorrows," "All the Way," and the bouncy title song to "Thoroughly Modern Millie," a Charleston Julie Andrews performed on the street during the opening credits of that 1967 film musical.

In conceiving their title tune for *Star!*, Cahn said, "I see a dark screen. Spotlight on Julie Andrews. Cut from her to 24 men in top hats, singing it."

Cahn sang it. " *'If the lady's da-dee-da-da-da . . .'* That's my image," he said. "Comes the moment of truth. We play it for him. Sollie says, 'Oh no, not in this picture.' I knew I was in trouble. You ever see the picture?" Cahn waved the memory away with his hand. "Forget it."

Cahn and Van Heusen's sprightly song about the lavish trappings of celebrity was made to sound tinny and scratchy as if the audience were listening to early movie sound. The number was played under a sepia-toned mock-Movietone newsreel of Gertie Lawrence's early years. In the middle of this historical account, the real Lawrence—that is, Julie Andrews—breaks widescreen color into the projected image. The initial sight of her, overly made-up and dressed to the teeth in a costume by Donald Brooks, bordered on the monstrous. Brooks's budget for Gertie's gowns alone was $350,000, yet the real money, $14 million, was eaten up during eight months on location in New York, Washington, and the south of France.

"We put together the same team we had for *The Sound of Music*," recounted Robert Wise. "What could go wrong after that?"

In test screenings with audiences to gauge reactions before *Star!* officially opened, indeed nothing seemed to be wrong. The musical scored high, which later gave rise to an industry warning. Since then, any time a producer grew cocky over a supposed excellent response to his film at a preview, he could be brought back to earth with the line, "Oh, yeah? Just remember *Star!*"

The movie became synonymous with the word "bomb" until Michael Cimino's 1980 unmitigated disaster about the early 1890s Johnson County, Wyoming, land war, *Heaven's Gate*. That picture, at least, garnered mounds of publicity, albeit negative. *Star!* disappeared without a trace, as far as the public was concerned. It however remained to haunt the studio.

"I remember the first review," said Robert Wise. "We opened in London, and *The Sound of Music* had played this one theatre, the Dominion, for three years. And the first review said that the Dominion had better be ready to play this picture for the next three."

Wise shook his head.

"I don't think the public was prepared to see Julie in an unsympathetic role," he said.

"I don't think the public was prepared to see me in an unsympathetic role," said Julie Andrews, five months earlier and a continent away. "Gertrude Lawrence was a bitch. I suppose she was a strange choice as the subject of a movie."

"With all her overacting and silliness," Noel Coward said of Lawrence, "I have never known her to do a mean or unkind thing." Of the finished film, Coward declared, "Julie Andrews was talented, charming, efficient, and very pretty, but *not* very like Gertie. Danny Massey was excellent as me and had the sense to give an impression of me rather than try to imitate me. He was tactless enough to sing better than I do, but of *course* without my matchless charm!"

Reviews of the film were not terrible. The New York *Daily News*, usually a fairly reliable barometer of public taste, awarded it three-and-a-half out of four stars. ("I was a sucker for the musical numbers," its then-second-string critic Kathleen Carroll said in retrospect), and Renata Adler, the critic for *The New York Times*, wrote nothing horribly unkind in her notice, but she did blithely dismiss the entire picture in a matter of paragraphs. Her move bruised more egos than hampered the box-office, with one promotions man recalling, "The morning her notice came out, I thought Darryl was going to march over to the paper and assassinate her." Adler, recalling her critique of the picture several years later, winked an eye and explained, "I just looked at the silly thing and thought, 'What the hell?' "

Reviews aside, *The Sound of Music* proved a Julie Andrews musical was that new-fangled word, "critic-proof." *Star!* would surely pick up the audience that was left waiting for more Julie Andrews. But it did not.

Fox was thrown into a panic. *Star!* had to be yanked from its roadshows, and one hour was hacked out. Robert Wise in 1986 would not discuss the butchery, other than to confirm he had no hand in it, he had not seen the film in nearly two decades, nor did he know if or where a print existed.

Taken out were the musical numbers, leaving the movie with its weakest ingredient, its story. Playing up Gertrude Lawrence's numerous affairs, although Julie Andrews was never shown going beyond a good-night kiss, the truncated version was retitled *The Loves of a Star*. (Universal attempted a similar maneuver with a pale biography of dancer Isadora Duncan starring Vanessa Redgrave, *Isadora*, which was tantalizingly renamed *The Loves of Isadora*, to continued lack of interest at the ticket window.)

The Loves of a Star produced scant box-office results, yet the fighting was not over. Playing up Julie Andrews' image of goody-goodness, the movie was re-retitled *Those Were the Happy Times.*

They weren't.

Star! never received an American network television airing, and it is not as of 1988, nor is it expected to be, available on videocassette.

X

Hello, Dolly! is fantastic, really fantastic, the best musical ever made, and that includes *The Sound of Music*, which is the biggest grossing picture ever made. But I wouldn't predict that *Hello, Dolly!* will outgross *The Sound of Music*, even though it's a better picture.

—Darryl F. Zanuck,
International Herald-Tribune,
October 25, 1969

The costliest and most challenging set was the 15-acre segment of New York City which serves as background for the film's opening and for many key sequences, including the parade. At one time this set was to have been built on the studio's Malibu ranch, but this would have created a fantastic transportation snarl, with as many as 5,000 extras and a crew of hundreds traveling narrow canyon roads. Eventually, production designer John DeCuir worked out an ingenious layout involving the disguise of 11 major studio buildings and the creation of many more on the studio lot. All told, 60 buildings, comprising sections of Manhattan's Fifth Avenue, Broadway and Mulberry Streets, 14th Street, the Bowery—including the old Grand Central Station, Tony Pastor's Theatre, and the Waldorf-Astoria and Fifth Avenue hotels—were constructed. The detail is exquisitely accurate, down even to the advertising billboards, except that some geographic liberties have been taken.

And over it, a three-car train pulled by a steam engine threads its way along 600 feet of elevated track, while horse-drawn trolleys glide along tracks on the street below.

133

Fortunately for the film's budget, animated electrical signs did not first appear in New York until 1891—a year after the date of our story. Hence the so-called Great White Way is not in evidence.

—from the *Hello, Dolly!* souvenir
program

Richard Zanuck announced that Twentieth Century-Fox had purchased the film rights to the Broadway hit *Hello, Dolly!* on March 9, 1965, six days after the opening of the studio's version of *The Sound of Music*. Within the year, the assignment of writing and producing *Dolly!* fell to Ernest Lehman, who tackled the problem of how to bring its slight story to the screen. Thought—and a budget—had been given during the conception stage to shooting the musical in Rome, to save millions of dollars. No way, said Richard Zanuck.

"Jesus," he told writer John Gregory Dunne, "you can get away with shooting *Cleopatra* in Rome, but *Hello Dolly!* is a piece of hard-core Americana. You shoot that in Rome and the unions back here will raise such a stink you'll have a hard time getting over it. It would have tarnished the image of the whole picture."

Still left to be decided was how the material would be handled. The two leads would be played by Streisand and Walter Matthau. "My knowledge of the project started before the casting," said Hugh Fordin,* who had been head of casting for Broadway producer David Merrick in New York before joining Twenthieth Century-Fox in 1966, when he cast *The Boston Strangler*. (Darryl Zanuck had asked Fordin to find a part in the movie, which was based on the true-life story, for his latest girl friend, Genevieve Gilles, only Fordin was forced to admit that Gilles's French accent was not suitable to the picture's setting.)

Of the gestating *Dolly!*, Fordin said: "Robert Wise came into

*David Brown, commenting in late 1987 on Fordin's quotes that appear in this book said that he did not remember any Hugh Fordin working at Twentieth Century-Fox.

my office and said, 'What do I do? I want to do it for Ernie Lehman, but I can't see myself in this place.' And Robert Wise got himself out of *Hello, Dolly!* I have the feeling, because of *The Sound of Music*, Dick and David got Robert Wise before they got the property."

Ernest Lehman held several meetings on the project. "He was the golden boy at Fox at that time," said Gene Saks, a director who had successfully adapted the Neil Simon Broadway stage comedies *Barefoot in the Park* and *The Odd Couple* to the screen. He had met Lehman through the television producer Norman Lear.

"Lehman had these big offices at Fox and he asked me to direct *Hello, Dolly!* We discussed it for hours. He'd already hired Michael Kidd to choreograph. Then Ernie and I spent days seeing each other and discussing it further. Like so many projects, we said, 'Goodbye' and I walked away thinking I had the job. I never heard from him again."

Hello, Dolly! had several European antecedents before American playwright Thornton Wilder spun a 1938 play out of one of the later versions and called it *The Merchant of Yonkers*. The work was revised in 1954 and retitled *The Matchmaker*, and it starred Ruth Gordon as Dolly Levi, the meddlesome Lower East Side matchmaker, and Sam Levene as Horace Vandergelder, a horse-and-feed store owner in Yonkers. She was widowed; he was eligible.

In 1958, Paramount filmed *The Matchmaker* as a vehicle for Shirley Booth, with Paul Ford (best known as television's Colonel Hall on the Phil Silvers "Sgt. Bilko" show) as Vandergelder and a young Shirley MacLaine and Anthony Perkins in supporting roles. *The Matchmaker* came out limp on the screen, because, played as a talky farce, it had been filmed in a realistic-looking period setting although its acting remained intentionally stagy.

"I said to Dick and David," recalled Fordin, "that they had to look very carefully at what they were going to do, because farce doesn't work onscreen, as evidenced by Shirley Booth in *The*

Matchmaker. And Dick said, 'What? Shirley Booth did a movie of *Hello, Dolly!*?' "

Fordin recommended they run *Hotel Paradiso*, a 1966 British adaptation of a Feydeau farce, starring Gina Lollobrigida, Alec Guinness, and Robert Morley. "See if that worked," he said. They did and it didn't. Fordin said he next suggested "making *Hello, Dolly!* as a great big M-G-M musical. And they did it. But they did it wrong."

Among other obstacles, Irene Sharaff's gowns were too cumbersome for the diminutive star to dance in.

The worst mistake, Fordin believed, was the hiring of Gene Kelly as director. "Gene tried," said Fordin. "He was a competent director and a great dancer, but he lacked the imagination to get up on the crane and block out the "Before the Parade Passes By" number. Michael Kidd did it, and by then he and Gene weren't speaking."

Neither were the stars. "Streisand was a dream," said Fordin providing a view that conflicted with her reputation for being difficult with director William Wyler on the set of *Funny Girl.* The new star had infuriated the Hollywood community by attempting to co-direct the picture with the respected veteran.

"She tried her damnedest," said Fordin, "and on *Dolly!* she didn't have a director who discussed anything with her. We didn't know if her performance was Martha Raye, Mae West, Marlene Dietrich, or Lena Horne. Vocally she was phenomenal, but Barbra couldn't talk to Gene. And Walter, from Day One, was impossible. His attitude was, 'I hate this movie. I hate being here.' "

"Me and musicals is a mistake," Matthau said in 1988. "The only music I like is Mozart. If they let me play Don Giovanni that would be the right idea."

"In order to get Walter to do *Hello, Dolly!*," said Gene Saks, who had directed the actor in *The Odd Couple*, "Fox had to buy his house in the Adirondacks. In those days Walter used to ask for the most ludicrous things, and they had to be in his contract. Walter and his wife Carol used to go visit this lake and then they

136

built a house there, and then a lodge. Walter hated it and moved to the West Coast. As one of the conditions of working on that movie, Twentieth Century-Fox had to buy this house. Walter's that kind of guy. He once wanted the two of us to have [producer] Jennings Lang make this particular movie we were going to do. When I asked Walter what was so great about Jennings, he said, 'He gets me free gas.' "

"Why Walter and Barbra were enemies, I don't know," said Fordin.

One of the legends to grow out of the confrontations between Streisand and Matthau was that, after his continued annoyance at her endless delays in showing up to the set, he announced to her: "I have more talent in my smallest fart than you have in your entire body." Her reply was to hand him a bar of soap, for his mouth.

"I never said that," Matthau insisted in 1988. He added sarcastically: "I would never say anything like that. I never use profanity of any sort when I'm mad. Only when I'm happy."

Asked to explain then how perhaps this story got started—the "fart" quote appeared in a question about Matthau and Streisand in the game of Trivial Pursuit—the leading man replied: "Well, we were fighting about something, and she was telling me that maybe I was angry with her because I had never met anyone who could give me competition in the acting department, and I told her, 'Yeah, you're probably right, you're such an accomplished actress that it staggers the imagination.' "

The Fox publicity staff was dispatched to Garrison, New York, which had been dressed to look like 1890 Yonkers, to keep word of any ego problems and delays on the set from leaking to the press. This maneuver had the reverse effect.

"The extras, everybody, would sit around for hours," remembered Fordin. Time, of course, was money. "Only nothing was happening. No one knew what to do."

A stickier situation developed with the finished film. According to the contract for the stage rights, the movie was prohibited from opening until the Broadway stage engagement had come to

an end. Because of the clever promotional gimmicks by its theatre producer David Merrick, that date did not look to be on the
near horizon, yet Richard Zanuck was so convinced that Fox had
a winner in the Streisand movie that he paid Merrick $2 million
so the movie could open before the Broadway production
closed, a decisive victory for the impresario.

"There were several ways around the dilemma without giving
in to Merrick," said Hugh Fordin, "without paying Merrick a
penny, in fact. But Dick wouldn't listen, even though I told him
I knew the contract with Merrick inside out."

By the time the movie had finished post-production, Merrick
had instituted all manner of gimmicks to keep his stage production alive, substituting the leading lady for one star after the
other. After the original Dolly, Carol Channing, came Ginger
Rogers, followed by Martha Raye, Betty Grable, Bibi Oster-
wald. Then came the clencher. In Washington, D.C., Merrick
had opened an all-black version, starring Pearl Bailey.

"That production was originally intended for the road," said
Fordin. "But Merrick looked at it opening night from the wings
and said, 'Forget putting this on the road. I'll close the Broadway production, put that one on the road, and put this one into
New York.' So the Broadway version with Yvonne DeCarlo shut
down, and ten days later, the Pearl Bailey version opened—
operating on a road contract. I told this to Dick Zanuck, who
hardly listened, then said, 'We'll pay Merrick. We don't want
any problems with blacks.' "

Fordin threw up his hands at such logic. There was another
out for Fox, Fordin had deduced, and he proposed it to Dick
Zanuck and David Brown.

"All right, you don't want problems with blacks? Then bring
that New York cast out here —you still have all the sets and all
the costumes and all the pre-recorded orchestrations—and re-
shoot a second version of the movie with the black cast. You'll
need new gowns for Pearl Bailey, maybe, but that's all. It
couldn't cost you more than $1 million. Shoot it, put it in the
can, don't touch it for four years, then release that."

Zanuck and Brown's reaction: "David said, 'The interest

charges would kill us,' " said Fordin. "The interest charges. Ha! They didn't even say it was a good idea."

Any sort of *Dolly!* movie at this time turned out to be a bad idea. Except for Streisand, too young but at least energetic, and Matthau, crusty enough to offset the silliness of the plot and dialogue, *Hello, Dolly!* was a lot of nothing happening, two-and-a-half hours of actors prancing about looking for a story. It had a famous title song, and Louis Armstrong, who turned it into a Pop Chart hit, sang it in the movie during a brief, engaging duet with Streisand that was the only thing in the movie that ended too soon. Beyond that, *Dolly!* offered nothing that would remotely interest any listener of a Top Ten, and proved to be the squarest movie in the most tumultuous year of the entire Youth Movement.

The roadshow engagement in Todd-AO went to popular prices within a month, 35 mm versions played neighborhood theatres on double-bills with *Doctor Dolittle* a few weeks thereafter, and the sound-track album on Fox records was reduced to 99 cents in clearance bins in cut-rate drugstores in time for the after-Christmas sales.

XI

"It was some anniversary of D-Day," said Hugh Fordin. "We were called into the Fox New York office screening room—oh, what a place that was. Classic Art Deco. It was a small movie palace, maybe 200 seats. Darryl did not get up in front of people much, but he got up before us and stood in the front of the room with his cigar and cane. He didn't need the cane to walk. He used it for show, like he used to wear riding britches to production meetings."

Zanuck greeted the crowd and then showed a clip from *The Longest Day*.

"We got a whole presentation that morning," said Fordin. "Then [producer] Elmo Williams got up, then [director] Dick Fleischer. Then the Japanese actor Toshiro Mifune got up, because he was going to be in it. Darryl said the company was going to embark on an important production, and this was going to be the definitive picture on the bombing of Pearl Harbor.

"I was going to be involved with *Joanna,* so I didn't care."

Others raised the question, to themselves, of why the company was going to produce a war picture in the midst of such widespread national anti-military sentiment over Vietnam. Later, others still questioned the budget of the movie, $20 million.

At least, that was the original budget of the movie.

XII

Paint Your Wagon is . . . one of the three or four most expensive musical films ever made, and I don't think it should just be ignored. It's probably one of the last of its breed—the super-gigantic blockbuster musicals, such as *Camelot* (15 million), *Sweet Charity* (eight million), *Star!* (14 million), and *Doctor Dolittle* (18 million), that have finally broken the back of the American movie industry. There is almost no way—short of a miracle—that it can recover its costs, and although there are several other movies of this kind awaiting to be released . . . it is highly unlikely that any new ones will be scheduled for production in the years to come, or, perhaps, ever.

—Pauline Kael, *The New Yorker*

"You know, I think I could make more money as an independent, producing two pictures a year and taking it a lot easier," Richard Zanuck candidly admitted to Leonard Sloane of *The New York Times* in September of 1968. The reporter referred to Richard as "a young man just two months short of his 35th birthday who grew up in the film business and in August was named president of one of its best known companies, Twentieth Century-Fox Film Corporation."

As for why Richard was not shirking his responsibility and abandoning Fox, he told Sloane, "My father founded this company, we're substantial stockholders, and I want to make this company move ahead."

In the first half of 1969, his and his father's company lost $13.1 million before an extraordinary gain of $11 million (from the sale of some South African theater holdings*). The sharpest decline was in film rentals for feature films licensed to television.

In the second quarter the company took a $12-million write-off on *Star!* and another $8 million on *Doctor Dolittle*. The quarterly dividend in August was omitted. The studio also was tip-toeing over another financial swamp by losing $2 million in interest charges annually because it could not release the $24-million movie version of the Broadway musical *Hello, Dolly!*, completed for over a year, owing to the contractual agreement with the show's producer David Merrick as to when the film could open.

The second quarter loss marked the first such since Darryl Zanuck became president in 1962. The company had in fact been paying dividends since 1963. It distributed four precent in 1963, 1964, and 1965, and two percent in 1966. It also paid 20 cents quarterly from the end of 1964 until 1967. At that time the rate was raised to 25 cents quarterly and paid until the recent revelation.

Rumors started to fly. Twentieth Century-Fox—that is, Darryl F. Zanuck—should gird for a takeover.

---

*These were 80 theatres that Spyros Skouras had bought for the company in 1957, after the U.S. Justice Department prevented Hollywood studios from owning theatres in America. Other properties were purchased through Europe and England. The South African holdings proved to be sitting on valuable pieces of real estate, so they were sold back to their original owners, the Schlesinger Brothers. Fox also had maintained a studio facility in South Africa, where it made some CinemaScope spaghetti westerns starring George Montgomery. Hollywood unions opposed the Fox South African studio, less for reasons of Apartheid (Darryl was credited by several sources as a staunch foe of racism) but because it posed a competitive threat.

XIII

DAUGHTER OF MOVIE MAN
PREFERS FASHION TO FILM

The distance between Hollywood and Acapulco is not very great, but while Darryl Zanuck presides over a huge movie enterprise, his daughter Darrylin spends her days in a tiny dress shop in the Acapulco Hilton.

However, it's debatable whose pace is more frenetic. Miss Zanuck designs the clothes she sells, designs the fabrics they are made of, and also runs a wholesale business.

In addition, she has five children who in turn own five dogs, numerous cats and birds and a newly acquired pet lamb. Her husband, Julio Piñeda, owns a large egg business, and the hens on his farm outside of Acapulco run into the thousands.

The Piñeda ménage lives in a rambling old house—"not on the farm, that would be too much," she said.

Miss Zanuck, who is in New York to show her line to store buyers, is a tiny, 29-year-old blonde who looks amazingly like her father, the Chairman of the Board of 20th Century-Fox. Although she grew up in the Hollywood studios, she says she never wanted to be an actress.

"I used to disappear into the wardrobe department and bother the people there," she said yesterday in the Seventh Avenue hotel room that serves as her wholesale headquarters.

"When I got home, I'd draw clothes designs and show them to my father," she continued. "He'd write on them 'great' or 'it stinks.' My former nurse found some of the sketches recently and sent them to me. This blouse is like a sketch I made when I was 11 years old."

—Angela Taylor,
The New York Times,
January 28, 1965

SUSAN ZANUCK IS WED TO HER PLUCKY PIERRE

PARIS, April 8—Susan Zanuck, 33, the daughter of American movie maker Darryl Zanuck, was wed today to an attractive and eccentric French sailor, Pierre Francois Savineau.

Zanuck was unable to attend the wedding in Cannes town hall, but Susan's mother, Virginia Fox Zanuck—daughter of the founder of Twentieth Century-Fox—was at the eight-minute ceremony.

As they were joined by Cannes Deputy Mayor Madame An-drée Boccoz, Susan wore a pale blue minidress and a white lace coat and Pierre wore a specially sewn blue Spanish shirt with lace collar and cuffs under a tuxedo.

It was the second marriage for both Susan* and Pierre. In ad-dition, Pierre enjoys a measure of fame throughout France for having undergone an appendix operation on nationwide televi-sion while under hypnosis and without anesthesia.

The 1962 operation, in which Pierre moaned a few times and retched a few more times shook France and caused thousands of letters to flood French TV offices from nauseated viewers.

Pierre, at the time, explained he underwent the experiment because he planned to sail a boat single-handed around the world and wanted to be sure he could withstand pain even if he had to operate on himself.

Susan met Pierre in Antibes last year when he went there to repair her rented yacht. "It was love at first sight," Susan said.

—Bernard Valery,
New York *Daily News,*
April 9, 1967

TV ACTRESS WED IN VEGAS

LAS VEGAS—Richard Zanuck, President of Twentieth Century-Fox Studios, and actress Linda Harrison, co-star of the television series *Bracken's World*, were married early today at the Sands Hotel.

The couple boarded a chartered plane after the ceremony for a flight to Los Angeles.

Zanuck, son of movie magnate Darryl Zanuck, met Miss Har-rison when she was a starlet in the Fox "New Talent School." She appeared in the film *Planet of the Apes*. It was his second mar-riage, her first.

—Associated Press,
October 27, 1969

*Susan's first marriage, in the early 1950s, was to Andre Hakim. After the wed-ding, Darryl made him a producer. Born December 5, 1915, in Alexandria, Egypt, Andre and his older brothers Robert (born 1907) and Raymond (1909) had worked for Paramount in Paris since their teens, and produced films in France during the 1940s. "When his wife left him" Jean Negulesco said of Andre Hakim, "Darryl still kept him around as a yes-man."

While Richard and Linda Harrison Zanuck were on their Christmas 1969 honeymoon in Acapulco, Darryl Zanuck went skiing in Switzerland with girl friend Genevieve Gilles. He broke his leg.

Early in these vacations, Darryl and Richard were forced to take a conference call with producer Elmo Williams, who related the sobering fact that in Japan veteran director Akira Kurosawa had squandered weeks of valuable production time only to shoot no usuable footage for their war epic, by now entitled *Tora! Tora! Tora!*

Tora! is Japanese for "Tiger!" and the three-word expletive was the code-word for the sneak attack on Pearl Harbor. The movie featured the novel idea of presenting the bombing from both perspectives. Richard Fleischer handled the American scenes and a memo went out saying that in order to assist audiences in recognizing which plane came from which side, American planes were always to fly right to left across the screen, while Japanese planes were to fly left to right.

Richard wanted to scrap the movie entirely and take a $3-million write-off then and there. The mere suggestion infuriated Darryl, who ordered production to continue and fired off Telexes to Williams instructing that the Japanese sequences be moved to Hawaii and reshot. Richard Zanuck not really wanting to, was forced to fire the legendary Kurosawa, which in America would have been akin to sacking John Ford.

"Dick and Darryl weren't getting along at all," said Elmo Williams. "Dick being head of production, that meant I was reporting to him. Darryl, on the other hand, was taking a very personal interest in the film and on several occasions said, 'Now look, you report directly to me. Don't report to Dick.' This made a very difficult situation."

The Kurosawa/Richard Zanuck dispute—indeed, the entire idea of making a movie about the bombing of Pearl Harbor—prompted a rash of jokes at the studio. The best had to do with planning the movie's premiere in Japan.

The line went, "Did you hear? They're not going to call it *Tora! Tora! Tora!* over there. They're going to cut out an hour and call it *Those Were the Happy Times.*"

XIV

"Me, a star-maker?" said Darryl Zanuck. "No. It's the public who makes the stars. I only decide to give people with talent and beauty the opportunity to use them. The man doesn't live who can say, 'Fine, I will make you a star.' Once a face is on the screen, the public takes over, and they don't always agree with me."

The first time Genevieve Gilles, née Gillaizeau, appeared before the cameras for Zanuck, it was for an ABC Television special, *The World of Darryl F. Zanuck*, an anniversary celebration of D-Day. Darryl hosted because he had produced the movie spectacle which celebrated the historical event, *The Longest Day*. Gilles, who was a model in Paris when Zanuck met her during a dinner party at Maxim's, was 19 or 17; no two sources on the freckle-faced honey-colored blonde furnish the same age.

By the time Darryl had assembled his crew for this TV special, the ranks had swollen to 36 people. "Large for television," quipped a production assistant, "but not large for Zanuck."

"It was a guide to the Normandy beaches," remembered Fred Hift, who was on hand. "Mornings before shooting, Darryl would go rabbit hunting in a helicopter. It was a real game of murder. The man must have had a death wish. He'd get ten feet off the ground and start shooting at these rabbits, and then he'd order the pilot to go lower, and lower. Why be in a helicopter at all? Anyway, the pilot refused."

During work hours the young Gilles grew restless on the set of the special, so Darryl wrote her into the piece. "It was a tiny scene set in a roadside café," said Hift. "He put her in a waitress outfit and had her carry a tray of drinks to some of the ex-soldiers

145

sitting around. It could not have been more than a three-second shot."

When the scene ended, Hift mentioned to Zanuck that he thought Genevieve looked good in it, and she, in turn, acknowledged Hift's compliment. "You're a sweetheart," she told him.

"Six o'clock the next morning my phone rang," said Hift.

"You up?" It was Zanuck.

"Not at six. No, Darryl."

"Well, when you are up, come over. I want to see you."

By the time Hift arrived at the hotel suite Zanuck was in his dressing robe. The morning newspapers were read and strewn about the floor. Zanuck walked over them and said, "You're right, she looked great. I'm rewriting the scene to include her."

The next take, Genevieve had lines. She still carried the tray of drinks, only this time she was stopped midway through the room and pulled over to the table occupied by Zanuck, who asked who she was.

"Monsieur," she responded, "I am an actress." The camera recorded Zanuck's mouth as it opened so wide that the cigar fell out. Then the mogul summoned Hift to the table and into the shot.

"Fred," Zanuck told him, as he pointed to Gilles, "make sure you get this girl's number. I think she has possibilities."

"It was awful," Hift said, "but who was going to tell that to Darryl? You didn't argue with Zanuck. It got worse as he got older."

Indirectly, ABC told Darryl. The network informed the representatives at Twentieth Century-Fox that the special would not air unless "that idiot scene" was deleted.

"Zanuck went berserk," said Hift. " 'If that scene isn't in the show,' he told the Fox people, 'you're all fired.' For a week nobody at Fox did anything about it. ABC remained intransigent, until finally Darryl unhappily gave in. But it was a black mark forever against the TV division."

Nearly everyone who paid witness to the Zanuck-Gilles courtship recalled how he babied her. "I once had to bring her some wigs," Anne Head said, "and was met by Darryl at the front door of the hotel suite. He told me to keep quiet because Genevieve was still sleeping. He made it sound as though he were guarding a baby. The poor guy was absolutely smitten with her."

Hift recalled the time Zanuck lost his temper because a hotel put a call into Genevieve before nine A.M. "Those bastards!" screamed Zanuck. "They know she's not to be disturbed!"

"I've never seen such a violent display of temper," said Hift. "He was going to have the entire hotel staff fired. They were instructed that Genevieve was not to receive any phone calls or be disturbed until after ten. For someone so young, she certainly slept a lot."

Genevieve's actual screen test, never shown to the public, was a 20-minute fashion short filmed in Paris and the South of France, mostly around St. Tropez. Anne Head had been hired to handle members of the press, who on Zanuck's instructions were to be kept away entirely.

"It's amusing to look back on that now," said Head. "We did this in 1968, and when we got back to Paris, the students were rioting in the streets. What a contrast between those kids fighting for a cause and the pampered babies on the movie."

Zanuck hired the best possible people for the fashion short. The set photographer was Francis Gaicobetti, who went on to direct the *Emmanuelle* softcore porn films.

Head said that for all of Zanuck's devotion to Genevieve, her reputation on the set was anything but that of someone who was loyal to Zanuck, especially since she was hitting him where he would be hurt the most.

"She was double-dealing him down the line," said Head, recalling Gilles's infatuation with an English photographer on the set. "One morning he needed bailing out after some rumpus in a bar. Genevieve knew he was in jail and had to be sprung. Poor old Zanuck didn't know a thing about it."

Others associated with *Hello-Goodbye* insist Darryl was aware of Gilles's activities. One person said, "And the kinkier they were, the more Darryl was turned on. He felt this reflected positively on his manhood, that he could tame this wild child."

Genevieve's shenanigans did not endear her to the staff, most of whom maintained a begrudging respect for Zanuck, if only because of his past accomplishments on film. Gilles was another matter.

"She was always being so grand and drinking champagne," said Anne Head. "When I'd finally had enough of her pretentions, I made a point of correcting her. I said there's really only *one* kind of champagne to drink, and she asked, 'Oh, and what's that?' 'Krug,' I told her, and Christian Ferri who was some sort of Zanuck assistant, told me to shut up, because Genevieve's champagne bills were high enough."

XV

"The history of *Hello-Goodbye* goes back before the movie," said its first director, Ronald Neame. "I had taken over a film for Fox in London, *Prudence and the Pill*, a [1968] comedy about birth control. Fielder Cook had been the original director, only he had had a falling out with Darryl F. Zanuck because Zanuck had cast a French girl named Irina Demick and Fielder had found her, shall we say, in his mind, not quite . . . adequate.

"So Fielder Cook wanted to recast, and Darryl Zanuck said through Richard Zanuck that there would be no recasting, that if Fielder Cook did not want her, then he's the one not on the picture. So Fielder took off for California," recalled Neame.

"I was in Canada at the time, visiting Expo '67 and some friends, when I received this frantic, surprise call from my agent: 'Would you finish the picture?' It had David Niven, Deborah Kerr, Judy Geeson, some others, and only had a few weeks of shooting to go.

148

" 'Are you sure?' I asked my agent. 'It seems stupid, the film is this far along.'

" 'No, no,' he insisted. 'Cook's left.'

"This was a Saturday morning and I said, 'O.K., I'll come back to London, but I want it clearly understood that I don't want credit on a picture that's two-thirds done.' The agent concurred."

Neame returned to England and was shown the material shot to date. "Tuesday morning, the movie resumed," said Neame. "Richard Zanuck and David Brown thought I was a genius because I continued working."

And Irina Demick? "Quite a nice actress," said Neame. "But she had problems with the language. She's French. The picture was in English. Anouk Aimee had a similar problem. She, too, is French. So what I did with Irina was read her her part line for line into a tape recorder and left a gap after each speech for her to read back. I worked hard with her, and she was an extremely nice girl. She was no longer Darryl Zanuck's girl friend at the time but they were still very friendly."

Demick, in fact, was long gone by this time. While on location in Rome for *Up From the Beach*, the actress had pointed to a handsome young Swiss swimming the length of the hotel pool and informed Fred Hift that she and the man were to be married. What amused Hift was that she was still living with Zanuck at the time.

"Isn't he handsome?" Demick asked Hift.

"Well, yes, he is, Irina."

"Tell me, Fred. Do you think he's a homosexual?"

Hift did not know what to make of her inquiry, but did ask where the wedding would take place. "Here in Rome, Irina?"

Obviously her hopes for the marriage were not high. "Fred, are you crazy?" she answered. "In Switzerland. You can't get a divorce in Rome."

Because of Neame's accomplishment with *Prudence and the Pill*, Richard Zanuck and producer Robert Fryer offered the director *The Prime of Miss Jean Brodie*, which turned out aces. Maggie Smith won an Oscar in 1969 for her role as the Scottish schoolteacher poseur who rears her students to be "Brodie girls," carbon copies of her unhappy self.

"The job was a sort of repayment," said Neame. "It was one of my better pictures. I certainly enjoyed it."

What happened next, said Neame, "was that Darryl F. Zanuck was going to make a film with Genevieve Gilles, and we had a meeting to do with *Hello-Goodbye*. Darryl thought I was rather good at handling French girls. Also, how shall I say this? I was no threat. I was then already an elderly gentleman. Of course, I don't think Darryl was much older. In any event, he was very protective of her. He had detectives surrounding her."

As Neame viewed the situation, "Darryl Zanuck had removed himself from Hollywood and was living entirely in Paris, though he was still nominally the head of Twentieth Century-Fox. Dick was handling the reins. Darryl was in Paris with Genevieve Gilles supervising *Hello-Goodbye*. The producer was André Hakim, who at one time had been Darryl Zanuck's son-in-law and also had produced a picture I directed, *The Man Who Never Was*, a film Darryl's wife, Virginia, had invested in. So, in fact, I'd always rather liked her. Virginia, that is. Anyway, Andre Hakim later died of a heart attack."

Hello-Goodbye served as an ironic choice of titles. "It became apparent that I could not work on the film without Darryl Zanuck's interference," said Neame. "I was not given the reins a director normally carries. So I asked if I could be relieved from the picture. Oddly enough, at the same time of my wanting to leave, Darryl was contacting Richard Zanuck, 'Can we relieve Ronald Neame?' "

As an example of Darryl's interference, a member of the production staff recalled that during the first three days of the picture Neame was shooting close-ups of actor Michael Crawford while Genevieve was feeding lines off camera. Darryl sat on the sidelines, observing. After Neame ordered, "Cut," Darryl walked over to the director and said, "She was very good in that one, don't you think?"and Neame would delicately point out to his boss that she was not on camera. "Yes," Zanuck would say to Neame, "but you ought to consider it."

"My agent, Christopher Mann of London," said Neame, "told me not to leave the film until he could get to Cannes, where we were shooting. He wanted to know if I had a copy of my contract there, which I did. It had specific clauses X, Y, and Z, which stated I had to be given conditions of work that were normally given to a director of my standing, sort of a director's bill of rights. So Chris went over to Zanuck and said, 'O.K., Ronnie will leave the picture but only because he's not been given the conditions of work that would normally be given to a director of his standing. He will withdraw. But he will have to be paid in full.'

"Then Darryl Zanuck, or maybe it was his legal man, said to me, 'We will pay you for the picture on the understanding that for the next three years you will not mention the circumstances of your departure at all. If you do mention these circumstances, you will not be paid. We will hold that money for the next three years to insure you do not break faith.'

"I did not break faith. Darryl said at the time, 'Ronnie, you will never again work for Twentieth Century-Fox,' I said, 'So be it, Darryl.' And we parted company."

Variety placed the news of Neame's departure on its front page, and Gordon Stuhlberg, then head of production for Cinema Center Films, a division of CBS, phoned Christopher Mann to confirm that Neame had indeed left *Hello-Goodbye*, and then Stuhlberg offered Neame the director's job on *Scrooge*, a musical version of Dickens's *A Christmas Carol* starring Albert Finney.

"I was very lucky," said Neame. He got luckier.

"Six months after I finished *Scrooge* [September 1971], Gordon called me to say he'd just been made President of Twentieth Century-Fox, and he had this picture in which the director had just walked out. It was a terrible script, he said, and he didn't know if there was anything I could do about it, but would I be interested?"

And that is how Ronald Neame came to direct the 1972 sinking-ship adventure *The Poseidon Adventure*, which set off an entire cycle of disaster movies in Hollywood and which made him very rich.

"It's a saga," said Ronald Neame, "one that taught me that nothing is necessarily bad."

XVI

Jean Negulesco, a Rumanian Renaissance man and old Darryl Zanuck crony, stepped in to direct *Hello-Goodbye*. He deemed the mission a simple act of mercy. "He did it as an act of love for Darryl F. Zanuck," said David Brown in 1987.

The team of Negulesco and Zanuck had survived more than 20 years of frequently rough road and clashes of artistic temperaments. They had met in February 1948, shortly after Negulesco had announced his retirement from pictures and the resumption of his career as a painter.

The reason for his disillusionment with Hollywood was that he had just directed Jane Wyman as a deaf mute in Warner Bros.' *Johnny Belinda*. She would win the Academy Award as Best Actress for the role. Negulesco's reward from the studio was a pink slip. Warners was undergoing another period of cutbacks.

A few days after the axe fell, Negulesco's agent, Irving Lazar, got word to his client at his Palm Springs home that Darryl Zanuck wanted to see him.

"I didn't run to see Zanuck," said Negulesco. "I flew."

At the meeting, Zanuck handed Negulesco a script that he said no one but Negulesco could handle.

"But I know you can," claimed Zanuck, and Negulesco chose not to argue. He made the melodramatic love triangle, entitled *Road House*, with Ida Lupino, Cornel Wilde, and Richard Widmark. Thereafter, Negulesco was a Twentieth Century-Fox director and one of "Darryl's boys," proving a vital part of Fox history. He helped popularize Darryl's technological baby, CinemaScope, by showing that the device could tell a contemporary story. The first was *How to Marry a Millioniare* with Betty Grable, Lauren Bacall, and Marilyn Monroe, and he then went on to make such popular entertainments of their day as *Three Coins in the Fountain, Daddy Long Legs, Rains of Ranchipur, Boy on a Dolphin,* and *A Certain Smile.*

When in 1962 problems flared up between Marilyn Monroe and director George Cukor on the set of *Something's Got to Give,* Negulesco was contacted with the hope of calming his former star. The comedy was a remake of the 1940 Leo McCarey movie *My Favorite Wife* with Irene Dunne and Cary Grant, in which a shipwrecked woman presumed dead for years returns home on the eve of her husband's second wedding.

Monroe loved the original script, said Negulesco. The problem was, Cukor did not, and the temperamental Monroe did not adapt to his changes. She walked off the picture, Fox sued her, she sued Fox. Her co-star Dean Martin refused to make the movie with anyone else, and Negulesco thought he could resolve the standstill by cajoling her back to work with one of his paintings and a bottle of champagne. "She loved champagne," he remembered affectionately.

Negulesco never made the deliveries. Fox lawyers stopped him from contacting her. "Peter Levathes said, 'Absolutely not!' The next day," Negulesco said, "she killed herself."

Not that Fox went without a Monroe picture. The next year, the company released *Marilyn,* an 88-minute documentary with Rock Hudson narrating clips from all of the movie queen's Fox films, from 1949's *Ticket to Tomahawk* to the few shots, including a nude swimming sequence, from *Something's Got to Give.* It also released *Move Over, Darling,* with Doris Day and James Garner, directed by Michael Gordon. It was the recycled *Something's Got to Give.*

July 20, 1969, Negulesco was sitting in front of the television set in his London flat, watching Neil Armstrong walk on the moon, when the phone rang. After what had been a friendly silence of nine years, Darryl Zanuck was calling.

"Johnny, what are you doing?" Zanuck asked Negulesco.

"I'm watching the man walk on the moon, what do you think?" Negulesco knew Darryl Zanuck was not a man for idle chatter. "Darryl," Negulesco asked, "where are you, in town?"

"No, I'm in France. Cannes. I'm doing a great picture."

"You always do great pictures, Darryl," said Negulesco, one eye on the television screen.

There fell an uncharacteristic pause from Zanuck's end of the phone. "I'm in trouble," the mogul finally said. "I need you. When can you come here?"

His full attention now devoted to the conversation, Negulesco answered, "Whenever you need me." Explaining his knee-jerk response several years later, Negulesco, sitting in the same Mayfair apartment said, "I loved him so much, if he had asked me to come clean the toilet I'd have done it."

Faced with the order to come to France, Negulesco said, "So Darryl, just send me a ticket."

"Be at the airport in two hours," was the command. Negulesco was there. Only there was no ticket.

"Instead, there was a private plane," said Negulesco. "I took an overnight bag. I didn't know what he wanted. A story conference, I figured. The pilot asked if I wanted to go directly to Nice or via Geneva. 'Oh, let's go to Switzerland,' I told him. 'I'd like to pick up some chocolates.' You see, I hate to travel alone."

In Nice, two cars met Negulesco. "One was for my luggage, only I didn't have any, just my overnight bag." Negulesco was also greeted by Zanuck's assistant Bill, who told Negulesco that Darryl wanted him to read the *Hello-Goodbye* script, for the usual reason: "It's in trouble."

Negulesco was tired and begged off the reading assignment until the next morning. But first he asked Bill some questions. How long had they been shooting?

Three and a half months.

The budget?

Eight million.

How much had already been spent?

Three million.

"Astronomical," thought Negulesco. "That is, for then. Of course, today that's a TV short."

Negulesco read the script. "It was nothing to yell about. It pretended to be a soufflé, but it was flat. Very. I looked at what had been shot. After three and a half months all they had was one reel. What Neame had put together was excellent, but it was only one reel. Then I met Darryl."

Negulesco found his old boss as dynamic as ever: Also, extremely generous. "Anything I wanted," Negulesco recalled, "I got double."

Negulesco accepted the offer to direct the picture. "My affection for Darryl was so that I started to work. I also got a call from Richard Zanuck, Richard who always admired and looked up to his father. Richard said, 'Thanks. You've made the old man happy.'

"In the end," said Negulesco, "I think I saved the production a couple million dollars, which the group resented. There's a certain machinery that's set up when you make a film, and it comes to resent the creative end of the production. They keep the books, the budget—it's a whole world apart. It's really better to come in a little over budget or a little under, but never on, because then it looks like you're not only doing your own job, but you're also doing theirs better than they can. You must never undermine the importance of these people."

XVII

"The sole excuse for the film appears to be that it provides a showcase for Genevieve Gilles, a former Parisian model who plays the enigmatic heroine. Chicly sheathed, dripping jewelry,

155

and mouthing her lines in a flat monotone, she certainly cannot act. She does display herself freely and easily, however. 'Pipple enjoy looking at her,' explains Curt Jurgens, as the baron, while Miss Gilles displays her backside."

—Howard Thompson, reviewing *Hello-Goodbye*, in *The New Times*, July 13, 1970

".... nonacting and frequently unintelligible . . . a gorgeous starlet in the hallowed Fox tradition of Irina Demick, Juliette Greco, and Bella Darvi."

—Kevin Thomas in *The Los Angeles Times* on Genevieve Gilles

"The dichotomy was ludicrous," recalled a then-junior publicist at Twentieth Century-Fox. "It was frightening. The older people at the studio were being fired. Efficiency experts came in and got rid of them, to save the company from going under. Meanwhile, millions were being spent on Darryl Zanuck's girl friend. The furs, the jewelry. Anything she wanted, we had to get her."

Jean Negulesco acknowledged that the wardrobe had been lavish on *Hello-Goodbye*, and that it included furs and jewelry. Asked whether these items were returned to the studio that had paid for them, Negulesco declined answering.

"The making of the movie was one solid party," said Anne Head. "It was dirty old men at play. Genevieve had a stand-in who was making it with everybody. All the hanky-panky . . . I quit."

One morning Genevieve was swimming, innocently but playfully, with a couple of good-looking, young production assistants as the cameras were being set up on the pool deck. "If Genevieve was working," said an observer, "then Darryl was there." But the partying in the pool did not amuse him. He quickly disappeared into a cabana, then emerged a few moments later wearing a pair of bikini swimming trunks.

"I don't know how old he was then," said the witness, "but he was not in the best-looking of shape."

Zanuck, his chest inflated to its full expanse, marched directly to the high diving board and took a flying leap into the pool.

"Everyone nearly shit in his pants," recalled Anne Head. "My God, here was the President of Twentieth Century-Fox swimming laps to show up these kids."

Negulesco persuaded Head to remain on the film, assuring her that life would settle down once the company returned to Paris. "Nerves were very frayed," she said.

Little by little, the crew came back to Paris, where shooting finished and post-production began. Said Head: "Negulesco started cutting the movie with an English editor, and the two would meet at the studio every day at ten A.M. Negulesco told me, 'It's not going to shape up too badly. We're saving things with these two actresses. When they work with Michael Crawford, it's quite good.' "

"Two English actresses," recalled Negulesco, "one was Ira Furstenberg, who was still left in the movie. I'm sorry I can't remember the other woman's name."*

"Exuding even more steam [than Genevieve Gilles] while clothed is a chesty brunette named Ira Furstenberg, shown briefly at a Cannes casino," wrote Howard Thompson in the *Times*. "The less said of Michael Crawford, as the skinny, toothy young hero of this jape, the better."

"It's not a favorite of mine," a heftier Michael Crawford said of *Hello-Goodbye* in 1987, as he sat in his dressing room at London's Her Majesty's Theatre, where he starred as the lead in *The Phantom of the Opera*.** "It was great to work with someone like Darryl Zanuck. I just think his judgment wasn't as good in his later years as it was when he was a young man. Not that being young necessarily contributes. We all make mistakes. If we all knew the right choices, wouldn't it be wonderful?"

*Vivien Pickles.
**The program does not list *Hello-Goodbye* among Crawford's credits. It does mention his supporting role in *Hello, Dolly!*

157

On the subject of Genevieve Gilles, Crawford said: "Has anybody heard from her?"

"Miss Gilles . . . possesses a lovely mouth and other attractive physical features so long as photographer Henri Decae keeps her in soft focus, which means every close-up. Without this there are scenes in which she takes on a hardness of feature. She needs experience or tutoring in acting," said *Variety*. The trade publication termed the box-office chances for the movie "slim."

"Genevieve was wonderful in the picture," Negulesco insisted in 1986. "Very cooperative. We did good material in the picture, but there were these two other women who were excellent, in wonderful scenes."

"Negulesco showed Zanuck a rough, rough cut," said Head, "and Zanuck said, 'I'll not have these other women. Genevieve's the star.' Negulesco pointed out to him that it is an old lesson, even if you have the world's greatest actress, you can't center on her. And Zanuck was no fool. He was an expert film editor himself. Negulesco was fired."

"Darryl did the complete cutting of the picture," was all Negulesco would say of the latter stages of the film's post-production. "He cut out the other women entirely."

Negulesco was philosophical: "Darryl never saw himself as anything but right. He was like Napoleon. He doesn't want to say he lost Elba. He'd say the French weren't good enough."

"Zanuck was worried," said Head, "that Negulesco would file a lawsuit, so Zanuck told him, 'Look, we'll pay you everything we owe you.' Negulesco had a loyalty. I told him he'd better call a lawyer, but he said, 'No, Darryl's an old friend.' And that was it. Actually, it was sort of a golden egg for Negulesco. He got paid off by Zanuck and bought himself an apartment in Paris, just as all of Darryl's old girl friends had been able to do."

Genevieve Gilles did not take the criticism lying down. "I want to tell the press some day I am going to be successful and powerful," she alerted columnist Earl Wilson. "To be powerful is more important then anything."

When Wilson asked her how she would exert her power, Gilles responded, "So I can tell the press."

"What?" Wilson wondered. He said her reply was French and consisted of five letters, though it was her description of *Hello-Goodbye* that caused the most talk.

"My screen test," she called it, and revealed further that the movie "cost five-million dolluh."

She meant dollars. And the figure did not sit comfortably with one of the major shareholders of the Twentieth Century-Fox Film Corporation.

Her name was Virginia Zanuck.

PART FOUR

I

Within the thirty-day deadline after Darryl Zanuck's emergency homecoming, the far-reaching future policies for the corporation as devised by Dick Zanuck and David Brown were melded with the statistics of the Stanford Research Institute, and presented by Darryl at the meeting of the board in New York on August 29, 1969.

"A month ago I informed you that Dick and I had for some time been working together on an original, radical, and progressive plan for the future worldwide operation of our corporation," Darryl F. Zanuck told the gathering this unseasonably cool morning. He read from a prepared speech.

"At that time we deferred presenting it for your consideration and—hopefully—for your endorsement until we were in a position to answer all your questions with factual replies."

The board of directors had been elected earlier in the year, at the stockholders meeting held May 20. They included David Brown, Vice President, Director of Story Operations of Twentieth Century-Fox Film Corporation; John P. Edmondson, consultant and former Executive Vice President of E.P. Dutton (the book publisher); William T. Gossett, formerly President of the American Bar Association; William Randolph Hearst, Jr., Editor-in-Chief of Hearst Newspapers; Harry J. McIntyre, Vice President, Administration and Secretary of Twentieth Century-Fox Film Corporation; Paul Miller, Chairman of the Board and Chief Executive Officer of Gannett Company (Rochester, New York-based publishing and broadcasting company); William Huges Mulligan, Dean of Fordham University School of Law; Jerome A. Straka, Chairman and Director of Chesebrough-

Ponds; and Richard D. Zanuck, Executive Vice President in Charge of Worldwide Production of Twentieth Century-Fox Film Corporation, a board member since 1966 and owner of 35,858 shares of common stock in the company.

In addition there was D.F.Z. himself, President and Chief Executive Officer of Twentieth Century-Fox Film Corporation, a board member officially since 1942, and in control of 258,236 shares, which included 100,000 shares owned by his estranged wife Virginia Zanuck, and an aggregate 102,658 shares held in trust for daughters Darrylin and Susan and another 35,856 shares held in trust for Richard. Darryl Zanuck maintained voting rights in all 202,638 shares.

This particular board had been formed to replace one deceased director, as well as William Rogers, who had resigned in order to become Richard Nixon's Secretary of State, and others who had withdrawn or else did not stand for re-election. Except for the flagrant touch of nepotism, by now too old a story with which to contend, and the seats occupied by Brown and McIntyre, who each had served in executive capacities at the studio for more than five years, this was an unusual board by Hollywood standards. Zanuck's assemblage showed no signs of the usual pals and associates from the entertainment industry.

The board's sole tie to the old-boy network was the long friendship that had existed between McIntyre and Dutton's Edmondson, although a case could be made vis-à-vis David Brown and William Randolph Hearst, Jr.

Brown's wife, Helen Gurley Brown, served as editor of *Cosmopolitan*, the Hearst Corporation's most successful magazine.

Overall, Darryl Zanuck looked upon his board not only with pride but as a safety valve, given that these business-world titans would no doubt have the wherewithal to help Fox—and thus Zanuck—stave off any prospective hostile corporate raiders, talk of which already was being fueled.

Hollywood attorney Greg Bautzer had been asked by what he would only describe as "a large private New York investment banking house" to prepare an economic examination of Fox.

Darryl F. Zanuck in his usual work attire, at home in his Hotel Plaza suite. The date was March, 1969, and the 66-year-old mogul had suffered a broken ankle. (Photo: Associated Press)

William Fox, founding father of the Fox Film Corporation. Not visible are his white athletic socks, which he wore as a matter of habit with his dark business suits. He claimed his feet hurt. (Photo: Culver Pictures)

Fox Movietone Studios, located on Pico Boulevard in Westwood and built by William Fox in 1928 as a sound facility for his newsreels. He had built his original Hollywood Studio on Sunset Boulevard in 1917, but was to consolidate operations in Westwood. Movietone City, as it was called, still serves the 20th Century-Fox Corporation.

D.F.Z. and Joseph Schenck, who ran Twentieth Century Pictures, welcomed Douglas Fairbanks back to New York after the screen star--and partner in United Artists, which released Twentieth's annual slate of 12 features--had been in Europe for 14 months. (Photo: Associated Press)

Darryl and wife Virginia Fox Zanuck (no relation to William Fox) attend a Hollywood premiere of a 20th Century-Fox picture in 1936. (Photo: International News)

Polo, one of D.Z.'s great passions of the 1930's, was so closely identified with the studio chief that his regular drinking hole at the Beverly Hills Hotel was renamed the Polo Lounge. (Photo: Associated Press)

Darryl, daughter Susan, wife Virginia, and 20th Century-Fox producer George Jessel depart for Paris in 1948. Zanuck was to check film locations in England and Italy, as well as vacation in Paris. (Photo: Trans World Airlines)

Bella Darvi--her last name a conjunction of Darryl and Virginia--in her dressing room at 20th Century-Fox. She is visited by actress Jean Peters (in hat). (Photo: Culver Pictures)

Richard Zanuck, age 24, and his first wife, Lili Gentle, who had starred in Fox B-pictures. Dick and Lili were married in 1958. (Photo: Metropolitan Photo Service)

Linda Harrison, Richard Zanuck's second wife. She too starred in some of the studio's pictures, including *Planet of the Apes*.

Director Robert Wise, his star Julie Andrews, and D.F.Z. at the 1965 New York premiere of *The Sound of Music*. Critics hated the picture; audiences simply adored it; and the studio grew rich. (Photo: Metropolitan Photo Service)

Pierre Savineau, the second husband of Susan Zanuck (age 33), shown after their civil wedding ceremony in Cannes, France, April 1967. (Photo: Associated Press)

Helen Gurley Brown and David Brown leaving the Plaza Hotel in 1982. One of New York's best-known couples, Helen, editor of *Cosmopolitan* magazine, was considered more famous than her husband until he and Richard Zanuck produced two of the highest grossing films of the 1970's, *The Sting* and *Jaws*.

Dennis Stanfill, hired by Richard Zanuck and David Brown in 1969 to set 20th Century-Fox on the road to financial recovery. (Photo: Associated Press)

Henry M. DeMeyer, consultant from the Stanford Research Institute, initially was hired by Dennis Stanfill to assist in modernizing the financial arm of 20th Century-Fox. (Photo: Irv Antler)

Virginia, Richard, and Darrylin Zanuck, in forefront, as they left Darryl's funeral at the United Methodist Church in Westwood, the morning of December 27, 1979. (Photo: Associated Press)

Genevieve Gilles, Darryl Zanuck's longtime companion, and divorce attorney Marvin Mitchelson in New York on June 26, 1980, the day she announced that she was suing the Zanuck estate for "palimony." (Photo: Frank Leonardo/New York *Post*)

"The object of the study," Bautzer admitted, "was a takeover." The attorney later told *The Los Angeles Times* that he declined to go ahead with the study because he would only have done it with the cooperation of the Zanucks, and they were not standing for any takeover.

It was also known that the shrewd Broadway producer and former St. Louis attorney David Merrick was interested in launching his own buy-out, to be handled by the law firm of Fitelson & Mayers. Those said to be aligning with Merrick and who had already requested a list of the movie company's stockholders included Bernard Cornfield, the Geneva-based American financier; Harry Brandt, whose family owned the Trans-Lux Corporation; Leonard Gruenberg, the former chairman of the television production company Filmways; Charles Allen of Allen & Company, the major Wall Street investment firm that had taken control in the house and an eventual force at 1960s of Warner Bros.;* and the brokerage firm of Bear, Stearns, and Company.

"We have called this presentation 'A Working Paper on the Future of Twentieth Century-Fox Film Corporation,'" said Darryl. "I will ask Dick to read the initial portions of this report which represent our joint effort and when we come to a portion of this report which represents my recommendations alone, I will ask Dick to turn the floor over to me."

"This working paper on the future of Twentieth Century-Fox Film Corporation is exactly what the title conveys," said Richard. "It is a report to the Directors of what Management proposes to do with this company as we approach the 1970s—in fact, as we approach the twenty-first century.

"What will Twentieth Century-Fox be like when it becomes Twenty-First Century-Fox? How will it cope with the problems and opportunities of the space age? How will it overcome the present problems which affect profitability? What will it do to increase its share, not only of the motion picture and television

---

*And would do the same with Columbia Pictures.

market but also of the entire and vastly growing market of leisure time pursuits?

"For an authoritative, objective analysis of the United States film industry," he said, "we have engaged Stanford Research Institute to make a survey. Much of what is contained in the preliminary findings of that survey is common knowledge to us, but the confirmation of many of our theories through the use of an outside research organization is of great value. We know we are not flying by the seat of our pants."

The major discovery made by Stanford Research was that the movie industry stood on the brink of many changes in the field, some positive, some threatening. Movie attendance was in decline. Average U.S. weekly movie-theatre attendance the previous year (1968) was only an estimated 18,100,000 persons, "about *one-third* of the 1950 level of 53,300,000 persons. This took place during a period when population increased by more than 30 percent," said Richard.

The once-loyal movie-going public was getting older and television was monopolizing its attention. Television was still treated as the enemy by Fox, indeed by most movie companies. They were as yet still hesitant to advertise their product on it. Equally problematic was that movie production costs were rising. Theatres were shutting their doors. Currency restrictions and political instabilities were having a negative effect on the once-lucrative foreign market. The new technology, which would include cable television and videocassettes,* needed to be confronted as either a healthy challenge or the last fatal blow to the movie industry.

Richard Zanuck emphasized that some technological choices would have to be faced sometime soon. "The annual frequency of attendance of teen-agers is from five to ten times the fre-

*Darryl eagerly anticipated the revolution promised by cassettes, predicting for a group of European industry insiders in 1970, a full dozen years before the video explosion: "I am very much for them, and my son Richard is keen on them. But films will have four or five years in domestic release before they are transferred to cassettes. I think cassettes will be a great boon to movies." Except for the five-year "window"—the average lapse between theatrical first-run and video availability became six months—Darryl was correct.

quency of attendance of persons over the age of 40," he said. "Sixty-five percent of the moviegoers in 1967 were between the ages of 15 and 29. Persons between the ages of 15 and 19 attended films the most, about 13 times a year."

The conclusion Richard Zanuck presented the board was that the movie industry, to be successful, "must depend heavily on a very small proportion of highly successful films targeted for the youth market.

"It is therefore imperative that companies become far more selective in their motion picture output as there is no longer any automatic movie habit which will take care of films of average or below-average appeal."

How had movies lost their audience?

Richard blamed "the large number of films available on television" and "the rise in recent years of leisure time activities such as boating, certain spectator sports, travel, etc."

What would bring audiences back to the movies? "An outstanding attraction," a "film [that] deals with subject matter not available on television."

Richard brought Fox into the picture. The previous year the studio released 19 movies, as compared to 37 from Paramount, 27 from M-G-M, and 23 from Columbia. Fox's share of the market, then, was 17.5 percent.

"Since in 1968 there was a total of 255 feature films released," said Richard, "Twentieth Century-Fox achieved its 17.5 percent of the gross billings of all companies with only .075 percent of the releases."

By comparison, Fox's share of the market in 1966, when *The Sound of Music* was tinkling in the studio's ears and 23 other Fox releases entered the marketplace, was 19.2 percent in a year. All told, in 1966, there were 243 new releases.

Richard said that in four of the previous five years, net earnings from the production and distribution of Fox pictures, plus the corporation's other activities, rose substantially year-to-year.

"Notwithstanding all this," he insisted, "management is not satisfied.

"With the advent in the foreseeable future of the four-day

working week in the United States and increasing currency restrictions and political instability in many areas of the foreign market, it is apparent to us that radical and inventive new approaches to our company's operations must be devised and carried out if we are to meet the challenge and the opportunity of the coming decade."

For the time being, said Richard Zanuck, "we believe we are far from achieving our potential. We believe many of our assets can be more profitably utilized. We believe it is time to depart from some of the time-honored procedures and policies of the past. As a beginning, we propose an immediate change in the corporation's name from Twentieth Century-Fox Film Corporation to Twenty-first Century-Fox.

"What does this new name mean? The fact that we have deleted the words 'Film Corporation' from our new corporate title does not mean we are getting out of production and distribution of motion pictures. . . . Our objective is to reduce the dependency of the corporation on film rentals by building up profits in other related areas."

Mostly these involved real estate.

A "vital negotiation connected with the plan" which Darryl had cited at the outset of the meeting as another cause for his one-month delay, was the proposed election of Thomas J. Scallen as vice president in charge of Corporate Development. He was to bring to Fox his own company, whose divisions included the Ice Follies live-entertainment show, as well as an advertising agency.

"We preferred him over many better known, more sophisticated organizational types who have never met a payroll," said Richard. "Mr. Scallen will work hand in hand with Lehman Brothers and others on the acquisition trail."

The word "acquisition" provided a natural segue into Richard's next topic.

"Our attitude toward a major merger has not altered," he said. "THIS CORPORATION IS NOT AVAILABLE UNLESS IT IS TO THE CORPORATION'S LONG-TERM INTEREST

TO MERGE—and in the absence of such an advantageous merger, we intend to build from within and make our own acquisitions."

The floor was returned to D.F.Z.

"Gentlemen," said Darryl, continuing to read from the pages prepared by his son and David Brown, "I come now to that section of our presentation that is mine alone. It is with emotion that I make this recommendation. Two years ago I came to the conclusion that Richard Zanuck was the logical choice to become president of this corporation. However, I refrained from proposing this for two reasons.

"First, Dick was deeply involved in the task of preparing and putting before the cameras the most ambitious and, in my opinion, the best production program in the company's history. Two, I wanted to satisfy myself that Dick was willing to take on these broader responsibilities without stepping away from his most important function: the creative job of supervising production. I have satisfied myself on both points. Dick's present creative team plus additions to the corporate echelon will make it possible for Dick to do both jobs. Whatever the fruits of diversification, the making of pictures—our source of greatest profit— most requires the rarest talents.

"As most of you know, Dick has, after seven years as production chief, earned a reputation of being one of this industry's most able young executives and selfishly I want to use him in an even more vital capacity *without* losing him as head of production. I'm convinced good organization and a great backfield will make that work. For myself, I intend no slackening of responsibility or effort.

"I ask to become Chairman and Chief Executive Officer, and that I retain the final executive responsibility for the affairs of the corporation. I need Dick in this post of broader responsibility to make our plan succeed. I will concentrate on corporate policy without the burden of worldwide day to day operation which Dick is willing and able to assume," said Darryl.

"Richard Zanuck will fortify his new office, if this board elects him, by a slate of top appointments which will be presented to this board next month for approval. A careful analysis has been made of the duties he will be required to perform and it is my conclusion that it is totally practical for him to operate in both areas with the delegation of duties that is contemplated and with the recruitment of a new young generation of executives. This is a business *for* and by the young and we intend to bring the age level way down without sacrificing the experience and expertise of our senior executives."

Darryl proposed that Richard be based in Los Angeles, but that he spend a considerable amount of time in New York. For that, a permanent office would be set up in New York for him.

"It is my recommendation that this board approve Richard Zanuck as President because he is uniquely qualified to take this corporation into the '70s and to embark on new and successful voyages in the world of entertainment."

The board approved Darryl Zanuck's plan as seaworthy. Darryl Francis Zanuck was elected Chairman and Chief Executive Officer and Richard Darryl Zanuck, President, although the plan to rename the company Twenty-first Century-Fox was never implemented.

II

The day after the August 29 board of directors meeting, Darryl Zanuck blew his stack. Darryl had been given the "Historic White Paper"—which some studio wags were calling the "Historic White Wash"—the very day of the meeting. The founder of the studio had received no time to prepare for the shocking news that his son Richard wanted him to step upstairs so Richard could assume the throne.

"What the hell does a chairman *do?*" Darryl demanded of Richard, whom he accused of "putting me out to pasture."

"The word spread like wildfire that Dick had fired his own father," remembered a former Fox executive whose New York office was down the hall from Darryl's. "Needless to say, all ears were glued to the walls. Darryl was telling Dick to stick to reading scripts, *he* was running the company."

"What am I supposed to do?" harangued Darryl. "What does Chairman of the Board *mean*?" He yelled at Dick: "Now you're running everything. Why don't you keep your nose out of the war?"

The day after the board meeting, Darryl let Richard have it full throttle. "In front of David, he told me that I'd perpetrated the con job of the century," said Richard. "We had stolen the company from him."

III

Post-production demands on *Hello-Goodbye* forced Darryl back to France. In Westwood, Dick and David sought to hire a financial officer to take charge of the weak link in the studio corporate structure. Relying on the advice of Michael Thomas of Loeb Brothers in New York, the Fox executives contacted the recently hired treasurer of the Times-Mirror Corporation, which published *The Los Angeles Times*. The newspaper's publisher, in fact, was a childhood friend of Dick Zanuck's, Otis Chandler. Both men shared the privileges of second-generation powerful Californians. The name of the *Times* money man was Dennis C. Stanfill.

A lunch for the three men to meet was arranged at Perino's, away from Fox and away from the *Times*. Dick and David were totally convinced Stanfill was the right man to set straight the studio's financial picture. Still, if they were to sense any hesitation at the lunch before putting forth a final job offer, a little plan had been worked out. David would put his napkin on the table, as a signal to Dick. If it were Yes, and Stanfill was to be hired, then Dick would remain at the table. If the decision were No, then Dick would excuse himself and go to the men's room.

Lunch was pleasant, although when conversation came around to business, as it quickly did, Stanfill could not believe his ears. He was told that Fox was broke.

Slightly incredulous, Stanfill still was not discouraged. He would be happy to work for Fox. Then came the moment of reckoning. David Brown placed his napkin on the table. Richard Zanuck did not get up.

"Not going to the men's room was one of the biggest mistakes I ever made," Zanuck said later. He was more than a bit puzzled too by Chandler's reaction when he rang up his old chum with the news that he was hiring away one of Chandler's choicest employees. The publisher did not seem the least bit upset.

Born April 1, 1926, Dennis Stanfill graduated in the top one percent of his class at Annapolis in 1949, and after joining the Navy competed for and was accepted for a Rhodes scholarship, which took him to Oxford University and courses in politics, economics, and philosophy. It was a long jump for a soft-spoken Southern boy who had grown up in a small town in Tennessee, even though his ancestors had been well-to-do farmers for the past six generations.

At Oxford, Stanfill's entertainment consisted of "large doses of Keynesian theory, practical economics, and movies." In 1959, after three years sea duty followed by a job in Washington, D.C., briefing the secretary of the Navy on world affairs, Stanfill joined the Lehman Brothers investment banking firm, specializing in corporate finance. From there he moved to Times-Mirror, and then to Fox. He started in October 1969.

"The industry got too much money too easily," was Stanfill's cool opinion of Hollywood. "The money market was soft to begin with. Then the movies became pets of the conglomerates. And then there was *Sound of Music*, which Dick Zanuck and everybody else agrees was the most expensive movie Hollywood ever made because it led everybody into those expensive carbon copies. And if there is anything that seems clear, it's that carbon copies don't work."

As for his home base, Stanfill said, "Fox has probably thought too specifically in terms of the word 'movies' for too long. We have to define what it is we do more broadly as audio-visual entertainment. Fox is into the recording and music business, for

172

example, but not nearly as importantly as it should be. All those royalties from "Raindrops [Keep Falling on My Head," the song from *Butch Cassidy and The Sundance Kid*] didn't fall on Fox, not nearly enough of them."

The western *Butch Cassidy and The Sundance Kid* premiered in the second half of 1969, and was a desperately needed hit for the studio, which was shelling out interest payments on the still-as-yet-unreleased *Hello Dolly! Cassidy* starred Paul Newman, made a household name out of Robert Redford, and helped create the genre of the "buddy movie," itself a unique situation: There developed so many plum roles for male teams at the time that actresses, even Oscar winners such as Ellen Burstyn, Louise Fletcher, and Jane Fonda, found it difficult to land suitable employment. Butch Cassidy and the Sundance Kid were heroic badmen in the Old West; audiences cheered as they robbed banks. The movie also proffered a Top-Ten music hit, "Raindrops Keep Falling on My Head," written by Burt Bacharach and Hal David and performed by B.J. Thomas, only the original soundtrack album was not recorded by Twentieth Century-Fox Records, but by A&M Records. This too got Stanfill's goat.

"But let's not downplay the movies, either," he said. "I'm fascinated by that movie market. It's still got an incredible potential."

Unlike other people fascinated by the huge potential of the movie market, however, Dennis Stanfill did not live in Beverly Hills or Malibu. His home had long been in San Marino, an old-money enclave adjacent to Pasadena.

Dennis Stanfill, who liked to say, "The movie business is no business to be in," never really brushed shoulders with the crowd from Hollywood.

IV

In the first five weeks of 1970, Twentieth Century-Fox opened three pictures, and two of them—*M*A*S*H* and *Patton*, both having to do with war as seen from two very different sides of the ideological scale—were doing great business.

*M*A*S*H* is a S*M*A*S*H was the buzzword on the Fox lot. Elliott Gould and Donald Sutherland starred in director Robert Altman's black and bloody absurdist "buddy comedy" about the 4077th Mobile Army Surgical Unit during the Korean conflict. With its obvious parallels to Vietnam, *M*A*S*H* clicked heavily with the younger generation, yet the studio publicity squad was so uninitiated at going after this particular audience that for the first time ever Fox's promotions department made contact with underground newspapers.

"I remember having to go below 14th Street to deliver materials on *M*A*S*H*," said one in-house publicist. It proved a fruitful journey. "I saw that the editor had on his desk a list of the underground papers across the country. Here was everything I needed, so I asked for a copy of it."

Upon closer inspection the publicist saw that the list contained no phone numbers, and inquired after this omission. "What are you talking about 'phone numbers'?" the editor snapped back indignantly. "These guys can't afford phones."

Fox's upscale war movie was *Patton*, subtitled, *A Salute to a Rebel*, as a lure to the youth audience.* A technically superb biography of controversial World War II General George S. Patton, it contained enough intelligent spectacle, history, and human drama to attract a diversity of crowds. Another selling factor was the lead performance by George C. Scott, deemed certain to win him an Academy Award, which it did the next year, though, part rebel himself, he declined its acceptance. Scott considered the awards ceremony "a meat parade."

Hugh Fordin said it was he who brought Richard Hooker's novel *M*A*S*H* to the studio. Richard Zanuck disassociated his father from the picture, saying that Darryl had not so much as heard of the novel until Dick presented it at a board meeting. "I don't know whether he read the screenplay or not," Dick added.

*It was also the last roadshow engagement in the history of the studio.

Director Robert Altman, in 1986, would not respond to questions about his most celebrated movie, which had become a touchy subject for him. "I got $75,000 for doing *M*A*S*H* and the studio made $1 billion from it," said Altman, most likely referring to the immensely successful albeit watered-down television version of the movie, which Fox produced in the 1970s. The $75,000 was his director's fee. Total budget for the film, which had been shot entirely at Fox's Malibu ranch, was a modest $3.5 million.

"You know why I never made more from *M*A*S*H*?" said Altman, his voice rising. "They tried to vote me a percentage [of the gross] but Grace Kelly went to the Board of Directors and said, 'Don't you dare give that man a penny for that terrible movie!' "

No one could confirm or deny Altman's accusation, except to say it was Dennis Stanfill who had become chummy with Princess Grace. (She joined the Fox board in the early 1970's.)

Patton, which cost $12 million and was shot against a vast European panorama, was unmistakably a product of the Darryl Zanuck school. He originally had commissioned a movie biography of the military man as early as 1950. By the late 1960s, in the final stages of preproduction, he had summoned to Cap d'Antibes the movie's producer Frank McCarthy and its director Franklin Schaffner. There, Zanuck attacked the script approved by Richard that had been written by a relative newcomer Francis Ford Coppola.

"I think [Darryl] was still trying to show he could run things by remote control," said McCarthy. "I became aware for the first time of the tension between him and his son." When Richard Zanuck found out about the clandestine story conference, he quietly quit the studio.

"I walked out over that," Richard Zanuck said. "I resigned for a few days. Then my father backed down, sent me a nice telegram, and things were patched up."

In some ways, the American public, even reviewers, did not know what to make of *M*A*S*H*. Within the studio there

175

arose debates on how best to sell the film. It did not open at Grauman's Chinese Theatre in Hollywood, as did *Hello, Dolly!*, nor did it enter any of the old roadshow movie palaces in Beverly Hills or those in New York's Times Square such as the Rivoli, which normally played Fox pictures.

Instead, marking a significant change in theatre exhibition, *M*A*S*H* was booked into theatres which up until then were mostly reserved for foreign and art films, on New York's East Side and in Los Angeles' Westwood, the latter with its heavy influx of U.C.L.A. students.

"There can be no doubt about it," wrote critic Archer Winsten in the New York *Post*. "We're well on our way into a revolution of feeling, taste, naughty words, sexual mores, private beliefs, and public behaviors. *M*A*S*H* draws a few more guidelines in a wham, bam, thank-you ma'am style."

George C. Scott, not really as right-wing as the real General Patton, still hated *M*A*S*H*, and on one inopportune occasion, in front of a reporter from the Philadelphia *Inquirer*, screamed at a Fox publicity man, "That goddam piece of shit is demeaning to the American military!" The publicity squad decided George C. Scott would not grant many interviews.

The New York Times took heavy swipes at both *M*A*S*H* and *Patton*, though the newspaper's critics also managed to finger what movie audiences were thinking. Roger Greenspun in his opening day review wrote that *M*A*S*H* is "the first American movie openly to ridicule God—not only phony belief; real belief. It is also one of the few (though by no means the first) American screen comedies openly to admit the cruelty of its humor. . . . All of which may promote a certain air of good feeling in the audience, an attitude of self-congratulation that they have the guts to take the gore, the inhumanity to appreciate the humor, and the sanity to admire the impiety."

Of the more traditional film, critic Vincent Canby observed, "*Patton: A Salute to a Rebel* is likely to strike terror into any rational person who refuses—perhaps absurdly—to believe that war is man's most noble endeavor. [The film opens] with an overture that liberals can view as pure Camp, and Patton fans will interpret as pure inspiration."

The Army and Air Force Motion Picture Services wasted no time in banning *M*A*S*H* from its service theaters, because, according to *The Army Times*, it "reflected unfavorably" on the military. That newspaper's critic John Greenwald, attacking the movie, called it "a brutal, biting, outrageous put-down of military life." Summing up what was to be his condemnation, Greenwald said *M*A*S*H* was " 'black comedy' at its best."

Further playing up the differences between *M*A*S*H* and *Patton* was *Life* magazine columnist Hugh Sidey, who reported that President Richard Nixon screened *Patton* not once but twice before deciding to send American troops into Cambodia.

"One of the best parts of the movie," Nixon said, "was when Patton said they needed good weather so that they could use their air power. The general sent for the chaplain. A prayer was written asking for good weather. Patton prayed bare-headed in the snow. When the weather cleared the next day, the general sent for the chaplain and decorated him.

"Now," said Nixon, "we have every chaplain in Vietnam praying for early rain. You have to have the determination to go out and do what is right for America."

Darryl Zanuck sent Richard Nixon a letter of support.

The third Fox release of early 1970 was the espionage drama *The Kremlin Letter*, about the U.S. and Russia's proposed annihilation of China. Its director John Huston thought the picture "had all the makings of success. The novel by Noel Behn had been a bestseller. It had, moreover, all the qualities that were just coming into fashion in 1970—violence, lurid sex, and drugs.

"In any event," said Huston, "audiences rejected it."

V

Henry DeMeyer had been with the Stanford Research Institute for five years, though he knew relatively few people on staff at general headquarters. The sprawling, tree-shaded offices were located in Menlo Park, in northern California, near Stanford University, although the two institutions functioned separately.

DeMeyer's work for the Institute, and as an independent business researcher for more than a decade, had carried him to various corners of the world, which explained why he was a fairly anonymous figure in the office.

The Institute, which would officially become known as S.R.I. International, had been formed in 1946 as a problem-solving organization that aided and abetted business and government clients globally. The business of S.R.I. was research and consulting, and DeMeyer, a 1934 business graduate of the University of Chicago, had gained experience in both fields.

In the 1950s, he had worked as a senior financial analyst— "troubleshooter" was his description—at the Ford Motor Company, ending up in the Lincoln Continental division when that luxury model was revamped in 1955. He then moved to Chrysler and worked in the Detroit headquarters until he was sent to the company's Caracas, Venezuela, plant.

DeMeyer, of average height, stocky build, and bespectacled, looked like a businessman from the Midwest, and, except for his fluency with languages, he resembled the sort of dry, respectable community leader one expects to meet at a Chamber of Commerce meeting in a midsized suburban town. His specialty was the development of systems and techniques for management controls, product-price analysis, and profit planning, and in the early 1960s he put this skill to work at his own consultation firm in Seattle. He and his small team reviewed and installed management and financial control systems in the Pacific Northwest for such diverse concerns as a ski resort, lumber and logging companies, and a mining equipment manufacturer, work that DeMeyer found rewarding and stimulating. Still, he also found the business of business—running his own company

178

while overseeing the problems of the others—eventually wea-
rying, and this helped explain why the consulting expert was intrigued the day in 1965 when the invitation came to pay a visit to
S.R.I., where the supervisor of the Stockholm, Sweden, office
met with and persuaded DeMeyer to join the Institute and
move to Scandinavia, which is where he spent the next four
years.

His projects covered all of Scandinavia, including a major consultation for Trige-Titan, considered the General Electric of
Denmark. The 1960s, particularly the latter portion of the decade, was a time of economic expansion worldwide, and it was
DeMeyer's discovery that most foreign companies were 30 to 40
years behind their American counterparts in the manner of con-
ducting business.

In Christmas of 1969, DeMeyer, age 57, returned to S.R.I.
headquarters in Menlo Park to begin the new decade Stateside.
He felt new but not uncomfortable in the home office, and his
reputation somehow must have preceded him, because shortly
after the first of the year 1970, a young researcher pulled
DeMeyer aside in the hallway. He knew DeMeyer's name, and
introduced himself, saying that he was at work on a project that
DeMeyer ought to keep an eye on.

"This fellow said he was doing his second project for Twentieth Century-Fox, some sort of long-range study on the film industry and Fox's possible position in it," recalled DeMeyer.
"Except he emphasized that he really wasn't contributing anything to Fox at all, because if the studio didn't move quickly, the
study he had just finished would not do them any good."

DeMeyer felt mildly interested but not yet hooked. The
young researcher's first assignment for Fox had been a study
commissioned by the studio's Dick Zanuck some months earlier,
during the summer of 1969. There was to be a board of directors
meeting and Zanuck required some facts to explain why Fox was
performing as poorly as it had been. S.R.I. verified that the en-

tire movie industry was experiencing a downturn, only now the researcher had further economic data on the company, and the figures were staggering enough to get DeMeyer to bite.

Twentieth Century-Fox, said the researcher, was preparing to go belly-up. The studio was about to default on a $25 million dollar loan, and the company was in the hole to its New York banks for $75 million.

VI

Henry DeMeyer had met Allen E. Lee, manager of the Stanford Research Institute's consulting operations, briefly in Sweden at the latter part of 1969, before DeMeyer had left that office. Their acquaintance had been casual.

Lee, a University of California, Berkeley, graduate and 1950 Harvard M.B.A., specialized in business management and organization, areas that brought him to Union Oil as a transportation rate analyst and chief instrument engineer, and then to companies in the United States, Europe, Japan, and the Middle East where he evaluated their organizational effectiveness.

In Menlo Park in January of 1970, DeMeyer approached Lee on the subject of Twentieth Century-Fox. Given what the young associate had divulged earlier, the studio could provide a project DeMeyer could sink his teeth into. Not, Lee was to understand, that DeMeyer was starstruck by the glamor of Hollywood. DeMeyer barely went to movies. In fact, over the coming months when he did become involved with Twentieth Century-Fox, he was innocently capable of referring to Barbra Streisand as Barbara Stanwyck.

Al Lee heard DeMeyer on the subject of Fox in his office, and he understood that any eagerness on his colleague's part was purely from a business standpoint. It could also set an important precedent. DeMeyer—and S.R.I.—had never before tackled a movie studio.

In January of 1970, appointments for DeMeyer and Lee were

set up with Richard Zanuck, David Brown, who since the summer's board of director's meeting had been promoted to Executive Vice President for Creative Operations, and Dennis Stanfill, who had been at Fox for three months.

The S.R.I. men took an early flight from San Francisco Airport, a 20-minute drive from Menlo Park, and they arrived at the Pico Boulevard gate of Twentieth Century-Fox by late morning. The beige-colored soundstages loomed before them and the setting seemed quiet.

The first actual sign of anything resembling a movie studio was a small billboard emblazoned with the *Hello, Dolly!* logo—a painted Barbra Streisand in a flowered hat and Walter Matthau in a striped Arrow shirt and dark tie. Both stars smiled cheerily. The sign was attached to the wire-mesh fence that surrounded the studio property. Next to the *Dolly!* logo was a large printed message about Fox studio tours, saying they had been halted until further notice. This gave rise to a joke on the lot: The financial situation at Fox was so bad that one day Dick Zanuck walked into the commissary and fired four tourists.

The Fox parking lot was gaily decorated by the turn-of-the-century New York outdoor street set that had been erected for *Hello, Dolly!* at a cost of $2 million. Total cost of the picture was $24 million, making it the highest to date for any musical and, except for *Cleopatra*, the most expensive movie ever made.

The elaborate plywood facades for *Dolly!* masked the executive offices of Fox. Beyond these buildings, the remainder of the backlot was slowly being eaten away. The erosion had started in April 1961, when to ease the debts on *Cleopatra* and *Something's Got to Give*, Fox sold its entire land holding to the Alcoa Aluminum Company for $43 million, with Alcoa leasing back 75.7 acres to Fox. On the land where Shirley Temple once danced with Bill "Bojangles" Robinson and Jennifer Jones once walked to church in *Song of Bernadette* had been built an office and shopping complex known as Century City.

In the stillness of this setting, Henry DeMeyer asked a security officer where Richard Zanuck's office was.

VII

It was an understatement to say that Henry DeMeyer and Al Lee were impressed by Richard Zanuck's mahogany-paneled office, where the five principals gathered before lunch. Sumptuous was the only word they could think of as they examined the three separate arrangements of furniture—coffee tables, couches, works of art, elaborate lighting fixtures, and Darryl's 1941 Oscar for *How Green Was My Valley.*

What struck the men most was Richard Zanuck's desk, not that it had three white telephones, one of which was permanently plugged into David Brown's New York office, but that the long, polished wooden plank rested on an elevated platform with tiny spotlights in the ceiling, so that Richard could bask in their glow.

Richard was still tanned from the vacation-honeymoon he had spent over Christmas and New Year's in Acapulco. The men all introduced themselves, and the two S.R.I. men outlined briefly what it was their organization could do. Lunch afterward in the studio's executive dining room was pleasant and remarkably social. David Brown did most of the talking, said DeMeyer, "for the entire afternoon."

"He was the one who told us about Twentieth Century-Fox, who gave us the background on the studio," said the consultant. "he told us about the problems the studio had had, although he skirted specifics. He talked a lot about *Star!* and *Doctor Dolittle.* About all the money that had been sunk into them. He said musicals were very costly. A lot of time is needed for rehearsals. Locations. Blah, blah, blah.

"*Hello, Dolly!* had just opened. He talked a little about that. *Butch Cassidy and The Sundance Kid.* That was a hit for them. He mentioned that. Mostly he said where all their money had gone, into those pictures, and he discussed what they had in production. *Tora! Tora! Tora!* That was expensive, too. *The Great White Hope.* That was the cheapest one they had going, and that was $12.5 million.

"Oh yes. They were very high on *Patton*."

From time to time, Dennis Stanfill would try to interject a comment about the possibility of utilizing S.R.I.'s resources, said DeMeyer. Neither Dick nor David acknowledged that.

VIII

"Dick and David were living in a dream world. Being with the two of them then," Hugh Fordin said 20 years later, "was like being in Las Vegas with high rollers who didn't know what they were doing."

Part of the reason Fordin believed he was hired by the younger Zanuck and Brown was because of his professional link to David Merrick and the Broadway stage. "Dick and David looked to the theatre as a treasure chest of properties to be unlocked." Fordin could see that the studio was in need of new blood. "In those days," he said, "the desks in the story department, and the piles of scripts on them, had gathered dust about an inch thick."

Much of the studio's thinking was equally dusty, Fordin thought. "If the period had been the 1950s instead of the late '60s, Dick and David's behavior would have been tolerable," he said. "Even Darryl's. When you have your girl friend do a movie and you see from the beginning it's embarrassing, it's lunacy. But they were thinking this was M-G-M or Paramount in the '50s. They had lost their focus. They kept saying, 'We're all in the film business,' but there was no company there, no *business* going on.

"They would buy everything in sight, and not realize their stakes. Suddenly you had to dish out $50,000 for the first draft of a script, and then that option would expire and you'd have to renew it for another impossible sum. They bought so much they didn't know what they had, and, because there was so much, they couldn't make all they had."

One property Zanuck and Brown let slip away, said Fordin, was the Woody Allen stage comedy about one man's sexual ineptitude, *Play It Again, Sam*, which went on to become a big hit for Paramount and put its author and star into the mainstream of moviemaking. "Originally it had been produced on the stage by Merrick," said Fordin, who brought the work to Fox, "and Woody Allen was set to sign a major multi-picture deal with the studio, because he liked David Brown's approach."

Fox's financial reversal doomed the development of *Play It Again, Sam* for the studio, one of many mistakes Fordin witnessed from his vantage point. "David had a red phone on his desk in New York," said Fordin, "and every time it rang it meant it was Dick. That was the signal for all of us to get out of David's office and run. The call didn't mean Dick and David were turning the company around. It meant there was another new crisis.

"Dick and David thought all they needed was one more big fat hit to make up for their flops—but they couldn't see that they were never going to get it, because right under their noses the stakes had become too high."

After lunch, S.R.I's Lee and DeMeyer and Fox's Richard Zanuck and David Brown adjourned to Zanuck's office, where David Brown continued his discourse. "He had a very slow, stiff way of speaking," said Henry DeMeyer. "And he talked very softly for the next three hours."

David Brown's manner of speech has been described two ways. One was that it was scholarly. The other was, "He was capable of throwing the same sort of Hollywood bullshit you always hear at the Cannes Film Festival."

In Fox's New York office, Brown's mood was said to be easy to decipher. "If he were calm," recalled an executive, "he would puff quietly on his pipe. But if he got nervous, his bushy eyebrows would begin going up and down like Groucho Marx's." Another employee recalled, "In the office, David treated Dick like royalty, always trailing two feet behind him in the corridors, practically tripping over him in some sort of deference."

To Henry DeMeyer and Al Lee's ears, Brown's speech was soporific.

"Twice in Dick's office I had to nudge Al to stay awake," said DeMeyer.

For three hours, David Brown spoke of his and Dick's capabilities in running the studio, how they selected stories, put packages together—everything that was required for an outstanding operation of a successful film company. Nothing was said about the approaching default of nearly $100 million in bank loans.

Their day at Twentieth Century-Fox completed, Al Lee and Henry DeMeyer agreed with the Fox executives to come up with a proposal on how to help the studio. They then returned to Los Angeles Airport and boarded a P.S.A. flight home. In those days, the airline advertised the best-looking stewardesses in the air, and it outfitted them in shocking pink and orange minidresses.

Such bold attire nevertheless could not take Lee and DeMeyer's minds off what they considered the blindness of Dick Zanuck and David Brown. The business consultants sat silently in their plane seats, and after takeoff they were served drinks.

Raising their glasses, as if on cue, each man turned to the other and said: "Those two will have to go."

IX

"February 18, 1970

"MEMORANDUM TO: Mr. William B. Bateman, Senior Vice President [Chase Manhattan Bank]

"FROM: Gladstone T. Whitman [Vice President, Chase Manhattan]

"[RE:] Twentieth Century-Fox Film Corp.

"As you requested, we have reviewed the 1963-1969 results from information previously provided by the company.

"In essence we have concluded that the company must change aspects of its operations if they are to be reasonably sure of generating regular profits and the cash flow necessary to repay bank debt in an orderly way."

The banks were applying heavy pressure on Dennis Stanfill, because, within their own organizations, the lending institutions were feeling the heat. For the purpose of the Chase Manhattan study, *The Sound of Music* was tossed aside as a freak accident, "a non-recurring phenomenon." By eliminating the profits its exhibition brought Fox, and then concentrating solely on each of the studio's other releases, the bank found "their aggregate theatrical operations were highly unprofitable."

Furthermore, the studio was on a suicide course: "Not only did the company suffer staggering losses in pursuing their basic business during [the past six years], but they also followed a strategy that resulted in increasing their assets more than two-and-a-half times," said Whitman's memo.

The stockpiling was financed by *Sound of Music* profits, borrowing from banks and the Metropolitan Life Insurance Company, and floating convertible debenture issues. Assets were also bought with money from selling the Fox film library to television, including the record 1966 TV sale of *Cleopatra* to the American Broadcasting Corporation for $5 million, a deal that reportedly at long last put the Egyptian epic into the black.

Whitman's memo failed to generate much optimism for his bank. He could see no source of income. "Recent, published operating results and current market conditions would seem to preclude tapping of public funds in the foreseeable future. . . . We might add that 1969 losses will not result in a cash tax refund since [Fox] used amortization tables for tax purposes."

What Gladstone could muster was a call for action. Required, said the banker, were "significant changes in the company's modus operandi."

Whitman's demands, which he had no power to enforce, included "closing the studio."

X

After the studio visit, DeMeyer and Al Lee entered into a protracted debate in Menlo Park. DeMeyer spent the next several days preparing a routine proposal for Twentieth Century-Fox, the sort which would lightly trim the fat and could have been plugged into most any type of business, but which he argued would do nothing to alleviate the drastic situation at Fox.

Lee reminded DeMeyer that an assault was not what either Zanuck or Brown had requested, and so the routine proposal was forwarded to Richard Zanuck at the studio, where, it seemed, the matter died.

Then, suddenly, Henry DeMeyer started hearing on the telephone from Dennis Stanfill, from both the studio and the New York headquarters, where Stanfill's financial division was located. Stanfill also started supplying DeMeyer with a constant stream of data about Fox, almost daily. Stanfill could sense the inevitability of the entire Fox operation being reviewed by the banks, and wanted his division clean as a whistle, said DeMeyer. Furthermore, Stanfill required no permission from Dick or Darryl Zanuck or David Brown for such assistance from S.R.I., and privately he struck a deal with the Institute.

No proposal was involved, or even a contract to assist in Stanfill's housecleaning. S.R.I. did not want to agree to such a procedure, yet, said DeMeyer, "it was eventually seen that this would provide a means for getting a foot in the door of what was obviously going to be one hell of a project."

S.R.I. would bill on an hourly basis, which generally amounted to $6,000 a month, plus expenses, plus 20 percent. Stanfill, extending an invitation for Henry to come to New York, ordered a limousine to meet DeMeyer at Kennedy Airport, and a room for the consultant was set up at the Americana Hotel, on Seventh Avenue, within easy walking distance of the Fox office.

IX

When Henry DeMeyer reached New York and began looking at the financial division of Fox, he was reminded of his initial reaction to companies in Europe during the previous five years: If the companies abroad were 30 or 40 years behind the times, then Twentieth Century-Fox, despite its name, had yet to come into the twentieth century.

"Dennis Stanfill had over 500 people in his division," said DeMeyer. "Technically, John Meehan, who was called the comptroller, was also involved in the studio in terms of the running of the day-to-day operations. Everyone on the lot in California reported to Meehan, who was in New York. But Meehan didn't have an administrative budget to deal with the staff, as such. Hell, the studio didn't have an administrative budget at all."

For example, if someone needed to have a sign painted in Westwood, a sign painter would be hired, at any cost, and the bill would be sent to New York. And New York would pay it.

Of greater amazement was an unpoliced petty cash fund at the studio. Presumably, there was $50,000 available at any given time, because whenever the fund ran out, New York would replenish it. The money would be charged to whatever production it was the person making the withdrawal was working on, only there was no pressure to pay back and no one to demand that any payment be made.

Open to question, thought DeMeyer, was why a certain macho superstar owed petty cash $5,000, which had been taken as a quick withdrawal at the start of a weekend. The unenforced loan

188

seemed particularly unnecessary to the S.R.I. man given that New York was paying the actor a staggering salary, plus a whopping percentage from his last picture.

Larger sums could be removed from petty cash by the studio's top brass, including $10,000 by Dick Zanuck in February of 1970. Virginia Zanuck also had access to the till, one month dipping in for $856.80.

As comptroller, John Meehan oversaw the treasury arm of the studio, which was separated from Stanfill's financial division. Meehan had come to Fox from one of the Big Eight accounting firms, and, as legend held, he replaced a man who had displayed the temerity to fly to the coast and tell Richard Zanuck that Fox had suddenly found itself with $100 million worth of pictures in production.

"That's absolutely not possible," the executive told Dick Zanuck. "You can't do such a thing."

Zanuck's reported reply: "It's not only possible but I can." The man was fired and replaced by John Meehan.

DeMeyer and Stanfill collaborated for several weeks, culminating in a total of two months' work, going over budgets and organizational charts and implementing DeMeyer's recommendations. Stanfill struck DeMeyer as a quick study, and a man who did not say much, although he did seem to overextend himself and get "too involved in other people's business."

During their work together DeMeyer believed Stanfill did not bother to tell Dick Zanuck and David Brown that S.R.I. was on the job.

It was now early summer, and Stanfill and DeMeyer had accomplished what they had both set out to do. DeMeyer could return to Menlo Park, which he did. Within little time, however, the phone in his home began to ring. Dennis Stanfill was calling.

After pleasantries were exchanged and several unrelated issues discussed, DeMeyer heard the purpose of the call: Could

DeMeyer return to New York, this time to meet with all the executives of the organization?

S.R.I. now had a foot in the door.

XII

The word on the floor of the red-brick, fortress-like Fox New York offices at 444 West 56th Street, according to staff people around at the time, was that this consultant coming in from Stanford Research was interviewing a whole strata and then substrata of executives in very lengthy sessions—only no one really knew what Stanford Research was trying to accomplish.

"It was strictly a Stanfill maneuver," said a former employee. "he told the office that he was bringing in this new system that had never been tried in the movie industry before. Stanfill made it seem that everything that had ever occurred in our business had happened that way by accident."

"Dennis was such a nice guy," said Patricia Rick, who was asked to serve as Stanfill's executive assistant in New York once he joined the company. She had been hired in March of 1969 and put to work as David Brown's secretary, a position she did not care for, because, she said, "David Brown was not an easy man." She found her first boss not only made continual demands, but was "totally self-absorbed and inconsiderate of others." Dick and Darryl, she said, "were wonderful to their employees and knew the movie business inside out."

Stanfill, in that last regard, "was totally green in the industry. He relied on me a lot, to show him around," said Rick. One request Stanfill made of the young woman was that she listen in on meetings and take notes for him. "He was particularly interested in story operations. He wanted to know how properties were acquired by the studio," said Rick. "He knew of my loyalty to him, and would send me to listen at David Brown's door and then file reports on what I'd hear."

Patricia Rick, as well as others in the office, thought that Brown had his own earpiece working in the office, too: his wife Helen, who would visit, sit quietly on the edge of a chair, and observe what was going on. One member of the staff likened the relationship between the Browns to that between Nancy and Ronald Reagan. "Helen was very much in control. She might have allowed David to select where they were going to eat every night—back then, it was usually Pearl's, the Chinese restaurant—but it was Helen who determined who their companions would be."

Henry DeMeyer, by making his own rounds of the executive suites, was instantly piped into the company's secrets and the frustrations of its key players, who seemed to take quickly to the S.R.I. man.

"Most people love to talk," said DeMeyer. "The guys at Fox were no different. We'd average two to three hours together each. The meetings were held exclusively in a business environment, their own offices usually. No lunches or dinners."

DeMeyer met one-on-one with Harry J. McIntyre, Senior Vice President, Administration; Donald A. Henderson, consultant and former Vice President, Finance; Jerome Edwards, Vice President, General Counsel; Frank Kelly, Vice President, Treasurer; Peter Myers, Vice President, Domestic Distribution; David Raphel, Vice President, Foreign Distribution, who was highly regarded; Jonas Rosenfield, Vice President, Director of Advertising, Publicity, and Exploitation; Sol Schwartz, Vice President for Foreign Theatre Operations; and H. Blackmer Johnson, Secretary.

"Each one talked about his experiences in the film industry," said DeMeyer. "then I'd invariably hear from these guys how screwed up they were because of someone else in the organization. They were always pinning the blame elsewhere, and because of the organizational setup, they were not fully able to exert their creative powers."

The one constant in these meetings: "Frustration over Dick and David running everything on the West Coast, and here they were stuck in New York, where Darryl was running the show. And most of the executives did not think those three men were running the operation the way it ought to be."

In the marketing division, DeMeyer heard complaints about the product the studio had to sell, "one lousy picture after another," blaming Richard Zanuck and David Brown for the movies in production. Several of the remarks were peppered with comments about David really being the one who was giving the orders and Dick being a slave to them. "And there were a lot of smirky innuendoes," said DeMeyer, "about *their* father-son relationship."

By Thursday Dennis Stanfill got hold of DeMeyer and asked after his progress. The response was mutually favorable.

DeMeyer had a question of his own. "Dennis, it seems there's only one executive I haven't met. Darryl Zanuck."

"You will meet him," Stanfill said, evasively. "Eventually."

DeMeyer later deduced that Stanfill knew it was not yet time to bother Zanuck with S.R.I. Besides, from Stanfill's remarks DeMeyer gathered that the finance man did not hold the head of the company in high esteem, or even felt he was a necessary component in the long-range management of Twentieth Century-Fox.

What Stanfill required immediately was an extension from the banks, so he could arrange a presentation to show that Fox was in business.

Stanfill requested from S.R.I. a proposal to undertake an entire review of the operations of Twentieth Century-Fox, clarifying one aspect of the package to come.

"The proposal will only work if it is addressed to Darryl and personally signed by the president of S.R.I.," said Stanfill.

This was something that Charles A. Anderson, president of Stanford Research Institute, usually never bothered with. DeMeyer told Stanfill such a request seemed not only unnecessary but unlikely to be granted.

"No, no, no," insisted Stanfill. "You don't understand. Darryl's like an emperor. Over the years he's become accustomed to addressing kings and presidents."

Communications from anyone less were likely to go unanswered, Stanfill underscored.

"I'll see what I can do," DeMeyer promised.

Stanfill had one last requirement. Could S.R.I. hurry? The presentation to the banks was not far away.

"And just how far away are we talking, Dennis?"

"Less than a month."

In Menlo Park, DeMeyer hastily rehashed his Fox education for Al Lee, who suggested Henry go ahead and write the proposal, and, in fact, lead the project. On that one important point stressed by Stanfill, Lee expressed doubts that Anderson would sign the proposal and send a cover letter to Darryl Zanuck. That was not the Institute's style.

"Christ, Charlie's a president himself," said DeMeyer. "It would be as though he and Zanuck were equals. A letter to Zanuck from anyone else is likely to go unanswered."

S.R.I. President Charles A. Anderson personally wrote Darryl F. Zanuck on June 19, 1970.

XIII

At the May 1970 stockholders meeting of Twentieth Century-Fox, a dark-haired man with a bushy black mustache and what remained of his hair combed strategically on his head strode proudly to the front of the auditorium and, enunciating precisely, made an announcement. The Zanucks, Darryl and Richard, sat on the dais, Darryl in the more prominent position.

"My name is David Merrick," the dark figure, hand on hip, said into a floating microphone. His voice reverberated throughout the large room. "I own in excess of 200,000 shares, alas and to my regret."

Standing at the foot of the stage, Merrick faced forward to see Darryl Zanuck and suggested that perhaps Zanuck would let him stand on the stage and use the main microphone.

"You have me at a disadvantage, you know," Merrick said. "Telephones always put me off."

The Broadway showman knew how to work an audience; he received the laugh he desired, though the reaction was strained and more than slightly forced. Merrick, like Zanuck, was a showman through and through, tough to boot; unlike Zanuck, however, Merrick lacked eloquence, especially in front of a crowd. Darryl Zanuck remained stone silent, formulating a reply. It came quickly enough. "I'm afraid you'll have to wait a few years before you'll be at this microphone," he shot back.

The crowd whooped and hollered.

Merrick attacked Fox for spending extravagant sums on its pictures, and was outraged to learn that one of the studio's summer releases, *Tora! Tora! Tora!* would carry a pricetag of $25 million.

"The film will not be inexpensive, " Zanuck said on his own behalf, "but it will also be a wonderful picture."

Merrick could not resist: "I've been assured before that some of your turkeys would be wonderful."

Zanuck shot back that Merrick himself helped damage Fox's financial picture, holding up for ransom the release of the movie *Hello, Dolly!* and then, once the picture opened, injuring it publicly.

"Look what you did when [the movie version of] *Hello, Dolly!* opened in New York," Zanuck said to Merrick in front of the stockholders.

"You took out ads against it on buses and billboards saying your *Hello, Dolly!* was still the only one in town."

Merrick contended that his stage version was better than the company's movie.

With that, Zanuck demanded that Merrick apologize to the other shareholders, one of whom had bellowed at Merrick, "Sit down you bum!" Another rushed up to the producer and shouted, "You're insulting the company and me!" Merrick finally acceded.

Afterward, Merrick held a press conference. He admitted to the reporters that he did think the Zanucks "had a chance to turn the company around," though he said he was planning to "watch them very carefully for the next few months."

If the overhead was not cut substantially by that time, vowed David Merrick, he would wrestle to take control of the company or—at the very least—file a mismanagement suit.

XIV

Proposal Number MSC-70-158, "A Proposal for Management Assistance, REVIEW AND ANALYSIS OF COST EFFECT-IVENESS," established that a Stanford Research Institute team had recently assisted the Finance division of Fox and was successful in creating an organizational structure and job definitions and responsibilities.

While it was overseeing this task, S.R.I. also determined that the Fox executive management lacked pre-established goals that would curb its massive spending in light of sudden income plunge.

During 1969, income at the corporation dropped 37.6 percent from its 1968 level, while costs in all areas equaled or exceeded those of the previous year. The adverse picture was blamed on, among several elements, the absence of preplanning and budgets based on a planned profit objective.

S.R.I. said substantial reductions were possible and promised immediate cost-saving discoveries as it prepared a long-range restructuring of the company. The areas to be covered were administrative services, advertising and promotion, studio operations, and foreign and domestic distribution. By 1971, S.R.I. vowed, Fox would be operating on or at least close to anticipated budget levels.

The same day Charles Anderson dated the proposal's cover letter for Darryl Zanuck, Charles E. Blackford III, Vice President for Morgan Guaranty Trust, wrote to Dennis Stanfill.

The gloomy message, although addressed "Dear Dennis,"

said in part: "It seems to us that Twentieth Century-Fox is at the stage in its corporate life when a fundamental decision must be made—whether to remain primarily in film production and distribution, or to continue and enlarge other activities as well, some of which might be quite unrelated." Blackford suggested the first path, provided a certain financial logic prevailed.

"When the company approached its banks to set up the $78,000,000 revolving credit in the fall of 1968, we were told that the funds were needed temporarily to make and carry an unprecedently high level of film inventory. Many of the films included in the high level of inventory have had extremely disappointing box-office results. Some, such as *Star!* and *Doctor Dolittle*, following the outstanding roadshow success, *Sound of Music*, generated much lower film rentals than expected, with the result that there was little cash generated relative to their negative costs.

"Consequently, the financing of additional roadshows, such as *Hello, Dolly!*, *Tora! Tora! Tora!*, and also a number of 1969 general release films, many of which had relatively high negative costs, came principally from the revolving credit borrowings and little from other released film revenues."

Blackford had all but notarized the death certificate for big-budget extravaganzas.

"Despite the successes of certain current releases, such as *Butch Cassidy and the Sundance Kid* and *M*A*S*H*," Blackford continued, "it is not apparent to us that the company will be able to make regular reductions in the revolving credit.

"Furthermore, we understand that in recent years your T.V. series production has not only been unprofitable but has also been a net cash drain. We question whether your current level of network contracts justifies your continuing in this business in your present manner or, indeed, if at all."

The letter was signed "Sincerely," and indicated that a copy was being forwarded to Darryl F. Zanuck, who had already decided to implement a cost-cutting plan of his own. As he had ordered Dick to do in 1962, Darryl on May 30, 1979, again wanted the studio closed.

THE FOX THAT GOT AWAY

RICHARD F. ZANUCK
TWENTIETH CENTURY-FOX FILM STUDIOS
10201 W. PICO BLVD.
LOS ANGELES, CALIFORNIA

IN ADDITION TO PREVIOUS ECONOMIES AND ELIMINATIONS OF
PERSONNEL AT THE STUDIO YOU WILL EFFECTIVE AS OF TO-
DAY DISPENSE WITH THE SERVICES OF ALL STUDIO EMPLOY-
EES THAT ARE NOT ACTIVELY ENGAGED IN FINALIZING THE
EDITING, SCORING AND RERECORDING OF OUR COMPLETED
FILMS STOP YOU WILL FOLLOW THE SAME TERMINATION PRO-
CEDURE WITH ALL PRODUCERS, WRITERS OR DIRECTORS WHO
ARE NOT NOW ACTIVELY ENGAGED IN FUTURE PRODUCTIONS
THAT HAVE BEEN APPROVED BY THE BOARD OF DIRECTORS
AND ME STOP YOU ARE NOT TO DISPENSE WITH THE SERVICES
OF ANY EMPLOYEE WHO HAS A CONTRACT BUT YOU ARE TO RE-
FER ALL THESE TO ME FOR CONSIDERATION AND DISPOSITION
STOP IF YOU ARE NEGOTIATING FOR ANY FUTURE PROJECTS
THAT HAVE NOT BEEN APPROVED BY ME YOU WILL SUBMIT
SAME TO ME FOR MY APPROVAL BEFORE CONCLUDING NEGO-
TIATIONS STOP IN ADDITION TO THE ABOVE FORWARD AT ONCE
THE NAMES OF ALL EMPLOYEES NOW ON STUDIO PAYROLL
WITH EXCEPTION OF MAINTENANCE PERSONNEL BUT INCLUD-
ING TALENT UNDER CONTRACT OR ON INDIVIDUAL PICTURE
DEALS OR ASSIGNMENTS AND THE DATE WHEN EACH INDIVID-
UAL WAS SIGNED AND TO WHAT PROJECT.

> DARRYL F. ZANUCK
> CHAIRMAN OF THE BOARD AND CHIEF
> EXECUTIVE OFFICER

Unlike in 1962, Dick did not follow orders.

Upon receipt of Darryl's telegram, the son was both livid and hurt. His reply did not assist in closing the widening gap between father and son.

JUNE 2, 1970

DARRYL F. ZANUCK
NEW YORK OFFICE

I AM SHOCKED BY THE CONTENT AND THE METHOD YOU HAVE
CHOSEN TO USE TO CONVEY YOUR MESSAGE DATED MAY 30,

197

THE FOX THAT GOT AWAY

1970. IT IS INCONCEIVABLE THAT IN ANY WELL ORDERED AND PROPERLY MANAGED CORPORATION THE CHAIRMAN AND CHIEF EXECUTIVE OFFICER WOULD ISSUE AN ORDER OF THIS MAGNITUDE WITHOUT FIRST CONSULTING THE PRESIDENT OF THE CORPORATION AS WELL AS ITS TWO EXECUTIVE VICE PRESIDENTS. IN REGARD TO ECONOMIES YOU ARE WELL AWARE THAT THE STUDIO HAS REDUCED ITS EXPENDITURES AND PERSONNEL TO A FAR GREATER EXTENT THAN ANY OTHER DIVISION OF THE COMPANY. THESE ECONOMIES HAVE BEEN ATTAINED OVER A LONG PERIOD OF TIME AND FURTHER DRASTIC CUTTING IS UNDERWAY . . . FURTHERMORE I AM SURPRISED TO HAVE RECEIVED THIS UNILATERÁL COMMUNICATION FROM YOU SINCE OVER THE PAST WEEKEND YOU HAVE REFUSED TO ACCEPT TELEPHONE CALLS NOT ONLY FROM ME BUT FROM THE EXECUTIVE VICE PRESIDENT OF CREATIVE OPERATIONS* WHO WAS TRYING TO REACH YOU FROM LONDON. ON EACH OCCASION THAT I WAS ABLE TO GET THROUGH TO YOUR ROOM AT THE PLAZA HOTEL YOU OR ONE OF YOUR ASSOCIATES HUNG UP ON ME. THIS UNNATURAL BEHAVIOR RESULTED IN THE LOSS TO THIS CORPORATION OF A MOTION PICTURE PROJECT WHICH BOTH THE EXECUTIVE VICE PRESIDENT IN CHARGE OF CREATIVE OPERATIONS AND MYSELF REGARDED AS A HIGHLY PROFITABLE VENTURE . . . AS CHIEF EXECUTIVE OFFICER YOU HAVE THE AUTHORITY TO ISSUE ANY ORDER. HOWEVER AS PRESIDENT OF THIS CORPORATION AND AS A DIRECTOR IT IS MY DUTY TO INFORM YOU THAT TO CARRY OUT YOUR ORDER IN THE MANNER YOU STIPULATE WOULD IN MY OPINION RESULT IN A LOSS OF PRODUCTIVITY INJURIOUS TO THE CORPORATION . . . YOUR LACK OF FAMILIARITY WITH THIS STUDIO ORGANIZATION IS UNDOUBTEDLY THE RESULT OF YOUR FAILURE TO BE PRESENT AT THIS PLANT FOR NOT MORE THAN THIRTY DAYS DURING THE LAST EIGHT YEARS . . . THEREFORE BECAUSE OF MY RESPONSIBILITY AS PRESIDENT I MUST DEFER ANY SUCH ACTION AS YOU HAVE ORDERED PENDING PROPER CONSULTATION WITH ME. IF THIS SUGGESTION IS NOT ACCEPTABLE TO YOU THEN I WILL BE COMPELLED TO DISCUSS THIS MATTER AS WELL AS THE LONG TERM FUTURE OF THIS CORPORATION AND MY ROLE AS PRESIDENT OF IT WITH THE MEMBERS OF OUR BOARD OF DIRECTORS. I FEEL IT IS ONLY CORRECT TO INFORM YOU THAT MORE THAN ONE OUTSIDE

*David Brown.

BOARD MEMBER HAS SPOKEN TO ME WITHIN THE LAST FEW
WEEKS TO DISCUSS THIS VERY SUBJECT.

RICHARD ZANUCK, PRESIDENT

Two carbon copies of Richard Zanuck's reply to his father
were made.

One was sent to David Brown; the other, to Dennis Stanfill.

XV

Henry DeMeyer waited out the period between submitting
the proposal to Fox and its acceptance at his home in northern
California. True to form, Dennis Stanfill called DeMeyer personally. Darryl Zanuck was approving the S.R.I. plan.

June 26, 1970
Mr. Charles Anderson, President, Stanford Research Institute
Dear Mr. Anderson:

This is an acceptance of your Proposal for Management Assistance dated June 18, 1970.

This acceptance is made on the understanding that the charges
for the professional services aggregating, $108,700, will be the
maximum required to cover the services outlined in the Proposal. . . .
Sincerely,
Darryl F. Zanuck

June 30, 1970
Mr. Henry DeMeyer, Stanford Research Institute
Dear Henry:

As you have already heard, Darryl Zanuck has signed the acceptance letter for your Cost Effectiveness Study.

Would you please have the monthly billing for this Study ad-
dressed to me at my Beverly Hills address. . . .
With best regards,
Dennis

DeMeyer and the S.R.I. team arrived in New York ready to take all steps necessary to review Fox's East Coast operations, although the real dissecting would have to be accomplished at the studios in California.

Stanfill met the S.R.I. squad in his 56th Street office, and it was agreed that a Management Action Program would be put together and presented to the banking group July 15, less than two weeks from then.

Stanfill said he had no other choice but to rush. The banks were ready to liquidate Fox's inventory.

"By the way, Henry," Stanfill said to DeMeyer, "you are going to meet Darryl this afternoon."

Stanfill was far more outspoken on the subject of the Chairman of the Board by now. "It was undeniable Dennis thought Darryl was a fool and wanted him out of the way," said De-Meyer. "He showed no empathy for Darryl, nothing about his years of contribution to the industry and to Fox. Smooth as Dennis was on the outside, he could not hide his ruthlessness."

Some members of Stanfill's executive staff, in reference to Dennis's no-nonsense attitude, came up with a secret nickname for the finance man, which they used in the office behind his back: Otto von Bismarck.* He had already taken over and had re-decorated the pink-leather upholstered office of former company Chairman Spyros Skouras. It was now a tasteful beige.

At two o'clock that afternoon, Stanfill and DeMeyer met with Harry J. McIntyre, the Senior Vice President for Administration and Darryl's legal handholder.

It was McIntyre and Stanfill who escorted DeMeyer into Darryl F. Zanuck's lair, an imposing wood-paneled chamber that, like most places occupied by Darryl, reeked of stale cigar smoke. The room was small but not unprepossessing, sort of like Darryl. There were Oscars resting on a bureau top, a bust of D.F.Z. that was lit by a spotlight controlled by a dimmer, a

---

*Dick Zanuck and David Brown also had office code names. Because of his stature, the young Zanuck was known as "Little Napoleon." Brown's mustache branded him "The Walrus."

prominently displayed copy of Zanuck's 1923 book *Habit,* and a framed photo of Irina Demick. On the walls hung paintings by Cezanne, Van Gogh, Matisse, and, Darryl's favorite, Picasso.

Actually, Jean Negulesco said, "Darryl knew nothing about art. Only movies." Anything Darryl did know about art, Negulesco suggested, was gleaned from reading the art column in *Time* magazine.

Each painting in the office would have been worth a fortune if only it was not a forgery that had been painted for a 1966 William Wyler comedy, *How to Steal a Million.* The frames around each Impressionist master looked to be from Woolworth's.

Darryl was quietly puffing on a new Havana—he had his supply smuggled in from Cuba, and on that rare occasion when he would run dry, he would begrudgingly settle for an 80-cent Dunhill—as the trio of gentlemen made their entrance. Darryl never bothered to get out of his chair; instead, he leaned back from behind his desk and looked at the newcomer speculatively.

Fred Hift, Zanuck's publicity coordinator on *The Longest Day,* had observed that despite Darryl's blustery reputation, "He was terribly shy around strangers."

DeMeyer's first impressions of the legendary filmmaker were "narrow face . . . bushy eyebrows . . . a little straggly mustache. To me, he looked like an eager beaver."

"Darryl, this is Henry DeMeyer from the Stanford Research Institute," said McIntyre. "He's in charge of the project which we hope will ease the situation with the banks."

Darryl eyed all three men, again concentrating on DeMeyer. He took a puff on the cigar and said out of the side of his mouth to the S.R.I. consultant, "You know, I am a pretty suspicious old man. All my years in the movie industry and I've seen a lot of guys like you. They never did Fox any good. All they did was take our dough and give us a lot of gobbledy gook."

Zanuck removed the cigar from his chops, leaned all the way back in his chair, and looked extremely satisfied with himself. He folded his arms behind his head.

DeMeyer decided accepting such guff would prove a dangerous precedent. His response came automatically: "Mr. Zanuck,
I don't know whether you realize it or not, but Fox is on the
brink of bankruptcy. The banking group is ready to blow the
whistle and take all the steps required to get their money which
they feel you, your son, and the studio have squandered. Furthermore, it is my opinion that my men know your problems
and we know what can be done about them. Now, if you are a
suspicious old man like you say, and you do not cooperate with
our program, then I will be forced to terminate the project. And
you, as Chief Executive Officer, can answer to the banks your-
self."

Stanfill and McIntyre looked to see how Zanuck would react.
Darryl repositioned himself at his desk, placed an elbow on its
top, and motioned to McIntyre.

"Harry," said Zanuck, sticking his thumb at Stanfill, "you take
the bookkeeper here and get out. I want to listen to this guy in
private."

Stanfill visibly flinched at Darryl's reference to him as "the
bookkeeper."

"McIntyre knew how to retire gracefully," remembered De-
Meyer, who then spent the next two hours with Zanuck, as had
been pre-arranged. To the researcher's surprise, it was not time
devoted to Zanuck asking whether the studio could be saved. Instead, Zanuck proffered no questions at all. The Fox chief rega-
led his captive listener with stories from his glorious past,
sharing his victories and his disappointments.

"The whole time," said DeMeyer, who enjoyed the session,
"I listened to him talk, his history, how he went back. He
started by writing. He worked on one-reelers because that's all
they were making in those days. He'd write a one-reeler a night,
take that down to the studio, then he'd be turned down. He said
he didn't have any power to heat or light his room, all he had
was the room. He had to use cardboard in the bottoms of his
shoes because he couldn't afford to buy proper soles. And every
day he faced another rejection."

DeMeyer asked Zanuck where he was born. "When he told me he was from Wahoo, Nebraska, I thought he was kidding. I didn't think there really *was* a Wahoo, Nebraska."

DeMeyer stifled his reaction. "I didn't laugh at him. I never laughed at those people. I always sympathized with them. But later I had to look up where the hell was Wahoo."

DeMeyer was intrigued by how Zanuck went from having cardboard in his shoes to becoming one of the most influential men in the world. " 'When did you finally hit it?' I asked. And he said, 'I'll tell you. I wrote an article for *Physical Culture* magazine, and I sold it for $500. That allowed me to stop just long enough to reorganize my thinking. And from then on I sold my one-reelers. That was the last time in my life I had that kind of problem. From then on I became very successful.' "

The problem Zanuck did have, he confided, was with his son Richard.

"Darryl said Dick had never hit it big the way Darryl thought he should, the way Darryl had. He was upset that Dick's pictures were such bombs. Darryl made the excuse of how unhappy he was when, after *Cleopatra* and the studio was so broke, he had no choice other than to send Richard out to run the studio—because he didn't have the money to send anybody else."

It was not a popular decision all around, Zanuck explained.

"Darryl said that Robert Lehman, of Lehman Brothers, was on the board at the time and so dead set against nepotism of any kind that Darryl knew he had to keep Dick's appointment a secret from Lehman. So for two years, Richard was doing his job and receiving his checks under an alias."*

Darryl's resentment over Richard's allegiance to David Brown was also uncovered. "Shortly after he sent Richard out to the studio, he sent out David, and that's where he made the mistake," DeMeyer recalled Zanuck's explaining. "David was the

---

*As time went on, and Darryl, as was his wont, repeated this and several other stories to DeMeyer, the version altered slightly. Rather than Richard Zanuck's actual name being changed to an alias, his title was.

Svengali, Darryl kept saying, very tricky, also several years older than Richard—and was behind everything wrong that Dick did."

To DeMeyer's ear, Darryl sounded remorseful through much of the discourse. Without elaborating, the old man did acknowledge that the Zanuck family was estranged. "He never mentioned the wife. I didn't find out until much later he had two daughters. Dick was the only one he still had contact with, and their relationship had hit a brick wall."

Just as he was embarrassed by his son's lack of accomplishments, Zanuck was proud of his own, on *The Longest Day* and, especially, on *Cleopatra*.

DeMeyer interjected that he had never seen *Cleopatra*. Without missing a beat Darryl answered, "Don't bother," and continued talking.

"Darryl believed he saved the picture after Elizabeth Taylor and Richard Burton almost killed it," said DeMeyer. "He also ran on about the pictures he made with Elmo Williams, like *The Blue Max*, and how they were creative enterprises that were successes, as opposed to the turkeys Dick was turning out. But the thing about Darryl was, everything he talked about was in the past, though you wouldn't think it to listen to him."

At the end of their session together, DeMeyer felt he'd formed a friendly association with Zanuck, "who was different with me than he was with others. He wasn't mean and rotten, as I'd heard he was to several people in a lot of instances. We seemed more on an equal plane."

Darryl extended himself so far as to offer DeMeyer a cigar, a rare occurrence considering the way the mogul hoarded his stash. (Zanuck once rapped the knuckles of George Jessel with a metal ruler, after catching him trying to lift a Havana from Zanuck's desktop humidor, then later in the studio commissary made a wisecrack in front of a group of producers about Jessel's bandaged hand. Fred Hift called the incident "typical of Darryl's cruel sense of humor.") DeMeyer, however, refused Zanuck's gesture. He'd just given up smoking.

"I think Darryl quickly realized I was there to help his company, and I could be of use on something else on Darryl's mind, splitting up his son Richard and David Brown," said DeMeyer.

Their meeting concluded, Darryl escorted the consultant out of his office, beyond the anteroom with his two secretaries, Bonnie McCracken and Vinnie Argentino, and into the hallway. The entire time, Zanuck's arm rested around DeMeyer's shoulder.

"I'm not very tall," said DeMeyer, "but Darryl was a real shrimp. He had to stretch himself to get his arm around me."

As the two new pals made their way from Zanuck's office, DeMeyer noticed that the eyes of both of Zanuck's secretaries were bulging.

"I guess," speculated the S.R.I. man, "Darryl Zanuck didn't put his arm around too many people."

XVI

Dennis Stanfill never asked what transpired during the meeting with Darryl and DeMeyer. For the week following, the S.R.I. team prepared for what researcher Al Boyd called "The Dog and Pony Show for the banks." DeMeyer and his men worked around the clock, continuing their endeavor over the weekend.

Jonas Rosenfield's staff referred Boyd to artists who could create imaginative story boards and graphs to illustrate the Management's Assistance Program and exactly what steps Fox would take. These artists were the same talents Fox used to create movie posters, which made what the researchers were doing a far cry from the make-do numbers and stick figures S.R.I. usually relegated to graphs. By the same token, S.R.I. was not accustomed to dealing with artists and artistic temperaments. Three times over the weekend, Al Boyd lost track of his illustrator, who was hiding out so as not to be called on the carpet for missing his deadline.

Early one Sunday morning, while overseeing the foreign and domestic distribution charts, Henry DeMeyer received a phone call in his New York hotel room, from Darryl Zanuck, whom he had not seen since their face-to-face meeting. Friendly but matter-of-fact, Darryl requested Henry come later that day and view an assemblage of *Tora! Tora! Tora!* in the Fox screening room. DeMeyer didn't know whether to look upon the preview invitation as a compliment or an intrusion. The meeting with the bankers was only three days away; sitting in the dark for half the afternoon and reliving Pearl Harbor did not seem a high priority.

On the other had, DeMeyer needed to confront Zanuck with S.R.I.'s first recommendation for Twentieth Century-Fox, an iron-clad corporate by-law to which Henry knew Darryl would not take kindly.

"What the hell," DeMeyer told an aide when he returned to the Fox offices, "I might as well see the movie and then slip Darryl the memorandum when it's over."

DeMeyer, like most people, was awed by the art deco splendors of the Fox screening room, although not by the sight of the stuffed animal presiding outside the entrance. It was the life-sized Pushme-Pullyou, the two-headed llama from *Doctor Dolittle*. Like the studio, the Pushme-Pullyou had seen better days. Since the premiere of the movie three years earlier, the animal's woolly coat had been picked at by visitors to screenings, critics mostly. There were a lot of bald patches on the Pushme-Pullyou.

By contrast that afternoon, the researcher was "impressed as all hell" by Darryl F. Zanuck, whom he found "sharp and observant, showing none of the signs of senility Dennis was constantly harping about."

As *Tora! Tora! Tora!* blazed across the screen—DeMeyer liked the movie, by the way—Darryl dictated to his secretaries, rattling off changes to be considered, cuts to be made, colors to be corrected. Darryl's prowess as a film editor certainly had not failed him.

After the final fade-out, DeMeyer thanked Zanuck "for the privilege of seeing you in action," and handed the mogul the memorandum which DeMeyer imagined would bring a crashing halt to the S.R.I. project. The memo said that the mandatory retirement age for both directors and executives of Twentieth Century-Fox be lowered from 70 to 65.

Darryl accepted the sealed envelope, entered into conversation with the others in the room, and DeMeyer left.

Nine-thirty that evening the phone rang again in Henry De-Meyer's hotel room. There was no "hello" on the other end.

"What the hell is this recommendation?" Zanuck demanded.

"Now, Darryl," replied DeMeyer, "I thought the recommendation was rather clear and simply stated. The retirement age will be dropped from 70 to 65."

"You're goddam right that's what it says—and you know goddam well that I'm going to be 68!"

"All right, just calm down. If you read carefully you'll also see that the recommendation contains a provision that the Board of Directors is able to issue an exemption if it believes an individual's services are required past his 65th year. We set it up this way so that nothing that might happen would affect you— although you will have the privilege of stepping down if and when you feel the time is right."

There was dead silence from Darryl Zanuck's end of the phone. DeMeyer began to wonder if something had happened. "Darryl," DeMeyer said, "you still there?"

More silence. Then suddenly Zanuck spoke. "By God, you are right. That gives me the right to hold the gun. You just tell those bastards that I'll approve your goddam recommendation."

XVII

On the afternoon of July 14, a rehearsal meeting minus the bankers was scheduled with the Fox senior executives and department managers, the S.R.I. team, and Dennis, David, Dick, and Darryl. The meeting was called for two P.M., and everyone was assembled in the conference room, save for the four top players and Harry McIntyre. They huddled in Darryl's office arguing over the very first element of the S.R.I. Management Program, Page One, Step A, under "Creative Operations," regarding the forthcoming slate of motion picture production.

Effective the following day, S.R.I. assigned the primary responsibility to review the balance of 1970 and 1971 production and release schedule (that is, a film-by-film dollar analysis of above-and below-line costs,* advertising and publicity, foreign and domestic distribution, administration, total estimated financial commitment, as well as projected potential return) to an Executive Committee consisting of Darryl Zanuck, Richard Zanuck, David Brown, and a brand new participant, Dennis Stanfill.

The secondary responsibility for creative operations would fall to S.R.I.

Dick Zanuck and David Brown violently opposed the directive, in particular Dennis's inclusion in the decision-making process. Their argument against Stanfill could be heard through the walls of the executive quarters and into the conference room, where the others sat waiting for the rehearsal meeting to commence. Stanfill's executive assistant Patricia Rick likened Dick and David's dismissal of Dennis to a "school-boy rivalry between preppies and jocks." Stanfill's reaction to this, she said, "would be to bite his thumbnail and say, 'Not bad for a 44-year-old country boy from Tennessee.' "

The younger Zanuck and Brown said Stanfill had no right being assigned responsibility for selection of stories for production, or what prices would be paid, or what salaries should be. They based their argument on the theory that what they did and how they negotiated was more often than not accomplished at night over long dinners and lengthy drinking sessions. How, they

---

*Generally speaking, "above line" refers to upfront fees, such as salaries to stars, director, producer, and writer. "Below line" encompasses costs on the picture from pre-production planning (e.g., location scouting) to editing.

wondered, could they convince a willing "seller" to sign a contract at two or three in the morning if they would first have to
track down and then check in with Stanfill?

From the sound of things in the outside room, Darryl pretty
much sided with his son and David Brown.

Stanfill, for his part, sat silent.

DeMeyer, at Harry McIntyre's suggestion, was called into
Darryl's office.

"We need to find out what the hell this is all about," was
Darryl's greeting. Richard Zanuck, David Brown, Harry
McIntyre, and Dennis Stanfill eagerly looked on as DeMeyer
stepped closer to the chief executive's desk, atop which was
spread open the well-handled copy of the Management Action
Program. It consisted of 12 pages, was spiral-bound, and,
though it had a mustard-colored cardboard cover, was referred
to as *The Gold Book*. It outlined studio operations step by step
and made short- and long-range projections on streamlining the
entire company.

"Just *why* did you put the Executive Committee and Dennis
Stanfill in charge of the Primary Responsibility position on the
Creative Operations function?" Zanuck, cigar waving, asked the
S.R.I. man.

"It's relatively simple," said DeMeyer. "If the responsibility
for future decisions on fund commitment rests with the same individuals who have put this company into its present financial
hole, then no way are the bankers going to approve the S.R.I.
program."

Dick and David, sensing the threat to their authority, started
to object, pleading their case for several minutes, and, according
to DeMeyer, said, in front of Stanfill, "Dennis is not part of our
crew."

"The decision is up to you, not me," answered DeMeyer. "It's
your neck and not mine."

Darryl cocked an eye, pounded his fist on his desk, and announced, "Then goddam it, if that's the way it is, then that's
that. Let's go to the meeting."

Proceeding quietly from Darryl's office, Henry DeMeyer, Darryl and Richard Zanuck, David Brown, Dennis Stanfill, and Harry McIntyre made their way into the board conference room. Seated directly around the circumference of the table were the Fox executives. The S.R.I. consultants were located against the walls. Brown, McIntyre, and Stanfill found chairs at the table, while three spots remained vacant at the head. Darryl took the left side; Dick, the right. This left the middle space wide open. DeMeyer took it. Then, because no one said anything, DeMeyer started to address the gathering.

"Gentlemen, this meeting tomorrow is probably the most important that any of you have ever attended regarding the future of this corporation."

Darryl raised an eyebrow but did not unclamp his cigar. DeMeyer continued, "The banking groups feel that Fox's financial situation is close to being irreversible. Some of the banks have gone so far as to make their own suggestions as to what Fox should do in the future. Frankly, in my opinion, they will do anything to get their money."

XVIII

When they first showed up for the rehearsal, the attendees had received a copy of the following day's agenda. Darryl would welcome the bankers and introduce the meeting at ten A.M., followed by DeMeyer's 90-minute explanation of the S.R.I. Cost Effectiveness Program. Lunch would take place at the Holiday Inn on 57th and 10th Avenue, after which subsidiary reviews would be handled by Harry McIntyre, Lewis W. Wolff, Sol Schwartz, Lewis Stein, and Malcolm B. Kahn. Kahn would report on Wylde Films, an independent film production arm of Fox he had created with his partner, Robert B. Bean, before their company had recently been absorbed by Fox.

DeMeyer and Al Lee had spent the days prior to the rehearsal speaking separately with the presenters, and the meetings went smoothly except for one with Kahn, who did not confine his comments to Wylde Films. Kahn, a former University of Buffalo football player and one-time practicing attorney, felt he should be head of production for Twentieth Century-Fox, and expressed this heartfelt belief to DeMeyer, who could do nothing but listen bemusedly as Kahn outlined his production plan. Bud Kahn and Bob Bean, it turned out, had been burned more than once by Dick Zanuck and David Brown.

"I had a company called Wylde Films," Kahn recalled in 1986, "and Fox bought us out. The whole point was, we were to be involved in making feature pictures."

Wylde was the first of its kind, and its aim was to bring directors of commercials into Hollywood production. The practice became commonplace a decade later, when men such as Ridley Scott (*Alien*) and Adrian Lyne (*Fatal Attraction*) turned their talents to the big screen. When asked in 1986 whether he remembered the Stanford Research team of consultants at Fox, Kahn replied: "Oh, those assholes."

Among the properties Kahn had access to in the '60s was one several people take credit for, Woody Allen's *Play It Again, Sam.* Kahn and partner Bean envisioned Allen as a writer and star.

"We were friendly with Charlie Joffe and wanted to do the picture," said Kahn, referring to Allen's manager. "Woody was willing to work for scale, but it seemed Dick Zanuck wouldn't move on it."

Another property was *Made For Each Other*, by the husband-wife comedy writing and acting team of Joe Bologna and Renée Taylor. It took place at an emergency group-therapy session in New York, with Taylor and Bologna playing two losers perfectly matched.

"Bob and I took *Made For Each Other* to Dick and David. Now, Arthur Jacobs also had a deal with the studio," said Kahn.

"It turned out," said Kahn, "that Jacobs was bidding against us on the property—at the same studio! I was furious, and went in to see David Brown. So, David sits back in his chair and tells me, 'Well, we don't control Arthur Jacobs. He's got chutzpah.' Chutzpah? I got so goddam mad that I jumped over David's desk, grabbed him by the necktie, and said, 'Oh, yeah? I'll show you chutzpah!' "

Recalling the incident, Kahn said, "I suppose if I had to do it over again, I'd be less abrasive."

At the time, however, "I was so pissed I couldn't see straight. Finally, a deal was made, with us, predicated on the condition that Renee would play the lead. But, without my knowing it, Dick and David paid her money *not* to play the lead. I got so pissed off again—"

Kahn arranged a meeting between Taylor, Zanuck, and Brown. "They met and liked her," he said, "but now we had to pay her *more* to do the picture. Then one day Renee and Joe came in and said they'd just been asked to rewrite *Play It Again, Sam.* Rewrite Woody Allen, if you can imagine. I told them, 'Forget it. You're in *Made For Each Other.*' "

Dick and David, Kahn said, told him not to worry over losing Taylor and Bologna: "We'll get Chuck Grodin."

"The hell you will," Kahn responded.

"That's when I called Dennis Stanfill and asked what the fuck was going on," said Kahn.

In reply to having Bologna and Taylor usurped by Zanuck and Brown, Stanfill told Kahn, "I can't control them."

"By this time," Kahn said, "Renee and Joe were missing from New York and nowhere to be found. I called Dick Zanuck in California, and he told me they weren't there. 'Then, obviously,' I told Dick, 'they've disappeared.' David Brown told me he didn't know where they were, either. I said, 'Listen. Aren't we all working for the same company?' "

After Al Lee and Henry DeMeyer listened to Kahn, Lee inquired what he expected them to do about it, and Kahn replied that with their influence they could put him in charge. Lee advised Kahn to stick to the topic of Wylde Films.

XIX

"You have seen the agenda," DeMeyer said to the men at the rehearsal. "Your participation is of the utmost importance. However, it is even more imperative that you know that I am going to ask the banking group not to ask questions until the entire presentation is completed. Then, if you are asked something, do not elaborate. You may be inclined to try and impress the bankers with your importance. Don't. Whoever does may find himself offering his importance to some other company."

Darryl completed a half turn of the head and stared at DeMeyer.

"Understand?" asked DeMeyer. "Now, any questions?" None from the table. "Darryl?"

Darryl posed no question, simply an observation. Removing the stogie from his mouth and placing an elbow on the table, he said, "I think this is the first time I've seen all the executives of this company in one place at the same time."

XX

INTER-OFFICE CORRESPONDENCE ONLY
To: Attendees, including Messrs. [Vice President, General Counsel Jerome] Edwards, [Vice President, Director of Production Operations Stan] Hough, [Vice President, Treasurer Frank] Kelly, [Controller John] Meehan, [Vice President, Domestic Distribution Peter] Myers, [Vice President, Foreign Distribution David] Raphel, [Vice President, Director of Advertising, Publicity, and Exploitation Jonas] Rosenfield,]Vice President, Televison William] Self, [Henry] DeMeyer

213

cc: Mr. Harry McIntyre
FROM: MR. DENNIS STANFILL
Gentlemen: Attached is a slightly revised agenda for the Wednesday bankers' meeting.

Attendees who are expected to give formal presentations have already been notified—but each attendee should be prepared to contribute generally and in his area of responsibility. Discussion should, however, be brief since there is a full agenda.

All attendees are invited to lunch with our banker guests.
Dennis.

Ten bankers attended. They were Chase Manhattan Senior Vice President William B. Bateman, Vice President Gladstone T. Whitman, and Second Vice President Richard J. Miller; First National City Bank Vice President Donald Roberts and Joseph F. Lord; Morgan Guaranty Trust Company Vice President and Office Head John Snyder, Vice President Charles E. Blackford, and Vice President Bruce Merchant; and Marine Midland Grace Trust Company Senior Vice President David Gile and Vice President Alan Legon. The mood was not as tense as several of the participants had feared in advance; the reason being that the consensus was that *M*A*S*H* and *Patton* were starting to ease the cash-flow deadlock.

Darryl behaved graciously, in his businesslike manner this morning, keeping his opening remarks brief. He quickly threw the spotlight over to Stanford Research, telling the bankers that he was sure they would be impressed by the Management Action Program that had been developed. Ten days from now, Darryl told them, the Program would be presented to the Fox Board of Directors.

DeMeyer was given the floor. In introducing the facts contained in *The Gold Book*, DeMeyer requested that the banking personnel hold their questions until the end of the presentation. "Interruptions can frequently cause a meeting to fall apart," he explained.

For the next two hours, the group thoroughly examined *The Gold Book*. When the floor was opened to questions, relatively few arose. Those that did were desultory, centering on financing, new pictures, and Dennis Stanfill's place on the Executive Committee. Some assurance was requested regarding strict adherence to budgets.

After lunch, Lew Wolff's report on the Fox real estate holdings was felt to be too long-range to have any direct bearing on the immediate crunch. Deluxe Labs, the film processing plant on the site of William Fox's original office, Norman Stein assured the room, was profitable, and was developing Fox's product as well as that from other studios. Next on the agenda, Bud Kahn spoke on Wylde Films. The first five minutes of his allotted 15 were devoted to a professional explanation of the division. Then came his oversell.

Kahn launched into his ideas of how the studio could be making first-class films on a tiny budget. For example, instead of using a plush, green carpet if one were called for in the script, Kahn would have the floor painted green, and he made similar substitutions down the line. This ad hoc speech upset the Fox executives. Counterweighing that reaction, the banking group was amused, and some of them goaded Kahn with silly queries, which he would answer. Some of the questions about spending money were clearly meant to embarrass Richard Zanuck and David Brown, who looked annoyed but not uncomfortable, said DeMeyer. Darryl finally would stand for no more.

"You're talking about what we did 50 years ago in one-reelers," he told Kahn. "Sit down and forget it."

XXI

The bankers made known their reactions to the meeting five days later, when they sent a letter to Dennis Stanfill.

The message, encumbered in "bankerese," included 12 demands. Among the most pressing were that: The Fox board approve the Stanford Research Institute "Management Action Program" as outlined in *The Gold Book*; $10 million in loans be paid back before September 22; no film be allowed a budget of more than $2.5 million; and that budgets be presented to the banks for review on a film-by-film basis.

In addition, should a film exceed its budget by five percent, a written explanation had to be submitted. Only $20 million would be provided for the *entire* slate of the Fox films scheduled for the remainder of the year, and any acquiring or disposing of assets was to be approved *first* by the banks. This also included creation of any new television programs. Here too, any permission granted by the banks had to be in writing.

To stress the need to stop the outflow of cash, the bankers said in closing, "Your banks would be very favorably impressed if you were to institute a meaningful salary deferred program to exist until after your bank debt has been satisfied."

The three-page letter was signed by The Chase Manhattan Bank (National Association), G.T. Whitman, Vice President; First National City Bank, Donald Roberts, Vice President; Morgan Guaranty Trust Company of New York, J. Snyder, Vice President; Marine Midland Grace Trust Company of New York, David E. Gile, Sr. Vice President.

The letter was considered an ultimatum, one which several quarters saw as having effectively "cut off the balls of the powers-that-be" at Fox.

To DeMeyer's mind, control of Twentieth Century-Fox unquestionably now belonged to S.R.I.

PART FIVE

I

FOX WON'T DISCLOSE COST STUDY FINDINGS
NEW YORK—Twentieth Century-Fox Film Corp. Wednesday refused to disclose the initial results of a cost-effectiveness study it
has launched.

The movie company announced on Tuesday that it has engaged the Stanford Research Institute to make the study of the
entire Fox operation. . . . Asked for . . . the reaction they received from financial institutions, Jonas Rosenfield, Jr., Fox Vice
President for Advertising, Publicity, and Exploitation, said:

"These steps are preliminary. We do not have to disclose
them. We do not have to give the stockholders daily bulletins at
this point."

Fox has failed to renegotiate the second half of a $50 million
borrowing and is in default of the first half of the agreement.

—The Los Angeles Times

Henry DeMeyer and Al Lee had viewed very little of the studio when they first visited in January, and, in fact, felt too preoc-
cupied to have taken proper notice of the mammoth *Hello,
Dolly!* set. Now, months later, the men got out of their car and
stood back to look at the setting's turn-of-the-century splendor.
Above and in the distance ran approximately half-a-mile of a perfectly duplicated portion of New York's Third Avenue El.

"Hey, Al," DeMeyer asked his colleague, "why couldn't they
have done that in miniature?" The two newly fashioned experts
made their way to the executive offices.

"Well, you had quite a triumph with the big shots in New
York," Richard Zanuck called to DeMeyer from behind his elevated desk. DeMeyer had been motioned into Zanuck's office by
the executive secretary, Mary Ann McGowan.

"I didn't regard it as that," answered DeMeyer, moving closer to Zanuck, who did not get up from his seat. "It seems to me that neither you nor your father realize the seriousness of your situation."

Zanuck leaned back in his chair. At one time he had been a chain-smoker. Now his most obvious sign of nervousness was his constant gnawing at his fingernails. DeMeyer mentally noted—somewhat surprised—that the young Zanuck's nails were chewed to the quick.

"Look, Henry," said Richard, "I know the situation. Just what do you want?"

"You've been president for nearly a year," said DeMeyer. "Actually you have not acted as president but have continued to maintain the majority of your interest in the studio. It is my expectation that this project will develop to the point where you are in fact president of Fox or you are no longer with the company."

DeMeyer really hadn't intended to blurt out so much, and so frankly, but it was the way he felt and figured that in any event it was healthy to get it out.

Zanuck flushed, but withheld comment. After a moment, he half-smiled and said, "Well, why don't we see what happens?"

The next stop on DeMeyer's office tour was to see Stanley Hough. It was Hough, a tall, imposing figure, who had accompanied Richard Zanuck back to the studio in 1962 when everyone on the lot was to be discharged. In DeMeyer's findings, it was Hough, and not Richard Zanuck and David Brown, who ran the studio.

Hough and DeMeyer chatted a few moments before the studio executive leveled with the consultant. "As far as you people are concerned," said Hough, "I will cooperate in every way possible. But let's get things straight from the start. As far as I am concerned, you are Henry the Ninth. There have been eight guys ahead of you in here, all who were going to be efficiency experts and organize the studio to their way of thinking. Let me tell you something. Dick and I played together here in the studio when we were kids, I don't think that anyone knows more about this place than I do."

Meaning? "I'm ready to listen to your suggestions," said Hough. "If they are good, we'll do it. But you are going to have to show us before we start listening."

II

No sooner was S.R.I. on the lot than Dick Zanuck flooded various divisions on the lot and in the New York office with memos aimed at saving money. The deluge continued for ten days.

July 20, 1970
Dear Harry:*
We must eliminate political contributions by the studio or most certainly do our best to keep them down to the absolute rock-bottom minimum. I know this is going to be very difficult in the cases of Ronald Reagan and George Murphy since you and I are both on their campaign fund-raising committees and I know they will expect similar contributions from the company as in the past. Both men, as we all know, have been *very* good to Twentieth, particularly Murphy who gave a speech on the Senate floor strongly supporting our case in the *Tora* incident.** We will just

---

*Harry Sokolov, Executive Assistant to Richard Zanuck. The day before dictating this memo, Richard put Sokolov on an employee "hit list" of those whose jobs were to be eliminated.
**In June of 1969, Rep. John M. Murphy (a New York Democrat and no relation to California Republican Senator George Murphy), introduced a bill in Congress to prohibit the use of armed forces personnel and equipment in the production of films made for profit. The bill was a direct result of the Defense Department's assistance in the making of *Tora! Tora! Tora!* Darryl Zanuck, infuriated at what he perceived as questioning his patriotism, ordered $15,000 worth of newspaper ads to defend his film. These appeared in *The New York Times* and the Washington *Post*. In addition, the studio dispatched a lengthy Telex to John Murphy, stating that the film "does not glorify either side," and defending the use of armed forces personnel as extras. Six off-duty servicemen were burned during filming in Hawaii as a result of "a sudden shift of wind [which] sent the fire in a direction that could not have been calculated, despite numerous safety precautions." Murphy responded that he feared Twentieth Century-Fox was "toying with history in portraying the Japanese of Pearl Harbor as nice people.

have to stall, make excuses, and do everything possible to avoid contributions.

Perhaps there are other ways that we could help, such as letting them use our facilities for parties, etc.

RDZ

P.S. I know Frank Sinatra is going to put a big bite on me in behalf of Reagan and I dread his call. I have decided to eliminate all charitable donations . . .

. . . all Wrap-Up parties must be paid for at the expense of the producer or director. It cannot be charged to the studio.

RDZ

. . . we will no longer pay for legal fees in negotiations with talent, etc. There is utterly no justification to pay fees to the very people who come in and try to out-negotiate us.

RDZ

. . . night screenings in New York are very expensive; therefore, they will no longer be permitted . . .
Naturally, DFZ will be an exception to this policy.

RDZ

Dear Dad:
I think we should give serious consideration to the out-right sale of our television station KMSP in Minneapolis.* I am well aware that the station is prosperous and showing increased earnings but I am also convinced (as I'm sure you are) that the value of television stations across the country will reduce proportionately with the ultimate increase in cassette viewing.

Love, see you later,
RDZ

*Stanford Research recommended retaining KMSP; the station was retained and continued to produce generous revenues.

In past years it has been studio practice to send cars to meet talent or executive personnel. Wherever possible we should urge these people to use cabs and we will reimburse them upon receipt of the amount of the fare.

RDZ

Dear Dad:
The following options with players have been dropped:
James Coburn—$300,000
Heather Young—$600 per week
As options with players become due for exercise we will give each case the utmost scrutiny. Naturally, we will not drop those that have a value on the market in excess of what our deal calls for . . . example, Mia Farrow, whose option we just picked up for $170,000 since we will utilize her in the next year and she is receiving anywhere from $350-$500,000 on the outside.

Love, see you later,
RDZ

In addition to the staccato bulletins fired off in July, Richard prepared for his father a highly confidential lengthy memo that was, in effect, an executive employee hit list that included longtime Darryl crony Elmo Williams, whom Dick was prepared to discharge after the August 7 screening of *Tora! Tora! Tora!*, which Williams had produced. Frank McCarthy, producer of *Patton*, was also to be let go. All told, Dick targeted ten executives, estimating an annual savings to the studio of $506,700 in salary and fringe benefits. Darryl was forced to accept the plan, believing it was wiser to fire these people than lower their pay and reduce their morale. In replying to his son's memo, Darryl dredged up the old days, writing, "I cannot resist mentioning that I had a seven-year straight contract with Warner Bros., at $5,000 per week, and at that time $5,000 per week had the purchasing equivalent of about $20,000 per week in today's market. There were no complaints because business was good."

Darryl signed the approval of Dick's hit list, "Love, see you later." Dick had one last matter to resolve, however, his own executive compensation with the corporation. "Frankly," he told his father, "I am sick of hearing that we wrote our own tickets."

Before Richard Zanuck became President of Fox in August of 1969, his seven-year contract called for a salary of $150,000 current and $150,000 deferred.

"I had spent considerable time with the Corporation prior to this contract," said Richard, "but it was decided by the Board of Directors that, due to my performance and increased responsibilities, my contract be re-negotiated."

When he assumed the dual role of Production Chief and President at the August 1969 Board meeting, it was voted upon that Richard receive an additional $50,000 a year, a provision that, when it came up for vote, Darryl Zanuck abstained from voting on. Nor did Darryl raise a hand for or against Richard's receiving 20 percent of a profit-sharing plan intended for executives.

The purpose of the memo from son to father, which was shared by the board, was to stem the tide of criticism leveled at Richard Zanuck's employment contract. "I'd like to think that I've earned it," said Richard, "not connived it."

The memo was signed, "Love, see you later, RDZ."

III

The July 1970 board meeting in New York opened as scheduled. The only absent member was William T. Gossett, who was traveling in the Far East. The agenda included items approving the minutes of the stockholders' meeting of May 19, where David Merrick had stepped forward; and an update on a contract dispute with George Roy Hill, director of *Butch Cassidy and the Sundance Kid*.

Richard Zanuck reported that he had been advised that Hill

was taking steps to bring a suit for reformation of his percentage arrangements on the film, and said that he had been told that the Directors of the Corporation, as well as the Corporation itself, would be made parties to this suit.

Richard continued to hold the floor as he outlined three films scheduled for production: *The Mephisto Waltz, Marriage of a Young Stockbroker*, and *Kyle*. The first was in the vein of *Rosemary's Baby*, about the possession of a journalist (Alan Alda) who had procured the last interview of a great musician (Curt Jurgens). The second was based on a novel by Charles Webb, author of *The Graduate*, and dealt with exactly what its title suggested. Richard Benjamin played the wandering young husband. The third film was never made.

On television matters, William Self announced a prospective animated series for Saturday mornings on NBC, based on *Doctor Dolittle*.

Stanfill handled item six, on corporate finances, before the two Zanucks and DeMeyer turned to item seven, the S.R.I. Management Action Program. The banks had demanded the Board approve it.

"Mr. DeMeyer," asked board member John Edmondson, "have you, the Stanford Research Institute, or any other members of your organization, ever been engaged in a study of this kind in the movie industry?"

"This could be a trap," thought DeMeyer. "Should I say: 'Yes, but we are not permitted to discuss other clients,' or would it be better to say, 'No,' except for some 'far-out studies' that had no relationship to our program?"

DeMeyer had learned years before that the only way to live with a lie was to have an exceptional memory. He answered, "No, but I believe that freshness is what's going to benefit this organization. We won't be prejudiced by traditions that might be costing Fox and other members in the industry excessive expenditures."

Edmondson appreciated the argument. "I'm going to approve your program," he said.

Dennis Stanfill presented the Board the banking group's letter, which the rest of the men also approved.

FOX FILM BOARD VOTES PROGRAM TO
CUT COSTS BY $11 MILLION A YEAR

NEW YORK—Twentieth Century-Fox Film Corp. said its directors approved a program that is expected to lower operating expenses at an annual rate of $11 million by the end of this year.

Included in the program is a restructuring of studio operations under which 12 to 16 feature films will be produced annually, instead of 18 to 24, the number the company has been making annually since 1966.

Darryl F. Zanuck, chairman, and Richard D. Zanuck, president, said the cost reduction program wasn't "the traditional cyclical industry cost-cutting action" but a positive series of moves to adapt the company's structure to new industry requirements and to achieve a stable portfolio operation.

. . . As previously reported, Stanford Research Institute is assisting Twentieth Century-Fox management in developing the cost reduction program.

—*The Wall Street Journal*,
August 4, 1970

Obviously with the lower number of films, a Fox spokesman said, "our overall manpower needs will be greatly cut."

It is clear that the stringent savings program is designed to satisfy Fox's two major creditors. Last month Fox revealed that it had failed to renegotiate a $25 million financing arrangement with Equitable Life Assurance Society of the United States. As a result, Fox Chairman Zanuck said, the film concern is in default on another $25 million borrowed last year from Metropolitan Life Insurance Co.

Negotiations are underway with Equitable to renegotiate one loan, while Metropolitan has agreed to waive the default on its loan, at least for now.

—*The Los Angeles Times*,
August 4, 1970

The big decision to trim production to 12-16 features per year parallels earlier policy statements by Metro, Paramount, and other companies. Decision to trim domestic sales staff follows cutbacks first at Universal, later M-G-M (now with ten domestic divisions in which several regional managers often work out of their homes), and lesser trims to date by Paramount and Warners.

—*Variety*,
August 4, 1970

Top management at S.R.I. still experienced trepidations about the Fox project. The Institute remained uncertain whether the resultant publicity of what was being accomplished was proper—or necessary. DeMeyer forged ahead.

IV

NEW YORK—Hollywood is making too many dirty movies, the mother of a 16-year-old charges.

Hollywood deceives the public by putting innocent titles like *Alice's Restaurant* on lurid films, another woman complains.

A third angrily asks: Why doesn't Hollywood offer more wholesome movies such as *The Sound of Music* and *My Fair Lady*?

. . . Are innocent titles such as *Bob and Carol and Ted and Alice* used to cover up sexually candid films?

—Stanley Penn,
The Wall Street Journal,
May 13, 1970

Jack Valenti, President of the Motion Picture Association of America . . . may be astonished to learn that he is the father of *Easy Rider* (rated R). In a speech before the M.P.A.A. in 1967, Valenti said he was weary, weary, weary of the excesses in drug and motorcycle films. He wished for theatres full of *Doctor Dolittles*.

Waiting in the wings, the next speaker (Peter Fonda) made a perverse resolution: to make a good movie about drugs and motorcycles.

—Stefan Kanter,
Time magazine

Richard Zanuck reneged on his vow to *The National Observer* about "big, family-type" movies and "responsibility as a person and as a filmmaker to put on things of which I can be proud." In the summer of 1970, Twentieth Century-Fox became the first major Hollywood studio to release a sex film—and not just one. Two.

"They were part of a series of disasters," admitted David Brown in 1986, "exciting, well-intentioned movies that somehow got out of control. *Myra Breckinridge*, which I loved—I guess Dick and I were the only ones who laughed, not even our wives laughed*—and *Beyond the Valley of the Dolls*. That one really did us in with the square and quite puritanical board of directors, and Mr. Zanuck."

Roger Ebert, the Chicago *Sun-Times* film critic, was paid $15,000 to write the *Beyond the Valley of the Dolls* script, replacing a previous draft, for which the author of the original *Valley of the Dolls*, Jacqueline Susann, had been paid $150,000. Her book, a sex-and-drugs story of show business, was made into a Fox movie. Critics hated it; audiences loved it. But that was not the point about the sequel.

Between the first *Valley of the Dolls* and the later *Beyond the Valley of the Dolls*, the screen was enjoying new freedoms. If, in 1927, the movies learned to talk, then, in 1967, they learned to talk dirty. The movie production code, a mainstay of Hollywood since the Fatty Arbuckle scandal in the early 1920s, became a strict ethics-enforcing constitution under first president of the Motion Picture Producers and Distributors of America, Inc. He was Will Hays, former chairman of the Republic National Committee and U. S. Postmaster General.

By 1930, the code was formally adopted, mostly as a measure to prevent the double-entendre humor of Mae West from corrupting public morals. With few exceptions, the Production Code would not bend, until, that is, the mid-'60s, when the

---

*In 1987, Brown recalled that while on location in Antigua for his and Richard Zanuck's 1980 movie *The Island*, a special screening of *Myra* was arranged for cast and crew. "By the time it was over," said Brown, "Dick and I were the only ones still sitting there."

floodgates opened. Then it was to hell with shutting bedroom doors on audiences and substituting "darn" when what the screenwriter really meant was "damn," or even "goddam." From time to time, a "fuck" would also slip in, and tended to be reported in the newspapers. To assist viewers in assessing the content of individual films, the M.P.A.A., as it had then evolved, called upon its newly appointed president, Jack Valenti, a former public relations man for President Lyndon Johnson, to develop a ratings code by which all releases would be reviewed by a board and branded—either "G" (for General audiences), "M" (for Mature audiences; this was later changed to "GP," which seemed meaningless, and then to "PG" for "Parental Guidance Suggested"), "R" (for "Restricted—No One Under 16 Allowed Unless Accompanied by a Parent or Guardian"), or "X" ("No One Under 17 Permitted"). In 1967, the new system was introduced to movie audiences in a promotional film starring Julie Andrews, whose once-sparkling star appeared to be on the wane.

Enter Russ Meyer.

> "I like women who enter into sex like it was a soccer match. I don't like all this protocol stuff, where a man is expected to make the first move. A woman should be terribly imaginative. Like she should be able to do a striptease at a very surprising moment. I want them to lead as much as follow."

> —Russ Meyer at Yale

Forty-seven years old, dubbed the "King of the Nudies" for the 20 grade-A stag movies he had produced, Meyer had long harbored a desire to go legit, said friends, although his earliest aspiration had been to become a Hollywood studio cinematographer. That changed after Richard Zanuck viewed Meyer's $72,000 *Vixen*, which grossed more than $6 million—an excellent return for a tale of lesbianism and incest.

"If Meyer can get that kind of production quality out of simple equipment and seventy grand, just *think* what he could do with proper equipment and budgeting," said Zanuck. Dick offered

Meyer the pick of any property in the studio inventory, and Meyer selected *Beyond the Valley of the Dolls*. (Susann had by then already written a treatment with that title, which her husband Irving Mansfield was set to direct.) Meyer also planned to film Irving Wallace's novel about censorship, *The Seven Minutes*, as well as Edward Albee's *Everything in the Garden*, and Peter George's *Final Steal*. Once Meyer took the *Dolls* project for himself, the deal with the Mansfields fell through and they subsequently sued Fox for $10 million, because, among other things, Meyer's version had nothing whatsoever to do with the original *Valley of the Dolls*.

"Richard Zanuck is a bright young man," said Jacqueline Susann, "but he is deceiving and defrauding the public if he brings out a film entitled *Beyond the Valley of the Dolls*. Already, the staid London *Times* has labeled me a pornographer because they thought I wrote it. The film contains nudity, orgiastic conduct, and is a sex exploitation film."

In *The New York Times*, Vincent Canby opened his review of Meyer's *Beyond the Valley of the Dolls* by saying: "Any movie that Jacqueline Susann thinks would damage her reputation as a writer cannot be all bad." And, indeed, the $2-million movie, which years later continued to play the college circuit, was only half-bad, a pop-art mixture of sex, drugs, and mock-violence. Populated by living centerfolds, *Beyond the Valley of the Dolls* was difficult to like or hate seriously, if only for its tone: when one of the characters was decapitated, the soundtrack broke into the Twentieth Century-Fox logo music, complete with drumroll.

This left *Myra Breckinridge*. It was pretty foul. "The director Michael Sarne was castrated by Dick and David," said Hugh Fordin, who had worked with the British filmmaker on *Joanna*, a kinky, surrealistic musical about an amoral art student (scratchy-voiced Genevieve Waite) in swinging London.

"Michael could have done a fabulous job doing little films for Fox, but Dick and David gave him *Myra* to fuck him," said Fordin. "They knew he couldn't fix it. Nobody could. It was a set-up. They'd paid Gore Vidal all this money to come up with a script, which was unshootable."

Gore Vidal's novel *Myra Breckinridge* was a novel of confused sexual identities linked to the Old Hollywood. It did not so much pass for literature as it did for controversy, which, fanned by Vidal's appearances on television chat shows, could light a fire under a book and propel it to the best-seller lists.

The split personality hero/heroine, Myra/Myron Breckinridge, sets out to destroy sexual oppression in Hollywood. In the film, John Huston played the whisky-soaked studio chief, and the two halves of the one person were played by Raquel Welch, a throwback to the Fox glamour girls of the past (except she was brunette and devoid of vulnerability) and Rex Reed, an actor-journalist who made his name writing acid-etched profiles of movie stars and then going on talk shows to promote himself.

Mae West, whose most recent professional outing prior to *Myra* was a guest spot in 1966 on the *"Mr. Ed"* television series, was paid $350,000 and typecast in the role of a man-hungry Hollywood agent, marking the septuagenarian's return to the large screen after an absence of 26 years. Her entrance at the film's New York premiere drew vast crowds; the film did not.

"A tired, smirking elephant with no place to go," is how Howard Thompson in *The New York Times* critiqued *Myra*, while *The Wall Street Journal* got down to business: "A major studio, Twentieth Century-Fox, has invested many millions of dollars to satisfy what it obviously sees as a mass-market demand for the distasteful, offensive, and dishonest. (Rated X, the bon-bon will be denied to all those under age 17.)"

Darryl was said to be displeased his studio had stooped so low, and roundly criticized his son. "It was one more nail in Dick's coffin as far as the old man was concerned," said one executive, although a publicity man for Fox at the time disagreed, believing that, had the positions been reversed, Darryl also would have sanctioned the X-rated features.

"Any stories that tell you a studio is embarrassed by sex and violence are lies—so long as the picture makes money. A lot was being made in the press in the '60s as to what actor or actress was taking off his or her clothes in front of the camera. Earl Wilson practically printed a daily list. But the studio didn't mind. In fact, when a script was being discussed and it was said that such-and-such an actor was willing to take off his clothes, the reaction was, 'Great. That's wonderful.' "

Myra contained its nudity; Raquel Welch strapped on a dildo and proceeded to rape a macho stud, himself strapped to a medical examination table. During the scene, antique Fox movie clips were interspersed with the sodomizing, as though the stars were acting as voyeurs. This included a shot of Loretta Young. The actress filed suit against Fox immediately, claiming that her reputation would be harmed if she appeared as part of a sequence allegedly depicting unnatural sex acts. Young filed suit in Cleveland because of the intention to show the film there. The scene was excised.

V

"The Zanucks, man and boy, ought to have their studio washed out with soap," commented *Los Angeles Times* critic Charles Champlin. David Merrick voiced his displeasure, though declined specific comment on Russ Meyer.

Suddenly the studio had a new nickname: "The Blue Fox."

Darryl went to work saving face. "We are finding certain groups are going to these pictures less and less," he said of the sex-violence genre. "Their popularity is declining, especially in the thousands of small American communities that we call our bread-and-gravy audiences."

Outraged Fox producers sought to disassociate themselves from the company. Paul Monash, who had brought *Peyton Place* to television and served as executive producer on *Butch Cassidy and the Sundance Kid*, latched onto the press and announced, "Hollywood used to cater to the tastes of the country. Now it is pandering to the sick fantasies of the perverted." Monash cited as his examples *Myra* and *B.V.D.*, and called the studio "a purveyor of unredeemed filth," going so far as to demand the resignation of Jack Valenti because the M.P.A.A. president was quoted as saying he personally enjoyed *Myra Breckinridge*.

Replied Richard Zanuck: "I am stunned by Monash's attack, as it is not only unwarranted and unjustified but obviously publicity motivated.

"Regardless of the fact that Valenti personally enjoyed the film this had nothing whatsoever to do with his determination in giving it an X rating. Valenti's integrity, which Monash has attacked, remains unblemished, whereas Monash's integrity, in my opinion, is open to question," said Dick.

"How any man can attack a company and an industry that has spoon-fed him year after year is beyond comprehension."

VI

By the late summer of 1970, Darryl and DeMeyer had become, if not intimates, certainly admirers of one another's power. Several people noted that at the time Darryl was lonesome for a friend, someone he could trust and who did not want anything in return. For the most part, the bill was fit by Elmo Williams, who used to sit with Zanuck and watch film rushes sent to New York by the studio.

"They'd run them two at a time on two projectors," said one observer. "It was a mad sight."

When Williams was not available, DeMeyer was called upon to lend an ear. For his part, DeMeyer enjoyed Darryl's stories, even when the mogul began to wander, and even when the research man was not particularly familiar with Zanuck's cast of characters.

"Darryl told me about this writer he knew, who used to come over to the Plaza and tell him a series of wild stories, and Darryl was just fascinated," said DeMeyer. The writer was obviously Truman Capote, author of *Breakfast at Tiffany's* and *In Cold*

Blood. He visited Zanuck over a period of three successive evenings in 1968 and related his upcoming novel, which Capote intended to call *Answered Prayers*.

"Darryl just loved it, and paid this guy $500,000* so he could
turn the stories into a movie," said DeMeyer. "And then that
son of a bitch never wrote one word! S.R.I. made him give the
money back to the studio, although Fox only got a part of it.
Darryl got a big kick out of the whole thing, though."

DeMeyer said Darryl thought Capote should have been entitled to keep the money, "just for being so goddam clever."

Whenever DeMeyer was not within sight of Zanuck, Darryl
kept close track of his whereabouts. Should the consultant be
called to the studio, Zanuck would ring him to inquire into
which phase of the operation DeMeyer was looking. One morning, DeMeyer was asleep in his room at the Century Plaza Hotel
next to the studio when suddenly the phone rang.

"Morning, Henry," Darryl said. "You getting ready to dig out
some more crap at the studio?"

"Darryl, it is three o'clock in the morning."

"Oh, shit," Zanuck replied, "I'm screwed up on the time
again. I'll call you back later."

"Never mind, Darryl," said DeMeyer. "What's on your
mind?"

This came to be routine during DeMeyer's California stays,
when he would speak to Zanuck at great length, no matter the
hour. "Darryl, invariably, would talk about breaking up Dick
and David. It became pretty redundant," said DeMeyer, who
additionally thought it strange Darryl was on the phone so often
"considering he was also sending so many letters. Most of the
time he'd begin the conversation by saying, 'Henry, you'd better take a walk.' That meant he wanted to talk but I had to call
him from outside the studio. He was convinced Dick and David
had my phone bugged."

Once DeMeyer was forced to leave Darryl's Plaza suite via

---

*According to studio records, Capote was advanced more than $200,000 and
given a deadline of December 31, 1970.

the service entrance because Dick was due in the front hall. "Darryl didn't want his son to know we'd been talking. It nearly came to the point that Darryl didn't think I'd be out fast enough and I'd have to hide in the closet."

A different type of incident took place in DeMeyer's room at the Century Plaza. "I got home from the studio around midnight," he recalled, "and five minutes later came this little knock on my door. Well, standing outside were these two babes, who said they were there so we could have some fun. I asked them how they had come to my room, and one of them said they'd been told to. Fortunately, I knew not to let them in."

DeMeyer added in a conspiratorial tone, "They'd been sent."

In New York, DeMeyer held a standing invitation to join Darryl at his ritual Sunday night dinner at Trader Vic's, the Polynesian restaurant in the basement of the Plaza. One such evening DeMeyer joined Darryl, Genevieve Gilles, and Elmo Williams for dinner.

Williams's conversation with Darryl predictably revolved around the old days. "They were talking about *Twelve O'Clock High* for the umpteenth time, and Genevieve looked bored to tears," said DeMeyer, who tried to engage her in conversation.

"Genevieve, I've never been any good with French names," he said. "Do you mind if I just call you Ginny?"

Gilles gave the consultant a cold stare, but before she could say anything, Darryl leaned over the table, removed the cigar from his mouth, and replied, "Henry, you can call her any goddam thing you want."

VII

Paris had served as Darryl Zanuck's general playground ever since he had fled the studio in 1956, living much like some exiled king who skipped out on his country with the treasury in tow. Younger daughter Susan Zanuck also took up residence in Paris, although never with her father. Once she married Andre

Hakim, Darryl employed him at the Fox office, at 114 rue La Boetie. That remained the only bit of contact between father and daughter.

"They never spoke," a Paris journalist said. "Susie Zanuck became an alcoholic by the age of 25, and there was always a party going on in her apartment. You could look up to her balcony and see the smoke, because she liked to throw California-style barbecues. Susie had a lot of interesting friends—writers, artists—but there was nothing between her and her father. Complete death on both sides."

It was generally believed Susan resented her father's infidelity to her mother, and Darryl regretted Susan's lack of character and ambition. At the Paris premiere of *The Longest Day*, a personal triumph for Darryl, Edith Piaf sang *La Marseillaise* from the Eiffel Tower, then at the banquet after the screening, shared the table in the Palais de Chaillot with Darryl Zanuck, Irina Demick, and the American ambassador to France, General James Gavin. Susan was seated in Siberia.

In good times, Dick was a party to his father's Parisian revelry. When events soured between them, Paris became a bone of contention.

"There was this big bash Dick and Darryl threw for Elizabeth Taylor," remembered Bud Kahn. "You've never seen anything like it in your life. They took over Maxim's."

"No, it wasn't Maxim's," recalled Barbara Bladen, a reporter for *The San Mateo Times* who participated in an American journalists' junket to European cities to visit Fox movie locations. "The studio *recreated* Maxim's on the Place Concorde. It was fabulous—except first we had to watch this lousy movie with Darryl Zanuck's girlfriend. Oh, what the hell was her name?"

The 1968 gala was tied into the Fox picture *The Only Game in Town*, based on playwright Frank D. Gilroy's stage drama about an aging Las Vegas chorus girl and a gambler. Gilroy's previous *The Subject Was Roses*, about a soldier son who returns from World War II to find his parents continuing the same old quarrels, won a Pulitzer Prize and was turned into a modestly successful 1968 film starring its Broadway leads, Martin Sheen (as the son) and Jack Albertson. Patricia Neal played the mother. On Broadway, Gilroy's two-character *The Only Game in Town* starred Tammy Grimes and Barry Nelson. It opened to dreadful notices in June 1968, and closed after 13 performances. Nevertheless, Zanuck and Brown paid $700,000 so Fox could acquire its film rights. The producer would be Fred Kohlmar, who chose as his star Elizabeth Taylor. Her salary was $1.125 million.

One of the conditions Taylor demanded in her contract was that the film, although entirely set in Las Vegas, be shot in Paris, to place her in close proximity to husband Richard Burton, who was shooting *Staircase* for Fox with Rex Harrison. The location was not chosen solely to guarantee domestic bliss for the frequently battling Burtons. Paris allowed the couple to take advantage of the tax situation of working abroad. Though *Staircase*, based on a Charles Dyer play, was set in London and had to do with the marriage of two elderly homosexuals (played by two notoriously straight cocksmen), the British capital was created on sound stages of Studio Boulogne in Paris, as were the streets of Las Vegas. More than one observer recognized that Fox had managed to reunite the cast of the still-notorious *Cleopatra*.

The first co-star announced to play opposite Taylor in *The Only Game in Town* was Frank Sinatra, who withdrew when the start date was pushed back owing to Taylor's emergency hospitalization for a hysterectomy. As Sinatra's replacement, Taylor chose Warren Beatty, fresh from his triumph producing and starring in the 1967 populist gangster movie *Bonnie and Clyde*. Beatty had his pick of roles in Hollywood, and had turned down *Butch Cassidy and the Sundance Kid*, instead choosing *The Only Game in Town*. Producer Kohlmar paid Beatty $750,000. To direct the film, George Stevens ventured out of semi-retirement; he had directed Taylor in her two best films of the 1950s, *A Place in the Sun* and *Giant*.

The production made headlines. Burton stampeded before the cameras and broke up a love scene between Beatty and Taylor. She threw out her back when her husband yanked her away from Beatty and two weeks of filming were lost. Another incident causing a delay happened when Taylor became convinced her pet Pekinese, whom she kept on the set, had swallowed a $40,000 pearl. A search turned up the gem elsewhere.

For her dance scenes as the showgirl, Taylor was never shown below the waist. She had begun an unsightly weight gain that would haunt her for the next several years, and *The Only Game in Town* marked the debut of her new heft. Critic Vincent Canby compared her new shape to "an apple balanced atop a pair of toothpicks."

Both *Staircase* and *The Only Game in Town* were complete box-office washouts that still allowed its stars to walk away with six and seven-figure salaries.

"The reasons for still having a Paris office were all wrong," said Hugh Fordin. "The World War wasn't still going on. You could get money out of France. You didn't have to make pictures there because you couldn't take away your cash. The same thing was true of the London Fox office in Soho Square."

Stanford Research had something to say about the Fox foreign offices and their operations, assigning primary responsibility of analyzing the situation to Darryl and Richard, Harry McIntyre, and Stanfill. Secondary responsibility was to be shared by S.R.I., staff officer Edward C. Leggewie (Darryl's former French teacher), Andre Hakim, and, in the States, foreign distribution vice president David Raphel, Stan Hough, and controller John Meehan.

Everyone knew the writing was on the wall, that the offices had to be closed. Richard Zanuck did not mind for a variety of reasons. First and foremost, the business people speculated, was that he knew Paris and London were creating the cash drains that were forcing him out of his job. Second, Paris was where Darryl invariably met and pampered his mistresses, including

Genevieve Gilles, who had just bombed out—expensively—in *Hello-Goodbye*.

Darryl naturally viewed talk of closure of the offices, Paris in particular, as a further attack on his power, and a maneuver obviously implemented by David Brown. "The fight," said Brown in 1987, "was all over the girl."

"Darryl was furious," remembered Helen Gurley Brown, "He thought Dick and David were plotting to wrest control of the company from him and that David, in particular, was the Svengali, as he put it. That was the beginning of the forcing out of my husband and—since he would not abandon 'Svengali'—of Dick Zanuck."

Richard Zanuck was no actor when it came to masking his distaste for Gilles. "I had a very large loathing for this girl," he said. "I had weathered, rather pleasantly in most cases, many of my father's other girls, so it wasn't that there was any rivalry or jealousy between son and girlfriend. It was just that this particular one was really bad news and caused him, myself, and the company a lot of trouble. When she knew that she had a real enemy in me, she did a lot of unfair and unfortunate pillow talk, which didn't help my father's and my relationship."

Darryl also lacked the stamina to face a showdown over the foreign office issue. "He went through a very bad period at that time, physically and emotionally," Richard says. "He was showing some very early signs of senility. He became paranoid, partly, I think, because he felt his power with women and in life generally emanated from that position at the studio. He felt that any removal of that power would de-ball him, not only in the business world but in his social life. He was scared things would crumble for him if he was moved aside."

"The old man was senile," said an executive. "You'd be sitting there, and he'd be talking about something, then all of a sudden he'd stop dead. The old son-of-a-bitch wouldn't say anything for five minutes, then he'd pick up the conversation again. Everyone around him just behaved as if nothing was wrong."

VIII

On July 12, S.R.I. assigned a member of its professional staff already in Europe to determine both the short- and long-range plans for the operations of these European offices. It is expected that a report will be issued on findings, conclusions, and recommendations by August 1, 1970.

—from *The Gold Book*

By summer of 1970, the staff of the foreign offices had already been pared to the bone,* yet that was simply for openers. To look into the Fox Paris office, DeMeyer contacted an old colleague of his at S.R.I. headquarters in Stockholm, Dr. Jean-Paul Gimon. Darryl was properly armed for Gimon's investigation; he himself was slated to arrive in Paris the first week in August. On July 24, 1970, Darryl ordered Edward Leggewie in the French office to write a Personal and Confidential report on the Paris office activities, six single-spaced pages of details on business conducted at the facility. Darryl also had Andre Hakim provide a full account of his meeting with Gimon, which took place in Zurich, as the location proved mutually convenient. Darryl wanted to use the information to oppose any notion of closing down the Paris office.

From Gimon, DeMeyer learned that Hakim was a long-time friend of Darryl's, had been his son-in-law for ten years, and still considered himself a member of the family. Hakim also told Gimon that he was "playing a mediatory role between Dick and Darryl," and Gimon told DeMeyer that Hakim was frustrated "because of the lack of decision concerning film-making in Europe and because of the decision process itself. Mainly, Dick

---

*It was at this time Fred Hift was relieved of his $200-a-week position in the London office. He found no sympathy when he broke the news to Fox National Director of Publicity Dick Brooks. "That's the way the cookie crumbles," Brooks coldheartedly told Hift. On the other hand, David Brown was as comforting as he could be to Hift, given the circumstances. "What was ironic," remembered Hift, "is that as I was speaking to David, I noticed a job hit-list on his desk. Number One on the list was Dick Brooks.

Zanuck makes a decision more or less by himself in New York, and Hakim feels that the distribution people's advice should be taken into consideration to a greater extent than it has been in the past. Hakim reports having a four-year contract with Twentieth Century-Fox and claims that if they don't want to make any films in Europe, he will not object to having his contract . . . bought off."

IX

On August 15, 1970, S.R.I. turned in a 14-page progress report, showing a potential of $5,727,000 in cost reductions on the corporate operations, with another $300,000 savings on the DeLuxe Color lab subsidiary, and yet another $35,000 on the music publishing division. That came to a grand total of $6,144,300 for this investigation alone.

X

An executive at Twentieth-Fox said to a newsman, "I hope to see you next week if I'm still here." This more than anything else reflected the attitude of Twentieth employees who are aware of the empty state of the film company cupboard and the commensurate need of cutbacks.

Actually, Twentieth might come out swinging in the fiscal area in a few semesters from now. But the word is out and retrenchment is the order of the day.

Morale of the personnel . . . is low.

—*Variety*,
August 27, 1970

FOX FILM POSTS
$17.1 MILLION LOSS
FOR 2ND QUARTER

NEW YORK—Twentieth Century-Fox Film Corp. reported a net loss for the second quarter of nearly $17.1 million, although it had returned to profitability in the first quarter with net income of $967,000, or 11 cents a share.

241

Darryl F. Zanuck, chairman and chief executive officer, and his son Richard D. Zanuck, president, said the movie production and distribution company had made "substantial provisions" in the second quarter for "all anticipated losses" on films currently in release.

They added that, "based on current estimates, it is expected that the next half year will mark a return of the company to profitable operations."

—The Wall Street Journal,
August 28, 1970

Darryl informed the press that his company's cash flow was more than adequate to maintain operations and that it should permit a reduction in Fox's bank debt. In the first half of 1970, he said, the company paid nearly $7.5 million, followed by a payment of nearly $6.3 million on July 30, expecting to pay $10 million more by the end of September. Darryl based his good news "on record-high U.S. film rentals, the second quarter provision for losses on films, and a recently announced cost-reduction program."

XI

Labor Day weekend, Henry DeMeyer toiled alone at S.R.I headquarters in Menlo Park, setting up an administrative budget program for Fox, something the company had never used, and planning a computer installation, something Hollywood had never used. The computer would help achieve $250,000 in annualized savings, and the budgets would implement controls at long last on the studio's runaway spending.

As it was a holiday, the air-conditioning was not operating in the office, and, except for DeMeyer, the only other soul on the premises was the security guard. "The hotter it got, and the more materials I ground out for the Profit Budget System, the worse my mood," remembered DeMeyer. That was when the consultant was startled to find the security man standing over him with a Telex long enough to be used as wallpaper. It was from Darryl. The message had been sent from Paris to Harry McIntyre in New York, with the request that copies be forwarded to Stanfill and DeMeyer. The S.R.I. man started to read the rambling message, and as he did his temper grew shorter. He was about to dash off an angry reply when he realized: "What the hell, there is nobody here to put it on the Telex. And you can bet that Dick and Stanfill are not around to get their copies." The reason for Darryl's lengthy emotional outburst was S.R.I.'s Recommendation Number Ten, formally presented August 27, 1970, stating that the Paris office be closed.

"I do not see how we can logically avoid a controversy with Stanford on Recommendation Ten which I have carefully studied," countered Darryl. "The confrontation is unavoidable in my estimation because the Stanford Report is inaccurate in innumerable respects." Darryl cited the importance of maintaining the foreign offices because in the past they had "aided and supplied personnel to the production or partial production of our Hollywood-based films." In part, Darryl was blaming the problems generated by the movies completed in Paris on Dick.

"As an example," he said. "*The Only Game in Town* was made in its entirety in France because the Hollywood studio signed a contract with Elizabeth Taylor specifying that the film be produced in France . . . a costly error which had no relation to any decision made by our Paris office."

Other films that lost money for Fox, *Staircase* with Burton and Rex Harrison, *A Flea in Her Ear* with Harrison, Louis Jourdan, and Rachel Roberts, *Two for the Road* with Audrey Hepburn and Albert Finney, and *How to Steal a Million Dollars* with Audrey Hepburn and Peter O'Toole "were originated at the Hollywood studio and contracts and terms of the films listed above were negotiated at the Hollywood studio," Darryl pointed out. "I do not criticize the Hollywood studio management for their judgment . . . but neither the Paris nor the London offices did anything except follow instructions."

David Brown recalled Dennis Stanfill's entering the fray. Said Brown, "He took me aside in the empty boardroom, which was to be our execution chamber at a later time, and he said, in an uncommon conspiratorial tone for Dennis, 'Do you think we can get Dick to fly to Paris and get this terrible thing patched up?' I said it would be wonderful if it *could* be, but I didn't know whether Darryl Zanuck should be flying to New York or *who* should be doing the patching up."

Inexplicably, Darryl shifted his stance, perhaps realizing it unwise to cross S.R.I. at this stage in the game, especially as he might wish to align himself with the Institute should a larger battle arise.

On September 7, 1970, after a week of trans-Atlantic messages and responses, he wired the responsible parties and approved "closing both production offices in Paris and London in spite of the fact that as a result of my experience in both foreign and domestic productions I am convinced that this closing down of both offices will in due time prove to be fundamentally and financially wrong and eventually lead to expenditures that will not be justified."

Admitting he was doing "an about face on my part," Darryl said it was because of "the Hollywood studio's action in refusing assistance from the Paris production offices,* and since Stanford Research recommended that both London and Paris production offices be eliminated, I do not wish as Chief Executive Officer to take a contrary view to the majority as I prefer to wait and let time prove the wisdom or lack of wisdom of the decision."

Dick Zanuck, however, would not let sleeping dogs lie. "Dear Dad," he wired back on September 9, 1970, "[I] do not wish to get into a debating contest with you, however, despite what you may think, I must repeat again Stanford Research Report had nothing whatsoever to do with anything regarding *The French Connection*. We would have handled *The French Connection* entirely from the studio if Stanford Research had never been en-

---

*Dick Zanuck stone-walled his father's attempt to assist in casting a proposed action-adventure to be filmed in Marseilles, *The French Connection*

gaged. The studio is certainly capable of shooting three days in Marseilles without the help of the Paris or London offices just as we are capable of shooting anyplace in the world. I completely agree with your decision regarding the closing of the offices and we can get into the details of exactly how this should be done when we meet in New York. I do not however share your apprehension in connection with the closing of the offices and I think you will find that most of the executives both at the studio and in New York agree with the Stanford Research recommendation. Love, see you later, Dick."

Both sides insisted on scoring points with Stanford Research, as if to prove who was running the show. Darryl did not put down his gun.

"Dear Dick," he wired September 10, "I also do not want to get into any debate regarding Stanford Research. . . .

"My decision regarding the closing of the offices was made very clear to you and all concerned and I wholeheartedly go along with it although it will eventually result in far more problems that I do not want to dwell on at this time. If you or Stanford or Dennis believe that I previously defended the necessity of our two foreign offices in order to protect the positions of Edward or Andre then I urge you to disabuse your mind of this idea.

"It does not surprise me in the least that most of the executives both at the studio and New York agree with the Stanford Research recommendation and that you do not share my apprehension as I have found in my career that I have usually been misled by the 'experts.'

"Since I have stated my position and agreed to the closing of the offices for the reasons stated in my earlier Telexes I prefer to keep out of the situation entirely from here on. I have a hectic schedule in New York during the nine working days I am present and I am compelled to leave for Rome in the morning following the board meeting. A decision has been made which I have approved in spite of definite reservations therefore my position is clear. . . . Love, see you later, Dad."

XII

The Paris and London offices of Twentieth Century-Fox were closed. Upon his return to New York from Europe, Darryl Zanuck mentioned the matter to Henry DeMeyer.

There were repercussions over the closing of the French headquarters, as Darryl had predicted, though not of the sort he would have anticipated. These involved Andre Hakim's swindling Twentieth Century-Fox out of hundreds of thousands of dollars and, according to the legal papers filed in California civil court, Hakim's handling of alleged "black money"—unaccounted for, untraceable cash—for Fox.

Hakim was charged with overbilling the studio on film properties he purchased between 1965 and 1970 and then diverting the excess funds into concerns he secretly controlled in Switzerland and Liechtenstein. In one instance, Hakim told Fox he had contracted for the company, at a price of $105,000, a director and a "hot writing team" to make a film entitled *L'Echelle Blanc* (*The White Ladder*). In actual fact, said the studio, the hot team consisted of two teen-age girls Hakim met in Paris and convinced into signing their names to a script. The girls received $100 each.

Hakim, in turn, told a prosecutor in Zurich, where he had been summoned to testify, that he had been handling "black money" for Fox, which is a general method for evasion of United States taxes.

Hakim was denied a trial in California on his lawsuit against Fox for $605,200 in back pay.

XIII

Twentieth Century-Fox paid $500,000 for the screen rights to Philip Roth's 1969 bestselling novel *Portnoy's Complaint*. The controversial and scathingly funny book had built up the reputation of being about masturbation, although it wasn't. It was about being Jewish, but it was no *The Jazz Singer*. Rather than show respect to the religion, the book satirized the faith and its cultural customs in the same black-humor approach *M*A*S*H* applied to war, even though Jewishness was not as universal a topic.

"The legend engraved on the face of very Jewish nickel," wrote Roth, "on the body of every Jewish child!—not IN GOD WE TRUST, but SOMEDAY YOU'LL BE A PARENT AND KNOW WHAT IT'S LIKE."

Roth's hero, 33-year-old Alexander Portnoy, was an orgiastic, mom-ridden, psychiatric cripple. Mother Sophie was a monster and Moby Dick seemed the only appropriate casting choice. As for Alexander Portnoy, although an eager and willing Tony Curtis, whose last choice role had been as *The Boston Strangler*, originally approached screenwriter-producer Ernest Lehman for the part, the field remained open and highly competitive.

"Are there any up-and-coming actors who aren't Jewish?" wondered Curtis as he surveyed the field at the time. The possibilities to play Portnoy? Elliott Gould, George Segal, Dustin Hoffman, Richard Benjamin, Gene Wilder, Ron Leibman, and Woody Allen. Lehman's single comment as to who might land the plum role: "I'll say this much, you can eliminate John Wayne."

The introduction of *Portnoy's Complaint* to the studio came during the September 1970 Board of Directors meeting in the immediate aftermath of Darryl's personal defeat suffered by the closing of the Paris office, the embarrassing negative press and the pressure from the board over Fox's X-rated summer with *Myra Breckinridge* and *Beyond the Valley of the Dolls*, and Darryl's by now psychotic need to dissolve the partnership of Richard Zanuck and David Brown, who had gone after the Roth property in the first place.

"*Portnoy's Complaint*, which, let's face it, never should have been made in the first place, was going to be made over Darryl's dead body," said one executive, who added, "which in one sense, it later was. Only Dick did not know that at the time he proposed *Portnoy* to the Board."

At the meeting, the younger Zanuck took great lengths to explain why Fox should produce *Portnoy's Complaint*. The Board members were nonplussed. For what seemed an eternity they listened to Richard's unusually pretentious psychological analysis of why the film would appeal to a large segment of film audiences. What Dick did not note was that, were one to strip away the novel's Jewishness, it was evident that Alexander Portnoy, a vitally ambitious young man in his thirties, totally lived in the shadow of his incontinent, ineffectual father.

Darryl listened patiently, sitting ready and armed with his reaction. One eyebrow was cocked during Dick's entire discourse, and Darryl's cigar was planted firmly in the middle of his mouth, tilting upwards. Usually it was slanted down.

Richard finished his presentation with the request that the Board approve the production of *Portnoy's Complaint*.

"Gentlemen," began Darryl, "as long as I am Chairman and Chief Executive of Twentieth Century-Fox, *Portnoy's Complaint* or any other film with the same degree of obscenity will not be produced." This was a deliberate sabotage, a revenge on Dick for closing Paris. In his last Telex to his son, the one in which he reluctantly approved the shutdown of the office, Darryl wired that the argument over the issue was closed, as "all our energies should be mobilized for our story conference on *Portnoy's Complaint* next Tuesday and our Board of Directors meeting."

Darryl was certainly mobilized. He informed the gathering that while he was still in Europe he had hired a secretary to go over the Philip Roth novel carefully and tally all of its four- and five-letter obscenities. It seemed an unusual move, yet with great sobriety, Darryl read the list, holding it delicately in his right hand, while his left elbow rested on the conference table, his cigar smouldering.

"Anus—3," said Darryl. "Ass—16; Asshole—2; Balls—24 . . ."
The secretary left off the Yiddishisms from the list, although she
did raise questions over *"pisher," "putz"* and *"rochmones."*

Darryl went on. "Beat my meat—1; Blow me—2; Boffed—1;
Boner—1; Cock—16; Cocksucking—2; Cocky doody—1;
Crap—2; Dick—5 . . ." Darryl did not look up but continued,
"Dong—3; Dork—1; Fart—1; Fellatio—1; Fornication—1;
Fuck . . ." Darryl looked up, ". . . and fucking—55; Finger
fuck—2; 'Fuck my pussy, Fuckface, till I faint'—1; Fucking
whore—2; Hand job—2; Hard-on—6; Gissum—2; 'Go down on
me'—1; Jerking off—2; My joint—1; Motherfucking—1; Muff-
diving—1; Nigger—1; Nuts—1; Penis—17; Poopie—4;
Prick—16; Pussy—10; Screwing—5; Shit—29; Bullshit and
Horseshit—2 . . ." Darryl cleared his throat, ". . . 'Shove it in
me, Big Boy'—1; Sucking off—8; Taking a crap—1; Tits—13;
Titties—3; Tough titties—1; Turds—1; Twat—1; and Wad,
Weenie and Whacking off—4."

The men were outraged. "Oh, yes," interjected Darryl. "One
more." His secretary being British, Zanuck explained, this left
her uncertain whether this particular last word, which appeared
in the novel six times, qualified. It was not to be found in the
British lexicon, he said. Darryl moistened his upper teeth with
his tongue and pronounced the word.

"Snatch."

There was an uproar from the Board members. Several said
that if Fox were to make films such as *Portnoy's Complaint* they
would resign.

XIV

By late August 1970, rumblings were reverberating through
the studio that the facility would close and Fox would set up
small offices in Beverly Hills and work from there. Richard
Zanuck had Stan Hough prepare for the onslaught of just such a

program, and Hough insisted "the numbers don't add up to me. Let's remember that even if the studio closed tomorrow, we are obligated to pay $1.5 million in rent, another $900,000 in taxes and additional expenses which will total at least $2.8 million in hard cash annually.

"We have discussed it many times, but the inescapable conclusion remains—a move to duplicate facilities elsewhere doesn't make economic sense at this time."

Dick Zanuck agreed. "Unless the studio is disposed of in a practical, economic, and logical way," he said, "it would be pointless to move into [Beverly Hills] and rent what we now have."

Darryl, however, privately discussed the possibility of closing down the studio, selling off the property, and establishing an entirely new concept in Fox's future operation, to function in the desert. Darryl also viewed this as a method to shut out the unions *and* Dick and David Brown.

Howard Hughes owned a considerable amount of property around Las Vegas, and it was Darryl's idea that a complete studio operation be established there, one that would be modern in every detail, air-conditioned, and not only a facility for producing films and television, but a tourist attraction for people on their way to and from the gambling center. In addition, he would build accommodations for the film workers, and non-union film workers at that.

Darryl was attempting to contact Hughes, but without success. He kept DeMeyer apprised of the situation and, after several phone calls to the S.R.I. man, fired off the following wire:

WESTERN UNION
DEAR HENRY
LOOK FORWARD TO SEEING YOU MONDAY IN NEW YORK ON THE MATTERS WE DISCUSSED STOP PLEASE CALL ME AT OFFICE OR HOTEL WHENEVER YOU ARRIVE STOP MEANWHILE I AM ATTEMPTING TO ADVISE THE GENTLEMAN WE TALKED ABOUT ON TELEPHONE TO BE SURE THAT IF NECESSARY I CAN REACH HIM MONDAY OR TUESDAY NIGHT AS MY BIG PROBLEM IN REACHING HIM IS THAT HE KEEPS VERY UNORTHODOX AND UNRELIABLE HOURS BUT AM REASONABLY SURE CONTACT CAN

BE MADE AFTER YOU AND I HAVE DISCUSSED SAME
AFFECTIONATE REGARDS
DARRYL

Darryl later discovered that the elusive billionaire had slipped off to Guatemala, thus killing the dream of the desert superstudio.

XV

September 15, 1970

Dear Henry:
I hope that you and your wife will be our guests and join the Management and Directors of Twentieth Century-Fox in New York for the World Premiere of *Tora! Tora! Tora!* on September 23rd. The tickets will be sent separately shortly.

It is customary, or practically mandatory, for wives to attend the Premiere, which is a gala event. I hope that Stanford Research would allow us to pay your wife's travel and hotel expenses. . . .

With best regards.

Sincerely,
Dennis

In addition to the preliminary affairs preceding the *Tora! Tora! Tora!* premiere, guests were presented seats to see Lauren Bacall in the musical *Applause** and tickets to David Frost's TV interview with two of the Japanese principals leading the attack on Pearl Harbor. The weather turned oppressively hot in New York on the day of the premiere, and Darryl, despite his many premieres over the years, developed a nervous stomach.

The elder Zanuck spent the entire day at home. Late in the afternoon, he called DeMeyer at the Fox office and asked him to

---

*A musical version of Joseph L. Mankiewicz's 1950 *All About Eve*, although he was not credited in the show's *Playbill*. Twentieth Century-Fox, however, drew a percentage on the show for owning the original material on which it was based.

come over, which DeMeyer did. When he arrived, Darryl was wearing only his pajama top.

Modesty was never Zanuck's forte. Besides the Corinne Calvet incident, there were stories left over from his days at Warners. Producer Milton Sperling, the son-in-law of Harry Warner, remembered the first time he spotted Zanuck on the Burbank lot: "He was carrying his polo mallet and was followed by his retinue of stooges. Suddenly, he stopped, walked over to the stage wall, and peed on it, all the while talking over his shoulder to the people he was with."

In the late 1960s, a producer of historical dramas accompanied a director to Zanuck's Plaza suite for the purpose of pitching a project. "Darryl was wearing a bathrobe and the meeting went terribly," the producer said. "When we got out of there I asked the director, who was usually an erudite fellow, what had happened, and he said he couldn't talk to anybody who was flashing his genitals."

"So there was Darryl, waving his plumbing," said DeMeyer, "and walking around in circles like a chicken with his head cut off."

"Henry," said the old man, "I'm going blind! The lights are flickering. I can't see a damned thing." The window air-conditioning unit was also fluttering. "Darryl," DeMeyer replied, "we're having a brown-out. The power company can't keep up with the demand during the heat wave." Darryl was also wearing a pair of dark sunglasses. DeMeyer settled him into a chair. Zanuck began pounding his fist on the arm, and started in again on Dick and David. This time Darryl assumed some of the blame himself. He said Dick was a spoiled brat, but that it could have been his own fault, giving Dick all the things he had growing up in Hollywood, all the things someone growing up in Nebraska could never have.

Anger veared Darryl off the nostalgia track. "Shit," he said, "how are we going to breakup Dick and David?"

"I don't know, Darryl," answered DeMeyer, "but I'm trying." DeMeyer further stated that separating the number two and three men in the company "should not be that hard to do."

"Henry," Darryl said now, slamming his fist into his hand, "by God, if you do that for me, I'll burn a candle for you. No, by Jesus, I'll burn the whole goddam church!"

XVI

The kingdom was crumbling. The studio commissary, with its Varga mural of Shirley Temple still intact, was ordered closed by DeMeyer after it was discovered that its manager, Nick Janios, was involved in kickbacks from food wholesalers.

Janios's attachment to the Zanucks ran deep; Darryl had hired him away from the Brown Derby years before, and it was Janios who, on Darryl's instructions one afternoon, brought Dick to his apartment over the commissary where it had been arranged— secretly, by Darryl—for Dick to lose his virginity to a professional. Dick was 13.

An inventory of unproduced film scripts totalling an investment of $5 million was also written off. "Everywhere we looked," said DeMeyer, referring to his S.R.I. team of 14, "we found money that could be saved." DeMeyer also came up with a bright industry-wide money-saving idea of his own and proposed it to Dick Zanuck: "Do away with the Academy Awards."

DeMeyer said that Dick listened attentively to the plan. "Look," said DeMeyer, "if you still want to keep them, just give awards to the actors. But when you start passing them out to film editors and cameramen, then you're going to find them coming to the studio trying to negotiate a contract with their prices going up."

Another plan DeMeyer threw Dick's way truly intrigued the younger Zanuck: Take the components of a movie, feed them into a computer, and sit back and wait for a definite formula for a box-office smash. That way you curtail financial risk. The dream got as far as Progress Report Number Two in the S.R.I. Management Action Program.

"Currently," the report stated, "at Institute headquarters, researchers are in process of analyzing the makeup and box-office results of in excess of 450 features. Coordinated with this analysis is one related to the effects critics may have on a picture's success or failure. At this time we do not know what the results . . . will be. We do expect that the results will certainly not enable all the successful ingredients to be put into a computer which then would write another *M*A*S*H* or *Butch Cassidy*, and not make another *Star!* or *Hello, Dolly!*

So what did happen? "The computer kept spitting back everything we fed into it,"said DeMeyer. "We never did come up with a formula."

XVII

Darryl's toy shed came next. The props warehouse was a three-story building, with a basement, and about the size of a city block. The place was jammed: chairs hung from ceilings and every square foot of floor space was utilized, mostly by real and bogus antiques that silently bespoke a potential cash value.

"Hidden Assets" were yet another element in *The Gold Book*. Richard Zanuck, Dennis Stanfill, and Stan Hough shared the primary responsibility, with S.R.I. having the second. The Institute's estimate was a potential $1.5 million to $2 million return come the liquidation.

As one S.R.I. examiner finished his tour of the warehouse in the basement, he jokingly remarked: "I've seen about everything except wooden Indians."

"Oh," the guide answered, "they're around the corner."

S.R.I. recommended their disposal, and Stan Hough was put to work. "Parke-Benet Galleries is certainly the most prestigious [auction house], although their commission of 18 percent is pretty stiff," he told Dick Zanuck. Hough was also alerted that Fox's period train, used in *Hello, Dolly!*, should fetch $100,000 and was a genuine museum piece. Overall estimate from the sale of inactive props, not counting Fox's fleet of model ships, was between $350,000 and $487,000. In May of 1970, M-G-M had staged an auction of its own, wherein props such as Judy

Garland's ruby slippers from *The Wizard of Oz* commanded $15,000 and Lana Turner's dress from *The Bad and the Beautiful* fetched $225. But that was M-G-M. The very idea of selling off the Fox trove incensed Darryl.

"WE SHOULD HOLD OFF ON ANY SALE OF PROPS AT THIS TIME," he wired his son. "I KNOW WE COULD USE THE MONEY BUT THE LONGER WE WAIT THE MORE WE CAN GET FOR THEM STOP HOWEVER MY BASIC REASON IS THAT IT WILL BE PICKED UP BY THE PRESS AND IT WILL GIVE THE OPINION THAT WE ARE REALLY SCRAPING THE BOTTOM OF THE BARREL AND I AM SURE WE WILL GET A LOT OF UNPLEASANT GOSSIP IN THE COLUMNS AND WE CERTAINLY HAVE HAD ENOUGH RECENTLY."

Darryl was panged by a combination of nostalgia and anxiety, as well as pride. Once again, however, he was forced to face the inevitable. He loosened his position on the sale, waiting some time to admit further in a later telegram to Dick: "I OBVIOUSLY AM SUPERSENSITIVE ON THE SUBJECT BUT [NOW] I AM WILLING TO GO ALONG WITH . . . YOU . . . I RECALL ONCE THAT WE SENT [STUDIO EMPLOYEE] THOMAS LITTLE TO NEW YORK YEARS AGO AND WE BOUGHT AN ENTIRE ESTATE IN WESTCHESTER AND THIS INCLUDED A TREMENDOUS AMOUNT OF ANTIQUE FURNITURE AND SOME RARE PAINTINGS, ETC. AS A MATTER OF FACT I RECALL THAT WE HAD TO RENT AN ENTIRE BOXCAR TO SHIP THEM TO THE COAST STOP I ALSO RECALL THAT WHENEVER I HAD EASTERN VISITORS LIKE HARRY OR CLARE LUCE THAT WHEN I TOOK THEM ON A TOUR OF THE STUDIO I ALWAYS STARTED IN THE PROP BUILDING AS LITTLE HAD THEM ARRANGED MAGNIFICENTLY STOP."

Thus did Darryl's fond recollections of days past end.

He signed the wire, "LOVE, SEE YOU LATER, DAD."

XVIII

"Frankly," Stan Hough informed Dick, "I am much more concerned with our inability to dispose of some 'visible' assets like the 25 planes from *Tora! Tora! Tora!* which we presently have on our hands at a cost of approximately $500,000. Thus far we have failed to come up with an insight or solution to this problem and I haven't been the recipient of such an inspiration from anyone else. The same problem exists with the miniature ships and carriers built for the same picture at a cost of approximately $1,045,000."

That bit of information provided fuel to Dennis Stanfill. In a confidential memo, Stanfill pointed out to DeMeyer that Stan Hough's memo to Dick was "revealing," especially concerning "the way money was squandered on *Tora! Tora! Tora!** Can you imagine $1,045,000 spent on ship models! We could have rented moth-balled Navy ships on the same amount.

XIX

One weekend in Menlo Park, DeMeyer spotted an ad in *The Palo Alto Times* about a "sneak preview" that night for "a Twentieth Century-Fox production," *The Great White Hope.* He and his wife got to the theatre as early as possible and stood in line.

The next Monday morning John Meehan asked DeMeyer how he liked the picture, and the consultant said something about having to pay to stand in a lengthy queue.

"What?" wondered Meehan. "You waited in line? The whole purpose of having the sneak in Menlo Park was so that *you* could see the picture."

"Well, forget it," said DeMeyer. "The thing's a bomb."

XX

Dear Henry:
I received your letter with the review on *Tora! Tora! Tora!* from *The Palo Alto Times.* It is a rather confusing review as at times I

---

*Critics noted that to stage the raid on Pearl Harbor in the movie, Twentieth Century-Fox spent $9.1 million. The Japanese during the real attack only spent $4 million.

think the reviewer is very enthused, and at other times I think he is disappointed or confused.

Naturally, we all like to receive good rave reviews. However, I prefer to see rave theatre receipts . . .

Best always,
Darryl

"Bosley Crowther went light on *Cleopatra*," a one-time Fox publicist recalled, "because Fox sent out word that if it bombed the company would go under."

The publicist went on to say that the same technique was applied to *Tora! Tora! Tora!* even though "everyone, down to the lowest clerk in the company, knew that film shouldn't have been made. But it was the pressure Darryl applied on his son. The old man couldn't get it out of his head that World War II was over."

"These things have the sound of an unofficial 'Be Kind to Fox Campaign,' " Vincent Canby wrote in his Sunday *New York Times* piece after the premiere of *Tora!* He told of "those news stories, which have been appearing in the trade press recently, to the effect that if the film is a box-office disaster, then, perhaps, Twentieth Century-Fox will collapse or, worse still . . . be taken over by David Merrick."

Canby said, "It does seem as if the way we were being prepared to blame a fickle public for any financial losses that might be sustained by *Tora! Tora! Tora!* [while] nobody seems to give much thought to what's really wrong with the movie itself."

In *Tora! Tora! Tora!* Twentieth Century-Fox claims to have "the most spectacular film ever made." The claim, like the production cost of the picture—around $25 million according to the producer—seems way out of line. What the studio probably has is a new albatross around its neck: It will be a miracle if *Tora!* returns its cost by, say, 1984; if anything, it is likely to be remembered as a financial disaster.

—Lead paragraph, Gary Arnold's
review of *Tora! Tora! Tora!*
in the Washington *Post*

Darryl dispatched word to DeMeyer: "I have just received a cable . . . that in Rome, as well as every key city in Italy, we have broken every record of any picture released by Fox, and this includes *The Sound of Music*. I must add, however, that musical pictures never do well in either France or Italy. Nevertheless . . . *Tora! Tora! Tora!* figures are simply unbelievable.

"I assume you know the fabulous business we are doing all over the world, and it is anticipated that our gross out of Japan alone will be in the neighborhood of $5 million".

Darryl was being unduly optimistic. As the Gary Arnolds and Vincent Canbys of the country knew, the prospects for *Tora!* turning a profit seemed unlikely during anyone's lifetime.

XXI

Before S.R.I.'s report on studio operations was released, Darryl issued the Institute a confidential report in his own defense, listing the number of successful films the company had enjoyed due to his instigation. The majority of the releases had had nothing to do with the Hollywood studio, he pointed out, adding that the idea to inform S.R.I. of this information had rested with Dennis Stanfill, and that as far as Darryl's profit and loss statement was concerned, "no one else has seen it except Dennis."

Zanuck's report was datelined Paris, October 6, 1970.

FOREIGN PRODUCED FILMS (Controlled by D.F.Z. & Elmo Williams) (Based on September 19, 1970 report.)
THOSE MAGNIFICENT MEN IN THEIR FLYING MACHINES
Net Profit to date: $10,683,000
Original story purchased, and screenplay written and film photographed entirely in England with second unit elsewhere.

THE BLUE MAX
  Net Profit to date: $2,830,000 and still producing revenue
  this week. Screenplay written in London, and produced in
  its entirety in Ireland.
ZORBA THE GREEK
  Net Profit to date: $2,565,000
  The production cost was $783,000
PATTON (D.F.Z.)
  Estimated profit: $2,192,000
  Original screenplay and revised screenplay written at Cap
  d'Antibes, and entire production photographed in Spain.
THE SICILIAN CLAN (D.F.Z.)
  Profit to date: $533,000 (this figure will be far exceeded).
  Story, script and editing done in Paris and New York.
THE AGONY AND THE ECSTASY (D.F.Z.)
  Lost $5,281,000
CHE!
  Lost $3,389,000
  The basic idea of this film was proposed by me. The script
  was written at the Studio but also approved by me. The
  production of the film was completely produced by the
  Studio.

TOTAL PROFIT: $10,133,000

FOREIGN FILMS PRODUCED BY HOLLYWOOD STUDIO

DR. DOOLITTLE:	Lost $11,141,000
STAR!:	Lost $15,091,000
SAND PEBBLES:	Lost $895,000
KREMLIN LETTER:	Lost $3,939,000
THE ONLY GAME IN TOWN:	Lost $7,557,000
A WALK WITH LOVE AND DEATH:	Lost $1,637,000
STAIRCASE:	Lost $5,201,000
JUSTINE:	Lost $6,602,000
THE PRIME OF MISS JEAN BRODIE:	Profit $831,000

A FLEA IN HER EAR: Lost $3,736,000

PRUDENCE AND THE PILL: Profit $513,000

You will note that I have not included THE BIBLE in either category although during the editing I made eight round trips to Rome in nine months.

TOTAL LOSS: $54,455,000

XXII

It has been concluded that the main studio property has a potential of substantial financial returns to the Corporation as a long-term, real-estate development. In view of this conclusion, it was also determined that, as the market value of the land increases, it will be increasingly detrimental to the Corporation's financial structure to continue production operations in the present facilities.

—from S.R.I.
"Studio Operations
Recommendation 15"

S.R.I. warded off shutting the Westwood lot for three to five years at least, or until the studio organization for feature and television production be restructured, overhead reduced, and the labor unions accept more efficient working methods. In any event, the Institute findings suggested, no decision would be made on the property until the existing studio became profitable. Only then should the decision be made to continue in the studio business.

XXIII

FOX FILM POSTED $5.2 MILLION LOSS IN THIRD QUARTER
NEW YORK—Twentieth Century-Fox Film Corp. sustained a third quarter net loss of nearly $5.2 million, but it was only about

a quarter the size of the loss sustained a year earlier. In the 1969 third quarter the company had a loss of $20.4 million.

The continuing losses reflect the company policy of writing off quickly the overly high costs incurred in the production of several recent films that haven't done as well as hoped at the box office.

. . . [A Fox spokesman] said, however, that "to date in 1970 the company has reduced its debt by $38.3 million—$13.7 million prior to July 21, $24.6 million since then with further payments to be made prior to the end of the year."

The company also said it "achieved a reduction in operating expenses at an annual rate of approximately $20 million, which will not be fully reflected until 1971." This is nearly double the annual rate of approximately $11 million, which the company announced as its goal earlier this year.

—*The Wall Street Journal,*
October 22, 1970

XXIV

Dennis Stanfill sought to exacerbate the touchy situation between the Zanucks over Dick's relationship with David Brown, at the same time cashing in on the fact that Henry DeMeyer had Darryl's ear. On United Airlines stationery, Stanfill handwrote to DeMeyer a letter dated October 27, 1970, marked "Private and Confidential." The envelope was not sent to DeMeyer in care of Fox in California or New York, but rather directly to Palo Alto. As a return address, Stanfill used his San Marino home.

"Dear Henry," wrote Stanfill, "I am being presumptive again and suggesting a way to respond to D.F.Z. on David Brown. Here is my suggested letter from you to D.F.Z. (at the Plaza) [parentheses Stanfill's]."

The suggestion, which DeMeyer did not take, played on Darryl's healthy ego and sought to smash David Brown's. Stanfill was asking S.R.I. to strip Brown of his decision-making power. "Dear Darryl," Stanfill wrote for DeMeyer, "Some time

261

ago you asked me to appraise the story operations of Fox. This appraisal would focus heavily on one individual, David Brown, since the Story Department has been drastically cut.

"I hope you can understand that S.R.I. as a matter of policy is reluctant to undertake formal assignments of executive appraisal. We do this on occasion but only with the express written request of the client. In any event I believe that you (and not S.R.I.) are uniquely qualified to make this appraisal.

"No one in American industry has more experience than you in judging story selection. Your seasoned opinion would be conclusive for any banker, director, or executive.

"I would like to suggest a procedure by which you could form your own appraisal on story selection. You could draw up a simple form as below and the[n] personally fill it in—for every picture since 1965 or some other recent year.

Name of Picture	Suitability of Story	Selecting Story Individual	Profit or Loss

"I think you will have an opinion (with facts to back it up) after you have made this historical appraisal.

"Now I would like to add my observations based on the data which has been supplied to me. Fox has written off over $15 million in story and scenario abandonments since 1963.

"This write-off was for stories never made into pictures. It is an additional loss to those picture losses sustained where the story solution was not suitable.

"I know you will agree that Fox cannot sustain such story and scenario write-offs in the future. We should bend every effort to reduce those write-offs. Again, you can be the best guide on how this should be done, since you have the greatest experience going over many years.

"I trust my observations have been helpful to you. I can discuss it further if you desire. Naturally, I will keep this matter confidential as you requested.

Henry DeMeyer"

XXV

Letters continued to exchange hands. Again marked "Personal and Confidential," a message found its way to DeMeyer from Darryl. "Dear Henry," it read, "Attached to this memo you will find a personal letter written by Genevieve to Dick at the studio. The letter speaks for itself, and the decision was made entirely by Genevieve." Gilles was asking to be relieved from her Fox contract, at a time when word was out Dick was prepared to fire her, despite her link to his old man. Darryl circumvented Dick's maneuver, and as he optimistically interpreted Gilles's decision, her request that her contract be terminated would not "prevent Genevieve from working in any of our future pictures . . . she feels that being under contract and not being used by the studio is detrimental to her. Therefore, she would prefer to be on her own as a free agent."

"Dear Dick," Gilles wrote November 5, 1970, on her private stationery, "According to my contract with Twentieth Century-Fox Productions Limited, I am to be notified by December 21, 1970, regarding my option for 1971.

"I would appreciate it deeply if you would not exercise my option.

"With my best wishes. Sincerely, Genevieve Gillaizeau."

XXVI

Once the Thanksgiving holiday had ended, in late November 1970, Gladstone Whitman of Chase Manhattan apprised Stanfill of the temper of the banks. Admitting S.R.I. had accomplished a great deal, Whitman believed the Institute "has just scratched the surface in many areas," and some of the bankers feared "the momentum of the cost-effectiveness program was slowing down."

Whitman sought more aggressive measures, with "additional, meaningful results," saying, "We must strongly encourage the company to stay on track if an explosive result is to be avoided."

XXVII

Yet already the pieces were being formulated to set off the explosion.

John Edmondson, formerly of E.P. Dutton, and Bill Gossett, the retired president of the American Bar Association, were the two leading outside members of the Board of Directors. During the months of the cost-effectiveness project, they had become closely associated with S.R.I. It was Gossett who realized the likelihood of stockholder lawsuits and the Board's potential liability. Among the examples of possible mismanagement was the money spent on *Hello-Goodbye*, of which $1 million was believed to be spent on the wardrobe that was not returned to the studio.

Following the board meeting of November 19, it was discussed what approach could be taken. Edmondson and Gossett felt that they had been grossly deceived, and their objective was to get Dick Zanuck and David Brown out of the corporation. Stan Hough, as a close associate of theirs, would also have been included.

The men set up a special committee made up of three outside board members, and on December 10, "RESOLVED . . . to consider the S.R.I. recommendations and to report to the Board its suggestions for implementing the S.R.I. reports including (without limitation) any executive managerial changes deemed necessary or desirable to effect a practical and realistic fulfillment of the S.R.I. reports, all in the best interests of the Corporation and its stockholders; and IT IS FURTHER RESOLVED, that said Special Committee shall consist of William Hughes Mulligan, Chairman, John P. Edmondson and William T. Gossett, the said persons to serve on said Special Committee at the pleasure of this Board."

Fordham Law School dean William Hughes Mulligan resigned from the committee after the second meeting, ostensibly because he wanted no part in the plot to axe Richard Zanuck. Mulligan was replaced by Jerome Straka, former chairman of the

Board of Chesebrough-Pond's. Bill Gossett became chairman of the committee.

As the leader of the S.R.I. project, DeMeyer was the first to be called before the troika. During the course of the interrogation he was asked about the relationship of Darryl and Dick, and the part that David Brown was playing. Considerable time was spent on Darryl's contribution to the corporation and to the film industry. It was pointed out that David and Dick probably had deceived Darryl on what was actually happening at the studio, and that the situation had been worsened by Darryl's relationship with Genevieve Gilles.

The opinion was expressed that Darryl's contributions and long record as a successful tycoon should not be destroyed, that the committee ease Darryl into a position where the Board would make the important decisions and Darryl would only be left to approve them. Then, after the contemplated changes in executive positions had taken place, Darryl would be asked to resign quietly from the corporation.

As for Stan Hough, he was merely a victim of association, rather than a power who was implementing actions that were imperiling the corporation's future. Hough should keep his job, stressed DeMeyer, particularly so he could provide continuity in the operation of the studio.

With the objective of disposing of Dick and David, the committee asked for some solid facts on which to move. Edmondson demanded the record on their regime.

DeMeyer's instructions were to handwrite this information, not to turn it over to a typist. "This way," said Gossett, "you will be the only one who will know where it came from."

John Meehan innocently supplied DeMeyer the necessary data, seven charts listing the breakeven for feature productions for the seven years, 1964 to 1970.* Each chart gave the name of the picture, the estimated dollar-figure film rentals required to break even, what the film ultimately earned (as of December 11,

*See Appendix I

1970, the day after the special committee made its request of DeMeyer), and the percentage of ultimate rental to breakeven.

Most of the movies DeMeyer had never heard of—*Third Secret, Male Companion, Deadfall*—yet that was not his concern. Of the 120 releases on the list, 84 lost money, nine were "just above" breakeven, 23 produced a fair to adequate profit, three did "outstanding" business (*The Sound of Music, Zorba the Greek*, and *M*A*S*H*, although they were deemed "nonrecurring exceptions"; *Zorba* did well because of its low price), and one release remained "questionable"—*Tora! Tora! Tora!*

This added up to a $161.3 million loss on features produced between 1963 and 1970, greater than either the $145 million profit on *The Sound of Music* or the $61.4 million made when Fox licensed its pre-1963 features to television.

As DeMeyer handwrote his conclusion for the special committee, "If it had not been for *Sound of Music* and sale of old features to TV, the corporation would have gone bankrupt on features produced during period 1963-1970," he thought to himself:

"So much for the record of Zanuck and Brown."

XXVIII

It was time to seal the gates. December 14, 1970, Darryl wired publicity vice president Jonas Rosenfield, "NO PRESS STORIES OF ANY SORT SHOULD BE RELEASED BY YOUR OFFICE OR THE STUDIO PUBLICITY DEPARTMENT EXCEPT PRESS STORIES RELATING TO FILMS WE NOW HAVE IN PRODUCTION OR HAVE BEEN COMPLETED AND ARE BEING PREPARED FOR RELEASE.

"THE ABOVE RECOMMENDATION, FOR OBVIOUS REASONS, WAS SUGGESTED TO ME BY THE SPECIAL COMMITTEE OF THE BOARD OF DIRECTORS."

No matter. Stories spread anyway.

FOX FILM PRESIDENT RICHARD ZANUCK
SAID TO BE FACING THE AX

NEW YORK—A recommendation that Richard D. Zanuck be replaced as president of 20th Century-Fox Film Corp. is widely believed to be under consideration by a special committee of three of the company's directors appointed to look into Fox's troubled financial situation.

. . . Fox itself declined comment on the report other than to say there haven't been any resignations among the top management to date. . . .

One source said it would be hard for Darryl Zanuck to oversee the firing of his own son—"fathers don't usually do this to their sons, no matter what. But it's hard to see how he would have very much choice except to act on the directors' recommendations."

—Stephen Grover in
The Wall Street Journal,
December 14, 1970

XXIX

Two days before Christmas 1970, William Gossett, Jerome Straka, and John Edmondson received a 13-page report at their respective homes: Subject: A STATEMENT CONCERNING THE PERFORMANCE OF RICHARD D. ZANUCK, DAVID BROWN, STANLEY HOUGH AND THEIR ASSOCIATES SINCE RICHARD D. ZANUCK WAS ELECTED PRESIDENT OF THE CORPORATION. It was from Dick Zanuck, David Brown, and Stan Hough.

Darryl was painted as the villain here. Richard took credit for the August 1969 Working Paper on Fox, which at the time "was suffering from inertia, lethargy, and a lack of positive, forward-looking thinking." Following presentation of that paper, the December 23 report said, "RDZ and David Brown developed in depth the plan contained in THE WORKING PAPER ON THE FUTURE OF TWENTIETH CENTURY-FOX FILM CORPORATION. Since DFZ was in Europe until the August Board Meeting, he was shown the plan just prior to the August Board Meeting."

The cat was out of the bag: "Reference is made at this point to the reported dissension between DFZ ad RDZ. In RDZ's view, this dissension developed primarily as a result of DFZ's reluctance to implement the Board's approval of RDZ's organizational responsibility as set forth in the Minutes of the August 28, 1969 Meeting. To repeat the pertinent sentence from those Minutes, 'DFZ will concentrate on corporate policy without the burden of worldwide day-to-day operation which Dick is willing and able to assume.' " Richard said that he was granted a $50,000 salary hike, proof that both the Board and he expected that he would fulfill this new role, and not be undermined by his father.

"DFZ has repeatedly expressed his understanding that RDZ's role in the corporation remained that of primarily a studio production chief. RDZ would never have accepted an increase in compensation during a loss year if he had known that it was DFZ's intention to restrict his duties to primarily what they had been previously.

"Another area of dissension developed early in June 1970 when DFZ abruptly and without notice sent an order by courier to RDZ at the studio directing RDZ to close down the studio forthwith. RDZ stated that to do so without consultation and careful planning would have resulted in great loss to the corporation and lawsuits from television networks, exposing the corporation to further damage . . . RDZ's decision not to comply with the directive was upheld months later by S.R.I.'s Studio Operations Report #15 which concludes that the studio must be phased out in an orderly fashion."

In conclusion, Richard, Brown, and Hough said in their own defense, "It is hard to imagine the rationale of even considering a change in production management when one takes into consideration that the hard-learned lessons of the past have been applied by this management." The report reminded the special committee that it was Richard Zanuck and David Brown's idea to hire Dennis Stanfill *and* the Stanford Research Institute.

"With respect to the engagement of S.R.I., it should be noted that RDZ and David Brown (both Stanford graduates) endorsed and with Dennis Stanfill, their appointee, hired S.R.I. to make a

'Cost Effectiveness Study.' Obviously, S.R.I. was not engaged as a tool by which 'executive managerial changes' might be instituted. Mr. DeMeyer has repeatedly stated that S.R.I. does not 'involve itself with personalities.' Never was S.R.I. engaged by RDZ and his team for the purpose of leading them to the execution chamber but rather for the benefit of the corporation's present management and in recognition of its problems."

XXX

Christmas eve 1970, Dick Zanuck sent wires to the homes of Edmondson, Gossett and Straka. "DEAR JOHN (BILL) (JERRY)," they read, "YESTERDAY I DISPATCHED TO YOU A SEPARATE REPORT DEALING WITH THE PERFORMANCE RECORD OF MR. BROWN, MR. HOUGH, AND MYSELF SINCE MY ELECTION AS PRESIDENT OF 20TH CENTURY-FOX. I WOULD LIKE TO ADD . . . THAT IN REGARD TO ALL STUDIO-ORIGINATED FILMS MADE DURING THIS PERIOD AS WAS THE CASE PRIOR TO MY ELECTION AS PRESIDENT APPROVAL WAS OBTAINED FROM DFZ. FURTHERMORE PRIOR TO THE ACQUISITION OF ANY LITERARY PROPERTY, PLAY, SCREEN TREATMENT, SCREENPLAY, SIMILAR APPROVAL, AND CREATIVE CONSULTATION WAS SOUGHT AND OBTAINED FROM DFZ. THE RECORD WILL SUBSTANTIATE THE ABOVE. I WOULD LIKE TO WISH YOU AND YOUR FAMILY A HAPPY CHRISTMAS AND A FINE NEW YEAR. BEST REGARDS. DICK ZANUCK."

XXXI

Ted Ashley, newly installed President of Warners, which just days before had purchased the screen rights to *Portnoy's Complaint* from Fox, called Richard Zanuck on December 28 to say, "DZ is starting a witch hunt against you." Ashley assured Zanuck, "If things go wrong, there's a place for you at Warners."

Darryl was being credited for putting his son's head in the guillotine. "Make no mistake," wrote *Los Angeles Times* gossip columnist Joyce Haber, "D.F.Z. still controls the directors." Her lengthier-than-usual piece ran December 23, under the headline "Zanuck to Oust His Son at Twentieth?"

"Darryl was in no position to fire Dick himself or even recommend firing," said DeMeyer. "Besides, Dick wasn't fired. He resigned."

An emergency board of directors meeting was called for December 29, 1970. Late the night before, in New York, Dick and David rang Dennis Stanfill at the St. Regis Hotel and asked him to meet them for a drink three blocks away at "21."

"We said that we knew that on the agenda of the board there would be a resolution asking for our resignations," David Brown said. "And we asked Dennis where his hand would be when that resolution came up. He said, 'Look, I'm a new boy here. I'm very appreciative of what you've done. But how long do you think I would last if my hand doesn't go up?'

"Dennis had never been with us," added Brown. "Any time we ever disagreed, he said, 'I'll just go to the banks.' "

"I asked him to do something much more simple," said Richard Zanuck. "There was just a bare quorum by one person. Many directors had stayed away—conveniently went to the Caribbean or wherever—didn't want to be involved in this. I said, 'Dennis, why don't you get a cold, get the flu, and don't show up? The meeting will have to be called off. Because if they don't have a quorum, they can't *fire* us.' But he didn't do it."

XXXII

In its confidential report, the special committee created by the Board of Directors of Twentieth Century-Fox asked for the resignations of Richard Zanuck and David Brown. Stan Hough was allowed to keep his job. Detailing the history of their decision, the committee said it had first met immediately after the adjournment of the December 10 board meeting, and between then and December 29 it had held seven meetings, each of three to six hours' duration. "Prior to and in the course of such meetings," the committee said, "members have given extensive consideration to the financial and management problems of the company and to the S.R.I. reports and the recommendations contained therein." Those consulted separately by the committee as it formed its opinion were, in order, Henry DeMeyer, Dennis Stanfill, Richard Zanuck, David Brown, Darryl Zanuck, Harry McIntyre, and Elmo Williams. Written statements from certain officers of Fox were also considered.

"Naturally," the committee conceded, what they heard from these executives were "factual recitations and arguments in contexts designed to support the position of the parties submitting them, and as such were somewhat less than objective. All of the executive officers of the Company who met with the Committee agreed, without exception, that the S.R.I. Reports were fundamentally sound, and they expressed the view that, with limited exceptions, the recommendations in the Reports should be fully implemented.

"On the basis of the foregoing, together with other information that has been supplied to it, the Committee has arrived at certain conclusions that are reflected in this report. Naturally, as directors and stockholders of the Company, the Committee has predicated its decision solely upon its evaluation and judgment as to what is in the best interests of the Company and its stockholders. In the circumstances such decisions are inherently difficult."

The three key decisions in the report were to be found in section I(a) and (b), under "Production," and II(b), under "Corporate Alignments," respectively. They were:

I(a) That the Board of Directors request the resignations, immediately, of Richard D. Zanuck, President and a member of the Board of Directors, and David Brown, Executive Vice President, Creative Operations and a member of the Board of Directors, without prejudice to whatever rights those individuals may have under employment contracts with the Company;

271

I(b) That, in the event that such resignations are not tendered forthwith, the Board terminate, effective as of December 31, 1970, the employment by the Company of Richard D. Zanuck and David Brown.

II(b) That Darryl F. Zanuck should continue, subject to the pleasure of the Board, for the term of his employment contract as Chairman of the Board and Chief Executive Officer of the Company with the same duties and responsibilities as are presently provided by the by-laws.

At the board meeting, the necessary signatures were committed to paper.

PART SIX

I

"When the Lord closes a door,
somewhere he opens a window."

—Maria, in *The Sound of Music*

"Everybody's ears were to the door the day Dick Zanuck and David Brown were being fired inside the board room," said Patricia Rick, who was sitting at her desk directly in front of the door once it opened and the two axed employees walked out.

"David came first," said Rick, recalling that "he looked as if all the blood had just been drained out of his face." Zanuck, she said, looked as though he had received a swift kick in the stomach.

"I didn't know what to say," said Rick, who still felt she had to offer something to her former boss, David Brown, though she realized full well that she had participated in building the case against him.

"I'm sorry," she said as Brown walked past her, as if in adaze.

"That's all right, Patsy," responded Brown. "Things have a way of working out."

II

RICHARD ZANUCK QUITS FOX FILM PRESIDENCY AFTER INDICATED RIFT WITH FATHER, DARRYL

NEW YORK—Richard D. Zanuck resigned as President and as a Director of Twentieth Century-Fox Film Corp. at a Directors'

275

meeting held yesterday. David Brown resigned as Executive Vice President, Creative Operations, and as a Director.

It was announced that Darryl F. Zanuck would continue as the company's Chairman and Chief Executive Officer "subject to the pleasure of the board for the term of his employment contract, with the same duties and responsibilities as he has had in the past." His contract expires in May 1973.

—*The Wall Street Journal*
December 30, 1970

FAST FADE

Resignations of 20th-Fox prexy Richard D. Zanuck and exec veepee for creative operations David Brown were effective last Thursday. Zanuck, it is understood, was ordered to be off the lot by noon, and Brown was locked out of his [New York] office, though he later was admitted to remove personal effects. Painters that day were erasing names from doors and parking spaces.

—*Variety*,
January 5, 1971

"I felt terribly let down that my own father could do this to me," said Richard Zanuck. "He was very cold ass at that meeting, very cold ass. Jesus Christ, it was brutal. And my father, talking, just sitting there, he showed absolutely not any ray of compassion for me. And that hurt me. It was an execution.

"Nobody was looking at me. It was like I had the plague, or something. And the loss of the company, my position. Everyone makes the mistake of assuming that their positions will go on forever, and it only came to me afterward that this was an occupational mistake, that nothing was permanent. Fox studios, which I had been controlling for so long, for nine years, a semi-demi king there, was suddenly no longer mine. It came as such a great loss that I no longer controlled it. And it made it no less agonizing that the man who had taken it away from me, who had replaced me, was my own father.

"Here was the great tycoon restored," he said, "proving to the world—and particularly to me—that he was still a power to be

276

reckoned with. But in a flash, I knew what had happened at that moment. If I had lost, so had he. He thought he had succeeded in getting everything he wanted. But I had heard a member of the investigating committee my father had set up insert a significant phrase into the resolution proposing that Darryl Zanuck be restored as President of Twentieth Century-Fox. He added what seemed to me to be fateful words: 'At the pleasure of the board.' I said to my father: 'Do you realize what that means? It means that at any moment they choose, they can dismiss you too.' Without more than a flicker of a glance at me, he shrugged his shoulders and casually said, 'It will never happen,' and went on to other business. I said, 'But it will. Watch out. You will be next.' He took no notice. He had won. I expect that night, when he told his girlfriend, she would be delighted."

Richard and David Brown returned to the Fox lot in Westwood. They were met by Dennis Stanfill. "I'll never forget his words," said David Brown. "He said, 'You know, there's a ritual to severance.' I'd never heard that expression before, which meant, 'Get your ass out of here before sunset because the longer you hang around, the more difficult it becomes." These, said Brown, were "executive posts we had for life."

"My car was parked at the curb with my name along the side in front of the building," said Richard. "I couldn't get into the car because the painter was down on his knees in front of the thing painting my name out. I couldn't open the door without asking him to stand up so I could drive off. And, of course, our secretaries were practically frisked when they left. We were treated badly in terms of this ritual of Dennis's."

"That's when Dennis shrunk in my eyes," commented Henry DeMeyer. "There was no reason on earth to give them the bum's rush the way he did. Dennis was the criminal, for his behavior."

"It gave me an extraordinary feeling," said Dick Zanuck. "From being a king, or a crown prince, suddenly I was made to feel like a criminal. The guard was watching me as if I was about to steal an ashtray."

"Dick's office was in shambles," recalled DeMeyer. "Nothing left in place except a large pile of papers on the floor, a bust of Darryl, and that Oscar for *How Green Was My Valley*. I often thought about it sitting alone like that. I wonder if someone ever took it."

III

"You are undoubtedly aware that your company has figured prominently in the news in recent weeks," Darryl Zanuck wrote in a letter to stockholders of Twentieth Century-Fox dated January 20, 1971. "Because much has been rumor and gossip, the shareholders are entitled to hear directly on these matters from the Chief Executive Officer.

"Shortly after our last annual meeting, we retained the services of the renowned business consultants and organization scientists, Stanford Research Institute. The Board of Directors instructed management to work with S.R.I. to analyze the operation of the corporation from top to bottom with a view to the attainment of maximum efficiency. . . .

"At the December 29th Board meeting the resignations as officers and directors of Richard D. Zanuck, President and David Brown, Executive Vice President, Creative Operations, were submitted and accepted effective December 31, 1970; and Dennis C. Stanfill, Executive Vice President Finance, was designated Executive Vice President Finance and Operations Control to assume primary responsibility for coordinating our continuing cost-effectiveness program. . . .

"We have made agonizing but necessary decisions. The decks are now clear. The organization is unified around the single objective of making our company profitable again. I am proud to head a team of professionals who are generally recognized as among the most competent in the film industry."

Part of the aftermath of the upheaval at the studio was serious talk that financier Kirk Kerkorian, who ran M-G-M, would stage a raid on Fox, or, at the least, merge with the Zanuck company. The name thought up for this combination of the two movie-making giants was "Twentieth Century-Lion."

The action did not take place.

IV

"You'd think those fellows Dick and David were criminals the way they've been treated," said Virginia Zanuck after the blood-bath. After nearly 15 years, the studio widow was emerging from the shadows.

"Dick had his battle and I have mine. I have 100,000 shares and I take care of a lot of my grandchildren. It would kill me if everything goes down the drain.

"I don't know what Darryl wants. He's built up this dynasty, and he's destroying it. He says we're legally separated. There's no such thing. I simply finally signed a property settlement in 1957 to protect my interests. He was involved with this Bella Darvi."

On January 10, 1971, *Los Angeles Times* columnist Joyce Haber reported that Mrs. Zanuck left for New York to consult with Milton Paulson, an attorney specializing in stockholder fights, and who had recently represented David Merrick in his unsuccessful attempt to wrest Fox from the Zanucks. Mrs. Zanuck decided not to stay at the Plaza Hotel, said Haber, because that was where Darryl lived. "I thought if I ran into him," said Virginia, "I'd konk him over the head."

V

Both Mr. Zanuck and his mother, the estranged wife of Fox's chairman, Darryl F. Zanuck, have indicated they support the dissident shareholders group, officially known as the Twentieth Century-Fox Stockholders Protective Committee. A vote to de-cide whether the insurgent challenge is successful will be taken at Fox's annual meeting in Wilmington, Del., next Tuesday. But it isn't sure that the outcome of the vote will be known immediately.

Richard Zanuck didn't volunteer the information he made in his claim. Rather, it was supplied by an anonymous tipster.

—*The Wall Street Journal*,
May 14, 1971

Virginia entered the fracas at the behest of an emissary who paid a visit to her Santa Monica home shortly after the firings of her son and David Brown. The representative had been sent by Charles M. Lewis, a New York investment broker (and the former son-in-law of Harry Brandt, the theatre exhibitor, with whom Lewis shared a pivotal role in Darryl's return to Fox in 1962), and Louis Powell, a New York attorney.

"I remember playing tennis with Bobby Redford, who lived in my building at the time," said Charles Lewis in 1987, recalling the events that led up to the proxy fight that pitted wife and son against Darryl Zanuck. "And I asked him, 'What do you think of Dick Zanuck?' because they had made *Butch Cassidy* together. And Bobby said, 'Oh, he's a super guy.'

"But the key thing with Dick," said Lewis, an energetic dynamo who talks nearly as fast as a ticker-tape machine, "was that things were getting pretty bad around New Year's Eve, the end of 1970. That's when I got a message from Don Henderson, the financial chief at Fox. First he said, 'I've got some bad news. We're bankrupt.' Then he said, 'They're going to fire Dick Zanuck at the Board meeting next Tuesday.' The stock by then was about eight dollars."

Lewis said that the first thing he did was to call his former father-in-law, whom he still referred to as "Papa." Brandt's reaction: "Well," he told Lewis, "you're going to have to start a proxy fight, because if you don't, I'm going to go bankrupt."

"He had so much Fox," said Lewis. "It was his major holding, and it was all banked and leveraged, which was why I had to get involved in this thing."

Lewis's next step was to contact Louis Powell. "He represented the head of Max Factor, and they owned 100,000 shares." Together Lewis and Powell went about gathering proxies, as well as the financing for such a fight, "Because," said Lewis, "the costs of a thing like that are enormous."

Because Darryl controlled the shares owned by his children—including Dick—the only major stockholder among the Zanuck family free to control her vote was Virginia, whose confidence was elicited and received. Her proxy would go to the insurgents.

Lewis's recollection of those days continued. "Dick Zanuck had a guy—we called him 'The Fly'—and The Fly was somebody who worked inside Fox, and for some reason or other he was able to secure documents." These were the papers necessary to build the case against what the insurgents' newspaper ads called "Fox's tired, old, and wayward leaders [who made] use of films as playthings for playmates." Using S.R.I. findings to bolster their arguments against Darryl, the Insurgents cited the statistics from the first S.R.I. operational review, that $20.4 million was needlessly spent running the studio.

"I'd find these documents on my doorstep," said Lewis. "Basically, I think The Fly started giving them to Dick, and then Dick would give them to me."

Lewis said that, although he eventually met The Fly once when Dick Zanuck introduced them at the Carlyle Hotel and the two "became kind of tight," the mystery person's proper identity was never revealed. When, later, the Security Exchange Commission looked into alleged unlawful practices surrounding the fight—allegations put forth by Charles Lewis—Lewis told his investigators: "There's no way, under penalty of death, I can tell you who The Fly is or where he lives."

"To this day," Lewis said in 1987, "I don't know who he was."

Lewis also said that although he was not sitting in the same suite at the Carlyle with The Fly and Virginia on the afternoon that the two of them met, he was located in the adjoining room. "I wasn't eavesdropping, but I couldn't help but hear their conversation. They obviously must have been involved with one another at one time or other, because he kept saying things like, 'Remember when. . . .' "

One of the incidents from long ago that Lewis heard The Fly asking Virginia to remember was his coming over to the Zanuck house and bouncing little Dick on his knee.

The proxy fight came to a surprise ending the night before the eagerly awaited annual board of directors meeting. "Ordinarily," said Lewis, "they used to hold them in New York, but on this occasion they moved it to Wilmington, Delaware, to make it harder to get to. It was a real pain in the ass."

The key to what happened next, said Lewis, "belonged to a fund in Kansas City that owned a very large block of stock, something like 300,000 shares, and the board of directors [in the person of Bill Gossett] said to Darryl: 'Unless you resign now, tonight, that fund is going to vote with Lewis.' So he resigned that night.

"Now, I get to Wilmington about 11 o'clock, and Harry Brandt's on the phone at my hotel, and he said, 'You won.' And I said, 'What do you mean?' And he said, 'It was on the radio: Zanuck resigned. You did it.' "

Lewis did not quite know how to interpret the turn of events, telling Brandt he would not believe anything until the next day's meeting. "When I see the vote," said Lewis, "then I'll know. So far, I haven't won anything."

"Well," posited Brandt, "you started right. Because he's o-u-t."

Lewis decided to call Dick Zanuck in California. "I wanted to let him know what had happened to his dad," said Lewis, who discovered that the younger Zanuck had already been informed. "Dick told me," said Lewis, "that the board made Darryl a deal so he could make three pictures, and Dick told him that they weren't going to honor that."

Dick advised Lewis that he should probably call Darryl himself. "He's in his hotel room right now," said Dick, who advised Lewis on contacting the elder Zanuck.

As to how the son knew of the whereabouts of his own arch-rival, his father, outsider Charles Lewis explained matter-of-factly: "Oh, they were very close, right up until the end, even during this fight, when Darryl knew Dick was going to vote for me and I got Virginia's vote. They may have been on opposite sides, but they never stopped talking to one another, or loving each other. Dick and his Dad always had a kind of family bond going between them."

VI

The Fox props, 2000 of them, went on the auction block February 25, 26, 27, and 28, 1971. The sale netted the studio $364,480. Henry DeMeyer wanted Lot #501, the Marilyn Monroe bed for *Let's Make Love*, only he was outbid.

Debbie Reynolds bought something from *Cleopatra*,* a pair of Roman Legion standards for $225. Lot #136, Shirley Temple's wooden soldier from *Captain January*, went for $450. Lot #407, Julie Andrew's *gros* point roses carpetbag from *The Sound of Music*, fetched $650. Lot #425, Paul Newman's *Butch Cassidy* bicycle, with chrome handle bars and a painted black frame, commanded one of the highest prices of all, more than $3000.

VII

Richard Zanuck filed a $14.5 million lawsuit in Los Angeles Superior Court against his father Darryl, William T. Gossett, chairman of the special executive committee, and Twentieth

---

*There were more props from *Cleopatra* in the auction—24—than from any other film.

Century-Fox itself, charging breach of contract in the loss of his job with the firm.

Suits were also brought by Richard Zanuck's wife, actress Linda Harrison, seeking $311,800, and by David Brown, asking $3.3 million. The 39-page complaint sought damages of allegedly inducing breach of contract, for alleged defamation, and for asserted affliction of emotional distress. It claimed that Dick was hired as Executive Vice President in Charge of Worldwide Production by Fox for a seven-year period, beginning January 1, 1967, and ending December 31, 1973, at an annual salary of $300,000.

"We were a couple of fellows walking along a beach at Santa Monica contemplating what we thought were the ends of our careers," said David Brown.

"I remember going down Hollywood Boulevard and wondering, will they take my star away from in front of the restaurant," said Dick.

"We were in such ego shock at the forced draft that nothing would do but that we resume executive life at another studio. So we went to Warners. When they gave us the job, we danced a jig that resembled Hitler's dance at the railroad car."

A year and a half later, the jig was up.

WARNER BROS. RELEASING
TWO OF ITS OFFICERS
FROM THEIR CONTRACTS

NEW YORK—Warner Bros. Inc. has agreed to release Richard D. Zanuck, senior executive vice president, and David Brown, executive vice president, creative operations, from their contracts with the filmmaker so that they might set up their own independent production company.

Both sides emphasized that the resignations were amicable. "We just concluded it was time to call our own moves," Mr. Brown said, adding that there is "nothing but friendliness" between Warner Bros. and the two departing executives.

—The Wall Street Journal,
July 10, 1972

Zanuck and Brown felt frustrated as executives at Warners, which did not seem like a family store. Their very first production as independent producers, *Sssss*, was a horror film about a snake. While still at Warners, however, Dick and David ingratiated themselves with producers Tony Bill and Julia and Michael Phillips. Once Zanuck and Brown set up shop at Universal, the three young producers brought them a "buddy movie" script by David Ward about two Chicago con men, called *The Sting*. Paul Newman and Robert Redford starred, it made everyone involved a great deal of money, and, along with six other Oscars, it won the Academy Award as Best Picture of 1973.

For their next film, Zanuck/Brown gambled and lost. The picture was captivating nevertheless, Goldie Hawn in *The Sugarland Express*, about a Texas mother who stages a prison break for her husband in order that they might reclaim their child from a foster home. The risk taken by the producers was on the film's untested director, whom they also employed on their next film. That one was called *Jaws* and the director was Steven Spielberg. The 1975 action picture about a shark who invades a Northeastern beach community outgrossed *The Sound of Music*, and launched Spielberg's career. The film also signaled the birth of Hollywood's marketing total escapist fare during the summer, and the "blockbuster or bust" mentality that quickly afflicted movie-making.

From *Jaws* on, if a picture did not pull in at least $100 million, it was considered a wasteful exercise.

VIII

After the emergency board meeting and the resignations of Dick and David, Elmo Williams was named temporary production chief. During this period Dennis Stanfill was solidifying his position in the corporation. The board, favorable impressed with Dennis and his actions, made him president of the corporation on March 18, 1971; however, that appeared to be only part of his ultimate objective as far as several saw it. Dennis's plans were to be the chief executive officer, and he was skillfully guiding the thinking of the board members toward this end.

Henry DeMeyer described his relationship with Stanfill as "close, and we freely discussed the majority of our plans and exactly what actions would be taken. In looking back, I do not think that Dennis and I were friends. Rather, I was a means by which Dennis could accomplish his ends."

"Dennis was the white knight as far as the banks were concerned," said Bud Kahn, who in effect was fired from Fox after S.R.I. labeled him an ineffective administrator because, Kahn said, he kept too much in his head. "They wanted me to create more paperwork. Dennis later tried to hire me back, so make of that what you will."

Kahn and his partner Robert Bean brought in *Made for Each Other* under budget, but were forced to back away from the *Play It Again, Sam* project. The hiring of the various writers pushed pre-production costs on the Woody Allen project up to nearly $500,000—beyond the means of Kahn's Wylde Films. Kahn, who smoked Zanuck-sized cigars, was not pleased with Dennis Stanfill over the turn of those events.

Stanfill became chairman of the board and in short order closed the Fox New York headquarters (and burned story files dating back to the days of William Fox, despite pleas to donate the papers to a college or university), cut studio overhead, and sold off assets such as Fox's 2,600-acre Malibu ranch. Fox paid no dividends in 1970 through 1972, and in 1973 its stock dropped to five dollars a share (from a high of $41.75 in 1969, the same year the Zanuck's problems became evident). In 1974, however, the company reported net earnings of $10.9 million on revenues of $281-9 million, despite a loss of $4.4 million on Wylde Films, which was discontinued. That same year Stanfill was credited with repairing the balance sheet, and by 1975 the company possessed no short-term debt and a cash flow sufficient enough to allow quarterly dividends (ten cents a share in the third-quarter).

Gordon Stuhlberg, a former television executive, became head of production under Stanfill from 1971 until December of 1974. Originally, said Charles Lewis, Stuhlberg was to be given a five-year contract; Lewis opposed the plan, saying that three-year contracts for top studio executives were long enough, and far more financially responsible in the overview. In any event, once Stuhlberg departed, Stanfill himself assumed the position of production chief, in addition to his duties as head of the corporation.

Business Week, in a laudatory feature on the executive, praised Stanfill for "taking an iron grip on operations, and tightening financial controls." Among the studio employees, however, he became known as "The Dictator,"* and in the film community, Fox gained the reputation as not so much a creative environment as a banking institution. "Artists did not want to work there," said publicist Bobby Zarem, who was one of several image-makers hired at the time to improve Fox's uncomplimentary profile.

In 1976, a major step forward was believed to have taken place with the promotion of Alan Ladd, Jr., from Senior Vice President for Production to President. At the same time, Stanfill fired David Raphel from his post as marketing chief; Raphel was considered by many as becoming too powerful within Fox's infrastructure, which probably posed a threat to Stanfill. (Simultaneously, the company also formed a new entertainment group composed of a record division, a music-publishing company, and a television-production operation.)

Ladd—or Laddie, as he was called—restored a creative atmosphere to the studio, bringing in a range of talent such as Mel Brooks (*High Anxiety*), Paul Mazursky (*An Unmarried Woman*), Fred Zinnemann (*Julia*), Herbert Ross (*The Turning Point*) and,

---

*One day in 1972, without any warning whatsoever, Patricia Rick was called into Stanfill's office, "and he fired me," she said. "He never gave me a reason. We always got along. He said, 'I have to let you go, and I asked, "When?"' Immediately! And I was out of there. I still don't know why."

in an announcement that surprised both coasts, the producing team of Richard Zanuck and David Brown.

When Dennis Stanfill greeted their return to the lot in 1979—more than nine years after he personally oversaw their "ritual of severance"—he ensured that Richard's new office was just as large as it had been "in the old days," and that Darryl's former desk be removed from storage in order that it might be used by his son.

Laddie's real coup was in bringing writer-director George Lucas's *Star Wars* to Fox (it had been turned down at Universal). The 1977 space epic, set a long time ago in a galaxy far, far away, sent the price of Fox stock soaring to $25 a share, and again made movie marketing tie-ins a viable retail force.

The success of *Star Wars* and the attention showered over Laddie and his tightly knit creative team were known not to sit well with Dennis Stanfill, whose own star was suddenly overshadowed. On July 25, 1979, Stanfill ordered Ladd and his two vice presidents, Jay Kanter and Gareth Wigan, off the lot. They formed their own independent production entity, the Ladd Company, and distributed their films through Warner Bros.

That same year, Fox staved off a prospective take-over by Chris-Craft industries, and it acquired Magnetic, a video-cassette company (which became the first to put Hollywood movies on the then-gestating VCR market), as well as a Coca-Cola bottling plant, and some resort properties. Stanfill also named Alan J. Hirschfield, formerly of Columbia Pictures, as studio boss.

Chris-Craft continued its takeover noises, but it was Denver oilman Marvin Davis who finally succeeded in buying Fox, in 1981, for $722 million. Davis, with his partner commodities trader Marc Rich, took the company private, at $60 a share.

Dennis Stanfill resigned as chairman and chief executive officer of Fox in 1981, reportedly in a power play with Davis ally Alan Hirschfield.* One legacy of the Stanfill era was that never

---

*Zanuck and Brown once again left Fox—this time by their own choice. Under Hirschfield, the producing team claimed, they could not get projects done.

once while the man was in power would he stand for nepotism in the corporation.

In 1984, Davis bought out Rich's share for $116 million when Rich was charged with tax evasion. Patti Davis, Marvin's daughter, was hired in the story department of Fox's New York office.*

In 1985, Australian-born publishing magnate Rupert Murdoch paid $250 million and became Davis's equal co-owner of Fox. Murdoch supplied the necessary influx of cash, given that in 1984 the company had lost $89 million. Murdoch and Davis then purchased seven Metromedia stations in 1985, with the purpose of setting up a fourth American television network, mirroring an S.R.I. recommendation in 1970 that Fox should take a bullish look to the small screen. Murdoch bought out Davis's entire interest in Fox by September of 1985. Price of the purchase agreement was $325 million. Fox's chairman of the board under Murdoch was Barry Diller, a movie executive whose strong suit was attention to the bottom line.

Fox's president was Leonard Goldberg, a longtime television executive. Upon joining the company in November of 1986, Goldberg told Aljean Harmetz of *The New York Times* he was particularly excited to be joining Fox, because, "There are no layers of management. Only Barry Diller and Rupert Murdoch, who owns the company."

For a while, it looked as though the Murdoch team was forsaking movies for television, launching its Fox Broadcasting Company to do battle with ABC, NBC, and CBS. By March of 1988, the Fox network was close to $80 million in the red, and it had suffered the humiliating defeat of attempting to take on the NBC late-night institution, Johnny Carson's *Tonight* talk show. Fox's version was *The Late Show* with Joan Rivers. She lasted seven months. Still, Fox TV was beginning to make inroads with its prime-time lineup, in particular its Sunday-night schedule of young-adult situation comedies.

*About the same time, the hyphen was dropped from the name Twentieth Century Fox.

As for the motion picture division, by the end of 1987 Fox had released three of the year's better films: the off-beat comedy *Raising Arizona*, the romantic satire of television journalism *Broadcast News*, and the drama set in the world of money trading (that also provided a heavy father-son conflict), *Wall Street*. While the last was something of a box-office disappointment— the film did best in New York, while having problems in Peoria—it was expected to perform well on cable television and videocassette.

IX

After his resignation in 1981, Dennis Stanfill wasted no time in suing Marvin Davis for $22 million, charging the corporation's owner with breach of contract, wrongful termination, interference with contract, bad faith, denial of benefits, and slander. In 1986, Stanfill received a settlement of nearly $4 million. Upon leaving Fox, Stanfill became a manager at Clarendon Capital Corporation, a Los Angeles-based venture fund, although in 1984 he came within a hair's breath of being named C.E.O. at Walt Disney Studios. Instead, the job went to Michael Eisner, formerly of Paramount, an executive who placed more emphasis on creativity than on iron-fisted economic controls.

The choice proved fortuitous. Under Eisner and his young head of production, Jeffrey Katzenberg, Disney achieved an enviable economic position, by instituting many of the exclusive-contract practices of the old studio system while still making sure, Katzenberg told *Time* magazine, to "watch every single solitary nickel."

X

Richard Zanuck was said to have accepted approximately $1.2 million to drop his $24.5 million lawsuit against Fox. David

Brown was said to have gotten $100,000 on his $17.5 million claim. Terms of Linda Harrison's settlement were never disclosed.

In some stockholders' actions, Richard and Darryl Zanuck were among Fox executives charged with "diversion and gross waste of the corporation's assets." Because of such, the suit said, "any payment by the corporation to Richard D. Zanuck, David Brown, or [Darryl] Zanuck should be enjoined as a flagrant waste of the assets of the corporation."

Among specific instances of waste, the suit referred to Darryl's production of *Hello-Goodbye*, starring "his personal friend, Genevieve Gilles, despite the fact that she had no previous acting experience that warranted such a role."

The Securities Exchange Commission began to investigate several irregularities stemming from the proxy fight. The request for just such an investigation was demanded by Charles Lewis, "because," he wrote S.E.C. Commissioner Richard S. Kraut, "there is substantial evidence of fraud in this matter, including altered proxies, false proxies, false proxy envelopes, and non-tallied proxies. There were also irregularities in the security precautions of the counting room which could have been permitted to such room when it was supposed to have been locked and sealed."

Among the targets of the S.E.C. was an unusual deal provided David Merrick, the largest single Fox shareholder, to turn over to management the proxies for his 202,700 shares and receive in return a negotiable note for $1.8 million for the movie rights to his show, *Hello, Dolly!* This was the amount still owed to the Broadway producer, who reportedly feared he would receive his "royalty" no other way. In an affidavit, Merrick denied any improprieties, stating, "I was free to make the bargain most favorable to myself." Merrick, before accepting the deal, had been asked by the insurgents' group to become President of Twentieth Century-Fox.

The S.E.C. also sought to explore the circumstances surrounding Darryl Zanuck's displacement as chairman on the eve of the May 18, 1971, shareholders' meeting in Wilmington, but suddenly, and without explanation, the investigation was shelved. "See, this was pre-Watergate," said Charles Lewis in 1987, "which makes it a little hairy."

Explaining his meaning, Lewis said, "Royall, Koegel, & Wells was the law firm that represented Fox. Otto Koegel was the lawyer. At one time it used to be Rogers, Koegel, & Wells. Now, who was Mr. Rogers? William. He used to be on the Fox board and then he became [Nixon's] Secretary of State.

"So, when this S.E.C. investigation started, I understand from Kraut, the commissioner of the S.E.C., that Rogers came over to the S.E.C. from the State Department and told Kraut, 'Shelve it. Don't stop it, just shelve it, until I tell you to go to work on it.

"If Watergate had taken place by then, that never would have happened. That did in the investigation, and it has never been opened since," said Lewis. "Actually, 'opened' isn't the right word. Because the case has never been closed."

In the final balloting at the annual directors' meeting, May 18, 1971, management won handily, 3.9 million votes to 2.4 million for Lewis's insurgents, and Darryl Zanuck was quietly eased into that netherworld once occupied by Spyros Skouras after *Cleopatra*, the non-position of Chairman Emeritus.

XI

Despite his maverick spirit and killer instinct, William Fox enjoyed few of life's blessings following his ignominious departure from his own studio in 1930.

"I do not know whether foxes ever run in packs, but I have read about wolves, and have learned that a wolf is not attacked so long as he is well and strong, and is running at the head of the pack," ventured William Fox's biographer Upton Sinclair in his 1933 volume *Upton Sinclair Presents William Fox*, which traced the recently lost fortunes of its subject. Continued Sinclair, voicing an observation that could easily apply to any ousted mogul: "It is only when something happens to him, so that he stumbles and falls, that the other wolves fall upon him and 'merge' him."

Contractually bound in 1930 not to produce any feature films for five years, Fox announced he would instead create educational movies that utilized the very sound-on-film process to which he still owned the patent. The courts struck down his claim. In 1932, the Chicago Title and Trust Company took over the Fox Theatre Corporation in an equity receivership: $410,000 remained outstanding on a note signed by William Fox.

The 175-house Fox Metropolitan Theatre chain then went bust, and in June 1936, in Atlantic City, William Fox, whose worth six years earlier had been estimated at $100 million, filed for personal bankruptcy. He listed his assets at $100, and his liabilities at $9,935,261.

During the legal proceedings, a skirmish developed in which it was determined that Fox, relying on his old Tammany Hall tricks, conspired to bribe U.S. District Court Judge J. Warren Davis with $27,500. A jury found Fox guilty of obstructing justice and defrauding the United States. On January 17, 1941, he was fined $3000 and sentenced to a year and a day in the federal penitentiary.

Exiting the Northeastern Federal Prison at Lewisburg, Pennsylvania, the morning of May 3, 1943, William Fox received a five-dollar bill from the warden, to start life anew. Fox was 64.

His wife and daughters extended a welcome home, although the great Park Avenue apartment was now devoid of its proud master's once-priceless art collection, which included works by Rubens, Gainsborough, Van Dyck, and Tintoretto. Mrs. Fox had sold them the previous Christmas at fire-sale prices. Fifty-two paintings went for barely more than $39,000.

With a few holdings intact, Fox opened a modest Fifth Avenue office with one secretary, and announced plans for re-entering the only industry he had known as an adult. His grand scheme included an option on 1,500 acres of land in Los Angeles, where he would build a new studio bearing his name. All he needed were investors. They did not step forward.

In 1950, Fox entered New York's Doctors Hospital, suffering from a variety of ailments related to complications from diabetes. There he was to linger for over a year before he died, May 8, 1952.

His funeral was held at Temple Emanu-El, on Fifth Avenue. Not a single industry representative was present.

The trade ad placed in *Variety* that week by Twentieth Century-Fox read, in part: "His daring, initiative, and courage enabled him to make a signal contribution to the growth and development of the motion picture industry.

"From the beginnings of his career he engaged in the production of films of magnitude and scope and blazed a trail for the industry in providing box-office attractions of wide popular appeal. He was truly a pioneer in foreseeing the present status of the screen as a medium of popular entertainment."

XII

The official announcement from the Board May 18, 1971, read as follows:

"He is a giant among filmmakers: Producer of some of the screen's most enduring masterpieces; innovator who has been identified with almost every motion picture development; a founder of Twentieth Century-Fox and closely identified for almost three decades with its achievements. It is unthinkable to us that he should not continue, in the years ahead, that close association, giving to the company the benefit of his creative genius, his wisdom and showmanship.

"Therefore, with affection and regard, we create the new position of Chairman Emeritus of the board with the hope that Darryl F. Zanuck will occupy that post."

Darryl was given an independent-production deal, and his contract still had until 1973 to run, but his career was over.

FOX FILM FEATURES BRIGHTER FINANCIAL NEWS
AND A GOODBYE TO DARRYL ZANUCK AT MEETING

Although he had been deposed as chairman in 1971, Mr. Zanuck remained as a director and his employment contract called for compensation of $150,000 a year, $60,000 of which was paid annually and $90,000 of which was deferred. Fox Film also had to supply Mr. Zanuck with a car, a chauffeur, office-hotel space, and secretarial assistance until his contract ran out yesterday.

Fox Film's chairman, Dennis Stanfill, took the occasion to wish the former tycoon "hail and farewell," but Mr. Zanuck was in Palm Springs. According to the proxy statement, Fox Film still must pay Mr. Zanuck "advisory compensation" for 10 years at the rate of $50,000 a year. Shareholders have filed a suit contesting this contract, and Fox Film legal spokesmen said discussions are being held on a possible settlement.

—Earl C. Gottschalk, Jr.,
The Wall Street Journal,
May 16, 1973

"He was always defending his flanks," said Richard Zanuck. "If you look at his history, you will see it riddled with number-two men, the closest men possible to him corporately and personally, being *axed*. Going back to William Goetz, who founded Twentieth Century-Fox with him. So when I became president, what he couldn't realize was that I was not doing it for myself."

In reply to his father's heated accusations, the son insisted that he and Brown "thought we had considered doing everything conceivably possible, including the changing of the name to Twenty-First Century-Fox."

In retrospect, the younger Zanuck agreed that such a change sounded "laughable, except the only thing that *really* seemed laughable was the prospect of ever getting there.

"I never *wanted* to be president," maintained Richard. "I felt that I was running the company anyway. But he never understood that. He took it as a direct challenge to the throne.

"And when there's a direct challenge to the throne, it has to be dealt with. Even if it's by one's only son. . . . "

XIII

Spyros Skouras died in 1971, two years after he resigned his honorary chairmanship of Twentieth Century-Fox. The retirement brought down a Roxy-sized curtain on a career that ranged from nickelodeon-theatre management in the days of the flickers, through his ascendency as a national theatre-circuit operator to the presidency of Hollywood's second-largest company.

"If I had it to do all over again, as a young immigrant from Greece, my choice would be—No," he said in 1969. Not that the memories were all *Cleopatra*-like. The fond recollections started "when my brothers and I bought the Missouri franchise for First National Pictures," then the second largest movie company. "Also, when I effected the merger of First National, the Stanley Company, Warner Brothers, and the Skouras Theatres. And when I was able to help with Greek War Relief. I could have died happy then."

Of Darryl Zanuck, whose legendary reputation long overshadowed Skouras's,* Skouras said: "I only hope that when the time comes young Richard Zanuck will succeed his father. He is capable and creative."

Skouras's departure from the New York headquarters was forced, recalled Hugh Fordin. "I remember the day he was asked to leave the premises. All of his stuff from this enormous office, including his desk, was packed and loaded onto a truck. The truck wasn't more than a few blocks away when the driver got called on his two-way radio. He was to bring back the desk. Remember, Skouras had originally bought *The Sound of Music*. The way he left the company, you'd have thought he was some kind of a criminal."

Among the mourners at Skouras's funeral were New York Mayor John Lindsay, W. Averill Harriman, former Postmaster General James A. Farlay, journalist Lowell Thomas, General James Van Fleet, Terence Cardinal Cooke, and Richard Zanuck.

---

*They both took credit for CinemaScope, which in any event was permanently displaced by Panavision in 1967.

XIV

"Darryl Zanuck took too long to die," said an old associate, intending to sound compassionate. "The proxy fight had taken everything out of the old man, forever," noted another executive.

"It was a very sour period," said Richard Zanuck of his father. "He never fully recovered from the blow of being eased into oblivion by the company he founded. There was a rapid deterioration, physically and mentally."

In early 1972, Zanuck became bedridden, explaining in a letter to Henry DeMeyer: "It was just another one of those things and adds up to the 'breaks' I have had in skiing and polo.

"For the second time in three years I broke my right ankle. The first time was when I was skiing in Megeve and this time I stupidly stepped out of the bathtub and slipped on a bar of soap."

Another setback to take place in his apartment at the Plaza was the theft of his art collection. More than $300,000 worth of canvases were stolen, cut out of their frames.

In 1973, *Variety* reported, "Darryl F. Zanuck has been commuting to Europe and elsewhere, looking for film properties with an eye to ultimate indie production. He also states he's 'been seeing a lot of my son,' meaning Dick Zanuck. . . . This cues reconciliation, following the legal imbroglio of two years back."

When Darryl slipped and fell while exiting the shower, face smacked against the bathroom wall, he broke five teeth which had to be extracted and which could not be replaced until his mouth fully mended.

Further disfiguration plagued him following 1973 surgery for cancer of the jaw, blamed on his years of cigar smoking. The operation marked the final turning point.

"Genevieve really took care of him when it looked as if he were dying," said Fred Hift. "She was the one who called Darryl's family and said, 'Something must be done. The man's very sick.' Dick, Darrylin, and Virginia thought that they should take him home. Virginia, astonishingly enough, forgave. All those years, Darryl never took off his wedding ring. It was Virginia who said, 'Bring Father home,' only the kids wouldn't come and get him. Genevieve had to put him on the plane to Los Angeles and accompany him home to this great reconciliation scene—where Genevieve was totally ignored. She announced how insulted she was and that she was going to leave on the next plane to New York, except that by then all her luggage had gone on to Palm Springs with Darryl's.

So Susie Zanuck said, "Come on, Genevieve. Our mother's had years of unhappy memories. What is she supposed to do, say 'Hello' to her husband's mistress? Come with us to Palm Springs, and if you're unhappy when you get there, we'll send you back to Los Angeles in a limousine."

"By the time Darryl got to Palm Springs," said Hift, "he was put upstairs and Genevieve was told, 'No. You don't have to say goodbye.' 'But I've lived with him all these years,' Genevieve protested. Then this burly guy picked her up and took her away.

"Genevieve filed charges, so the police took her back to Darryl's house, where the Zanucks said, 'We don't know this woman, she's a little crazy. . . . Here are her bags.' And Genevieve went back to New York. Later the Zanucks got upset. She was in Darryl's will."

"Dick said to me, 'Go with the luggage,' " Gilles told a *Time* reporter. "When I walked into the living room of the house, it was filled with people, most of them drunk. They were having a cocktail party. Darryl was a sick, sick man—he was supposed to be in bed. I walked out in the garden and cried. I went back in to say goodbye, and Dick wouldn't let me."

Gilles referred to the 1973 episode as "the kidnapping." She never saw Darryl again.

"Zanuck was all I had," she said. "He was my first deep relationship, the most important person in my life—and then he was taken away."

ZANUCK'S WILL CONTESTED
BY FORMER FRENCH MODEL

INDIO—A woman claiming she was the late Darryl F. Zanuck's mistress has filed a lawsuit in Superior Court here contesting the filmmaker's will.

Genevieve Gillaizeau, thirty-five, a former French model, claims in her suit that the will admitted into probate after Zanuck's death in 1979 is not his "true will."

She is charging Zanuck's widow and children with fraud and is seeking $2 million in damages and a court order compelling the Bank of America, as executor of Zanuck's estate, to present the "true will" for probate.

The current will in probate does not mention Gillaizeau. Her suit contends the "true will" was executed in 1973 before three witnesses and leaves her 40 percent of Zanuck's securities. . . .

—*The Los Angeles Times*,
June 3, 1981

In the suit, filed by attorneys Marvin Mitchelson and Harold C. Rhoden, Gilles claimed that Darryl Zanuck was senile and unduly influenced by his son when the senior Zanuck signed the October 31, 1973, will that disinherited Gillaizeau and reinstated Richard Zanuck as an heir.

"I never discussed any will with my father as long as he lived, so I don't know what she is talking about," Richard Zanuck told *The Los Angeles Times*. "There are hundreds of people who would be happy to testify that he was far from senile."

XV

"I hope it's forever," Virginia Zanuck said of the reconciliation with her husband. "He was sick in New York: When he got here, he weighed 115 pounds. Now he's at 130. I don't treat him like a patient—but he doesn't let me out of his sight."

299

"You know what my typical day consists of?" Darryl admitted in 1975. The interviewer, Lloyd Shearer, found the old mogul "small, smiling, blue-eyed, soft-voiced . . . mellow, mild, at times different, halting, and forgetful." Gone was the jack o'lantern smile, replaced by dentures.

"I get up about 8:30 and take a quick shower," said Zanuck. "Then I head for the main house and breakfast with Virginia. Usually it's fruit and hot cakes. I glance at the morning paper. The world right now doesn't seem to be in very good shape to me. Then I rest for an hour and walk the dogs."

Darryl cherished his two Yorkshire terriers, Tina and Lisa, a legacy from his life with Genevieve.

"In the afternoon I start watching TV for a few hours. Every now and then they show an old movie of mine, and it brings back memories. I go a long way back. I started writing scripts for Rin Tin Tin, the dog star, in 1923. Harry and Jack Warner paid me $125 a week. I think I wrote 20 scripts the first year.

"A few years later they put me in charge of production at $5000 a week. I was a kid, 25 years old. We did the first talking picture, *The Jazz Singer* with Al Jolson. Al used to live down here in the desert, just a few houses away. Then I embarked on the idea of using journalism, daily journalism, for story ideas. I turned out *Little Caesar*, then *The Public Enemy*—that was the one in which Jimmy Cagney pushed half a grapefruit into Mae Clarke's face. The films they show on TV today—in a way that's the story of my whole working life.

"Every time they show something like Eddie Robinson or Marilyn Monroe or Betty Grable or Ty Power or Dick Widmark—the so-called Golden Age of Hollywood—it conjures up memories. I don't want to sound immodest. People have accused me of being a lot of things. But a lot of that Golden Age of Hollywood—it was of my making. And while I don't live in the past, I'm proud of what I did."

And the future?

"If someone," he said, "were to bring me a great package, top story, two superstars, an outstanding director, a package with a potential of $100 million, you know what I would say? 'Take it to my son, Dick.' "

XVI

On December 22, 1979, United Press International's Vernon Scott received a phone call from Dick Zanuck. "I thought you'd like to know," Dick told Scott, UPI's Hollywood correspondent, "that my dad has died."

Said Scott: "No matter what had come between the two of them, Dick wanted to make sure his father's place in history was properly acknowledged."

At the funeral held five days later at Westwood's United Methodist Church, Scott noticed "that Dick was crying like a baby." During the service, the theme from *The Longest Day* was played.

In his will dated 1973, Darryl left the bulk of his estate, valued at $4.5 million, to daughters Darrylin and Susan and to Richard. Nothing had been left to Virginia, although it was made clear in the document that this was not due to lack of affection; rather, that Darryl had provided for her while he was still alive.

Genevieve Gilles maintained that as a result of the jaw cancer, circulation to Darryl's brain had been affected, leaving him mentally enfeebled. In her legal papers against the Zanuck estate, Gilles charged that Darryl's family kept the aged mogul under heavy sedation the final seven years of his life. When Gilles filed the suit to contest the will, she submitted a statement by a friend of the Zanuck family, Thomas L. Shirley. Shirley said that Darrylin Zanuck had admitted to him that she had forged her father's name on the 1973 will after conferring with her mother to keep her father's fortune from going to his one-time mistress.

Gilles eventually lost her bid to make claim on the will, because, said Jean Negulesco, "The poor girl filed too late, after the statute of limitations had run out." Gilles subsequently sued her attorney Marvin Mitchelson for malpractice; Mitchelson's challenge to the Zanuck will was indeed filed too late—by one day.

"Missing the statute of limitations is a classic example of negligence which any person can understand," Federal Judge John F. Keenan ruled on Gilles's behalf in her case against Mitchelson.

Thomas L. Shirley, meanwhile, went on to sue the estate of Virginia Zanuck for $20 million in damages for slander and invasion of privacy. He claimed that once he spoke on Gilles's behalf that Virginia and Darrylin had "conspired to forge the will of Darryl F. Zanuck," the two women falsely accused him of stealing money from the Zanuck family. Shirley said this was Virginia's and Darrylin's effort to discredit him.

XVII

Susan Zanuck was found dead in her Palm Springs home June 10, 1980, at the age of 46. A family spokesman said death was due to "natural causes." Sources close to the Zanuck family, however, told of occurrences of drug and alcohol abuse.

Besides her mother, sister, and brother, Susan was survived by her children Andre Hakim, Jr., Raymond Hakim, and Sharon Hakim by her first husband Andre Hakim, and Craig Savineau by her second husband, Pierre Savineau, from whom she was divorced.

XVIII

Virginia Zanuck, after herself being bedridden for years, died at the age of 83 on October 14, 1982. Her estate was valued between $10 million and $12 million, the bulk of which was the result of the large property settlement with Darryl in the late '50s. Virginia's will dated April 27, 1982, left virtually everything to Darrylin and nothing to Richard; an earlier document

302

signed December 21, 1981, equally divided Virginia's wealth between her surviving daughter and son. David Brown filed suit against Virginia's estate on behalf of Richard's boys, Harrison and Dean, claiming Darrylin had exerted "undue influence" on her mother to alter the will at a time Virginia was not of sound mind. Among the evidence Darrylin was prepared to present in court to prove Virginia's mental acumen were two video tape recordings. In one, Virginia was shown signing the 1982 will. In the other, Virginia looked full face into the camera and told Richard Zanuck he was being disinherited because he was wealthy and Darrylin was not; he had rarely visited his mother, while Darrylin waited on her "hand and foot"; and he had been harsh to his two estranged daughters by his marriage to Lili Gentle, Virginia and Janet.

Richard charged that the women in his family were impractical in matters of money. "I was the only working member of the family," he said. "My two sisters lived off the residue of the family fortune. I, being a workaholic for many years, was apart from their whole philosophy. What was disturbing to my two sisters, and even, strangely enough—and I'll never quite understand this—to my mother, was that I was becoming more successful than my father. There was a basic, almost unrealistic resentment when the receipts from *The Sting* and *Jaws* came in and they realized that I had amassed more money with one or two pictures than my father had in a lifetime of work. They never were able to understand it. I didn't change. My bank account changed, but I didn't. But their attitude toward me changed. It went beyond envy. A *dislike* set in. They looked upon me differently, as if they were dealing with a different person."

XIX

After five years, the marriage between Richard Zanuck and Linda Harrison dissolved. In 1974 she sought a divorce on the grounds of irreconcilable differences. Two months after filing,

Harrison asked the court for an order restraining Dick Zanuck from contacting her, following an incident in which she claimed he had violently beaten both her and her spiritual adviser, a 65-year-old man.

"He struck me, sat on top of me, and after restraining me with his legs and arms he repeatedly and viciously struck my face with his forearms in karate fashion, causing me extreme pain and suffering," her affidavit stated.

The elderly companion, whom Harrison identified as her "minister and spiritual adviser," was Vincentii Turriziani of the Risen Christ Foundation of Vincentii Turriziani. Harrison claimed that her husband punched and kicked Turriziani, smashed a statue, and struck the spiritual advisor on the head with it.

"He pulled several paintings from the wall, breaking the glass of some of them and also deliberately kicking his foot through a painting entitled *The Risen Christ*, which he knew had a special religious significance," she said.

Harrison said that starting in 1972 the marriage had become "difficult" due to Zanuck's "extremely violent disposition." Harrison had sought spiritual guidance from Turriziani in an effort to save the union. The Zanucks had two sons, Harrison Richard and Dean Francis.

In 1977, Richard Zanuck, age 42, married 24-year-old Lili Fini, who was barely older than Zanuck's two daughters from his first marriage. Richard and Lili II (as she was informally dubbed out of the couple's earshot) settled into the Santa Monica beach house that originally belonged to Darryl and Virginia Zanuck. Richard had purchased the property from his mother in 1970, and Lili converted it from a bachelor's pad into a family home.

"I think this house is reflective of me," said Lili. "I believe that what becomes you is a certain style, and that style is something I would carry with me to any home."

The Zanucks allowed writer Nancy Guild of *Architectural Digest* inside the house at the time they and David Brown were promoting their first venture as a triumverate, the fantasy *Cocoon*. The scenario proposal about a group of elderly couples who are rejuvenated thanks to a visit by space aliens had been discovered and developed by Lili, who said of the movie business: "It's something in your gut. It takes a certain personality, and it's very innate."

As for working in tandem with his third spouse, Richard Zanuck said, "Frankly, I couldn't have done it with my other wives, even though I loved them at the time. Of course, there is a certain amount of ego that has to be displaced when you're in a working situation with your wife. I can't fire her."

XX

In 1983, Thomas L. Shirley appeared on a television program hosted by attorney F. Lee Bailey entitled *Lie Detector*. He recounted the events surrounding Darrylin and Virginia's alleged forging of Darryl's will. Immediately after the broadcast, Darrylin filed a $60 million slander suit against Shirley, the program's producers, and Bailey for allegedly announcing that handwriting experts found the signature on the will to be forged.

In October of 1986, Darrylin filed a $10 million malicious prosecution suit against Genevieve Gillaizeau/Gilles, claiming the former mistress falsely accused Darrylin of forging Darryl's will. Darrylin's papers also said she was wrongly accused by Gilles of exerting undue influence on Darryl to exclude Gilles from an October 1973 will. The suit sought $5 million for the alleged malicious actions, citing mental anguish to Darrylin as well as harm to her reputation. Another $5 million was asked in punitive damages, with the surviving daughter claiming that Gilles was jealous of Darryl's filial love for Darrylin.

XXI

"I always enjoyed D.Z.'s confidence," said David Brown, "and that became a very dangerous thing later on, as my relationship with Dick progressed. I'll never forget D.Z. saying, 'I always thought you were basically loyal to me.' And I said, 'I didn't know I'd ever have to make the choice.' He was suspicious of Dick's and my relationship, and perhaps even jealous. He wanted the relationship for himself.

"I've always thought that at a certain point," Brown continued, "Dick became the father, and Darryl in a strange way became the impetuous son. Darryl had the capacity to make every picture, even the most modest, minor little thing, into the Second Coming. And Dick would have the difficult job of bringing him back to earth. He was dealing in the real world of the studio, fretting for the absent D.F.Z. I always detected in the relationship between D.F.Z. and Richard something resembling sibling rivalry, between a young man and a man who never wanted to grow old."

In 1986, Brown said that the reasons he and Dick Zanuck initially "brought in Stanford Research was because we wanted to consolidate our base of operations, and bring all the financial services to the West Coast, where they belonged. We wanted to restructure the company, bring Fox into the twenty-first century."

Where it went wrong, Brown figured, "was that when Stanford Research studied our track record, they failed to take into account non-recurring phenomena. We had *M*A*S*H*, *Butch Cassidy*, and *The Sound of Music*. Take those out of the equation and what are you left with? I told them at the time, 'Idiots, this *is* a business of non-recurring phenomena. Make ten films, and if two work, then you have glory and profit.' "

Asked whether he missed the glory days at the studios, Brown waxed nostalgic for only a moment.

"When you came through the gate to your office, you were in your own kingdom. You were protected by your own police and your needs were taken care of down to your home. In fact, the studio *was* your home. Your secretary brought her own coffee pot when she was assigned to you, and *she* worked on a seniority system.

"Dick and I," he said, "have not lived at a studio for years, but we planted the seeds for others. *M*A*S*H*, which we did, generated more money for the studio than *Star Wars*, when you count the television series.

"The bones are still at Fox. The *Hello, Dolly!* set is still standing, being slowly replaced by office skyscrapers. What's changed inside is that there are no more major departments. You can't even get a script mimeographed on lots anymore. Today they're just largely TV production centers."

Brown said what made movie studios attractive to people like Marvin Davis and Rupert Murdoch was what was accomplished over the past 50 years. "What they are buying is the past. That is not to say that today's catalogue—*E.T.*, *The Kiss of the Spider Woman*—is any less important than *M*A*S*H* or *Star Wars* or *The Sound of Music*. There are just as many good movies made today as were made before. What we still have to see is whether they can stand the test of time, like *Casablanca*."

As an aftereffect of S.R.I.'s foray into Fox, Hollywood became marketing mad. As 1987 dawned, newly-installed head of production at Columbia, David Puttnam, announced that his studio would adapt a policy whereby one executive would follow a particular project through from idea inception to the marketing of ancillary rights, and that astronomical star salaries were fiscally irresponsible and would not be tolerated at his studio."* No one was more aware of the trend than David Brown. He observed, "It arrived with the television executives. They were the ones with the marketing expertise. Barry Diller and Frank Price came from TV, and they brought the marketing executives in with them."

As a result, said Brown, "the production people who ran the business were suddenly being restrained by the financial people."

The marriage between the worlds of creativity and commerce was never a smooth one. Beginning in the early '70s, studios over-reacted, giving the green light almost exclusively to movies

*Puttnam was quickly ousted after antagonizing the Hollywood establishment.

based on potential audience, frequently at a cost of proper assessment of content, characters, or reputations of the participants or the property. Such greedy irresponsibility explained the rash of youth movies in the '80s, which, causing its own rippling effect, drove thinking adults from movie theatres once and for all.

The lucrative videocassette market, as Darryl Zanuck had portended in 1970, may yet reverse that trend. As *Newsweek* film critic David Ansen claimed in late 1986: The home audience is older than that for a theatrical feature, and it still nurtures a hunger for Hollywood product. A movie that may lose money theatrically can still move into the black thanks to ancillary rights earnings, such as going to video. This, without improving the artistic limitations of the endeavors, eventually proved the case with *Doctor Dolittle*, *Hello, Dolly!* and *Tora! Tora! Tora!*

In the '60s, Brown reflected two decades later, "There was no marketing—just movie ads. You had your own studio advertising staff. After a while we went to outside agencies. We did that with *M*A*S*H*.

"And it," he added proudly. "was a smash."

XXII

Rouben Mamoulian never directed another film after his aborted attempt to make *Cleopatra*. Walter Wanger never produced another film. Michael Sarne never directed another film after *Myra Breckinridge*. George Stevens never directed another film after *The Only Game in Town*. Jean Negulesco never directed another film after *Hello-Goodbye*. Russ Meyer never directed another film for a major studio after *The Seven Minutes*, which, under Stanfill, the studio buried upon its release.

"You could see it before your very eyes time and again," observed Hugh Fordin. "The Philosophy of Hollywood: 'You're too talented. You're too good. So we're going to give you something

that will not only fuck you here, but fuck you in the entire industry.' "

After *Cleopatra*, Joseph L. Mankiewicz made three more
films, for general release: *The Honey Pot*, a 1967 update of Ben
Jonson's *Volpone* starring Rex Harrison and Susan Hayward (it
pleased critics but not audiences and was retitled *It Comes Up
Murder* for general release), a 1970 western, *There Was a
Crooked Man*, and, in 1972, an adaptation of Anthony
Schaeffer's London and Broadway stage smash, *Sleuth*, starring
Laurence Olivier and Michael Caine and released by Twentieth
Century-Fox.

"Supposedly, you're as good as your last picture," Mankiewicz
noted ten years after the fact. "My last one was nominated for
Best Picture, I was nominated, and it was the only time in the
history of the Academy that the entire cast of the picture was
nominated." He shrugged and added, "I haven't worked since."

Richard Burton died in 1984. Elizabeth Taylor shed weight
and a new fiancé that same year, and created headlines worldwide when she paid a visit to Burton's gravesite. She seldom
makes feature films anymore.

For Barbra Streisand and Walter Matthau, the feud must
have ended. In 1986, Matthau and his wife Carol were one of
those personal invitees of Streisand to her one-woman concert
on her Malibu ranch, to raise money for nuclear disarmament.
Tickets were $2,500 per person, and the Matthaus were conspic-
uous in the audience. "I can like her politics, can't I?" said
Matthau in 1988. "She has a good instinct for the right political
side. I'm 100 percent behind that. Besides, I was never mad at
her. Just because you have a fight with someone doesn't mean
that you're mad at them and don't talk to them. You can wait 30
minutes, and *then* you can talk to them."

"The Sound of Money" was meant to tinkle again for Robert
Wise with the proposed screen musical *Zorba*, to star Anthony
Quinn and John Travolta, based on the 1964 film *Zorba the
Greek*. Wise's producer was to be Saul Chaplin and his

screenwriter Ernest Lehman; however, the project disintegrated in early 1987 when its studio, Cannon, was staving off bankruptcy and an S.E.C. investigation following a run of flop movies and overzealous expansion. Wise, then 72, announced he would commence work on another project with his same team; on April 21, 1987, columnist Liz Smith reported that this would be none other than the sequel to *The Sound of Music*. By October of the same year, Wise said that the studio had contacted his agents and that a search was on to see who owned the rights to such a sequel. "It would be an interesting idea," Wise speculated.

In 1978, Frank Gilroy took his experiences as the playwright-screenwriter of *The Only Game in Town* and concocted *Once in Paris*, an independently made, gentle satire of events surrounding the earlier production. Purely as a matter of coincidence, Wayne Rogers, leading man on the TV series *M*A*S*H*, starred as the thinly veiled version of Gilroy; at the time, the actor was keeping company with Sherry Lansing, then the head of production of Twentieth Century-Fox, and the first woman in Hollywood to achieve such a high-ranking position.*

Writer-director-producer Blake Edwards also lampooned Hollywood games, more savagely, in his 1981 *S.O.B.* It starred his wife Julie Andrews as a sweeter than sweet movie goddess whose latest release—directed by her husband—turns out to be the *Heaven's Gate* of musicals. To save face (and $40 million), the husband re-edits the movie, infuses sex scenes, and the goddess goes topless.

"I thought I would get all kinds of fallout, but no," said Andrews. "Everyone said, 'Right on, Jules—go for it, gal.' I was rather thrilled."

In the movie, the remake strikes gold; in real-life, *S.O.B.* did not. Julie Andrews' bare breasts did not attract lines at the box-office, but they did make a statement of sorts.

The star went into a self-imposed retirement in the 1970s, re-

---

*She later left to form her own independent company with one-time head of Paramount Pictures, Stanley Jaffe. After a sputtering start, they produced the 1987 shocker about marital infidelity, *Fatal Attraction*, a runaway hit of immense proportion.

turning to the screen in the supporting role of Dudley Moore's pal in the sex comedy *"10,"* again directed by Blake Edwards. Although the film's greatest distinction was that it presented a new pin-up girl named Bo Derek, its success bankrolled several other Edwards movies, invariably starring his wife.

"Very few people other than Blake go beyond the usual image of me," she remarked in 1986. Would she say that being typecast as governesses and nannies had plagued her for two decades? "Yes," said Andrews on the set of the somber drama, *Duet for One,* in which she played a concert violinist stricken with multiple sclerosis, *"Still."*

Did she mind that her box-office high-water mark with *The Sound of Music* had been topped by *Jaws* and *Star Wars?** "Do you mean, did I think, 'Shit, it's made more money than we did?' " She scrunched her lips. "No, Not at all. Things like that are hardly important."

In late 1986 word made the rounds that the executors of the Moss Hart estate were seeking Julie Andrews to star in a Broadway revival of *Lady in the Dark,* the musical about psychoanalysis written by the playwright Kurt Weill, and Ira Gershwin. Originally it served as a stage vehicle for Gertrude Lawrence; in fact, two numbers from it, *My Ship* and *The Saga of Jenny,* were re-enacted in *Star!* Should she bite, Julie Andrews would be stepping on a Broadway stage for the first time since she left *Camelot* to go to Hollywood, and thus began the entire '60s spate of musicals. Yes *Lady in the Dark* was not the only offer to provide a special sense of *déjà vu.*

Although Julie Andrews had not committed to the project, Walt Disney Studios commissioned a sequel to *Mary Poppins,* calling for Andrews to reprise the 1964 role which served as her launching pad to *The Sound of Music.*** The Disney sequel, as of

---

*As it was, *Variety* reported for years that the biggest box-office take of all time, though it was never properly accounted, belonged to the movie that started it all, D. W. Griffith's *Birth of a Nation.*

**In a readers poll published in *People* magazine on February 9, 1987, the question was: "What do you miss most at the movies?" An impressive 58 percent of the respondents expressed the "wish that, more often, theatres were alive with the sounds of sentimental musicals." The statistic was illustrated by the familiar shot of Julie Andrews singing atop the mountain in *The Sound of Music.*

autumn 1986, was to be written and directed by Howard Ash-
man, the author and composer of *Little Shop of Horrors*, an off-
Broadway musical hit that record mogul David Geffen independently released as a movie through Warner Bros. It opened
Christmas of 1986, and was reputed to have cost overruns, putting its final price between $45 million and $50 million.

As for the post-*Cleopatra* syndrome of the press showing an
abiding interest in the why and how much of movies, filmmakers
continued to complain about such snooping. The only surprising
element, given that the situation had existed for more than a
quarter century, was that some reporters were still treating
these reactions as something new.

LUCAS BLASTS MEDIA OBSESSION WITH B.O.

CANNES—George Lucas, executive producer of Cannes' closing-
night film *Willow*, sharply criticized the American press for creating an "unfortunate trend" in the United States of dwelling on
the financial rather than the creative side of moviemaking. . . .

Dodging a question about the budget of *Willow* and why his
own films are so costly, Lucas said, "The cost of a film is
irrelevant—it's very expensive to make movies."

—Claudia Eller,
The Hollywood Reporter,
May 24, 1988

XXIII

Irina Demick and Juliette Greco retired into private married
existences in France. Genevieve Gilles never starred in another
film after *Hello-Goodbye*. Her name, however, continued to
crop up in the news from time to time. Earl Wilson reported of
her impending American citizenship in 1974 at the same time
she was promoting a proposed $1 million movie based on a chil-
dren's story, *Julie of the Wolves*, about an Alaskan girl who jour-
neys across the tundra to San Francisco. Frozen en route, she
joins a pack of wolves. "This book will become a family picture

with a lot of taste," said Gilles, whose role would be that of producer, not star. "I don't want to be involved in any sex, blood, or
violence films for my first production." The film was never
made.

"A few years ago, Genevieve called me in California," said
Jean Negulesco in 1986. "She wanted to have lunch, and we did,
at Ma Maison. She came in wearing jeans and a white silk
blouse. She looked great."

"You know, Johnny," Gilles told Negulesco, "our picture has
been an enormous success in one place." It was news to
Negulesco. The place? "Saudi Arabia."

"I don't know how," said Negulesco, "but she said she had
gathered the millions to put into another film. All I had to do
was come up with the property. So I decided to remake my
Mask of Demetrius, with Genevieve in the role originally played
by Peter Lorre, the newspaperman, made into a newspaper-
woman from London who goes to Istanbul. Orson Welles was
very interested in playing the Sidney Greenstreet role. But instead, Genevieve decided to sue Virginia Zanuck and the estate
for palimony."*

A paternal expression overtook the veteran director's face.
"She was a nice girl," he said of Gilles, "a lovely girl."

XXIV

When *Jaws* was still fresh out of the water in 1975, Richard
Zanuck and David Brown made the interview rounds. New York
journalist Tom Topor observed, quite astutely: "A four-hour
conversation with Zanuck and Brown is about as revealing as
watching a stripper through a sheet of frosted glass. They have
been through so many corporate skirmishes, they have negoti-

---

*By 1987, with the litigation continuing, Gilles assigned her claim over to
Yeshiva University. "That was very odd," noted David Brown. "Genevieve
isn't Jewish. And neither was Darryl Zanuck."

ated so many intricate deals, they have done so much personal promotion that they have raised to the level of an art the knack of answering questions frankly and sincerely without ever letting themselves show.

"The whole effect is something like watching a very bright fighter and his very bright manager. Zanuck, who is 40, is small, muscular, tense, and gives the impression that if he needs to get his way by punching somebody out, fine. . . . Brown, who is 59, is large, avuncular, casual, and gives the impression that lounging in a chair is his most urgent mission in life."

"It's a very tight partnership," Zanuck told Topor.

"We don't keep score," added Brown. The journalist noted that a secret smile passed between the two men, then it was Zanuck who had the final word, and perhaps explained the special ingredient that accounted for the successful partnership.

"David lets me score all the ego points."

DAVID BROWN EXITS ZANUCK/BROWN SLOT

Effective this fall, David Brown, half of the Zanuck/Brown Co. production team, which produced such critically and commercially acclaimed films as *The Sting*, *Jaws*, *Cocoon*, and *The Verdict*, will withdraw from active participation from the 16-year partnership to pursue other solo activities.

—*The Hollywood Reporter*,
March 24, 1988

Mr. Brown said Mr. Zanuck, 53, with whom he has been associated for 30 years in various enterprises, intends to retain the Zanuck/Brown name. Currently, the company is producing films for MGM/UA Communications Co. and television shows for New World Entertainment Ltd.

Mr. Brown is working on what he described as "informal memoirs" and two other books, but also intends to pursue film and television properties for a new New York-based production company he hopes to call "The Manhattan Project." While the name is "associated with the greatest bomb in the world," he said, "I think we'll be foxy enough to overcome that connotation."

Competition with his former company shouldn't be a problem, Mr. Brown added.

Mr. Brown's earliest association with the movie business was with mogul Darryl F. Zanuck, Richard's father. After leaving Hollywood for a New York publishing job, however, he returned to Twentieth Century-Fox Film Corp. when the Zanucks were there.

—The Wall Street Journal,
March 25, 1988

Reliable sources revealed that the cause for the break-up, beyond the natural passage of time, was that David Brown, age 71, found his personal tastes too genteel for modern audiences, while Richard Zanuck, as aggressively ambitious as ever, was still enjoying the game. On the other hand, several insiders were crediting the split to Lili Zanuck, who saw no need to hold on to the partnerships of the past.

The parting was described in the [press] release as amicable, although neither party was available for comment.

—Variety,
March 30, 1988

EPILOGUE

Henry DeMeyer continued consulting for Twentieth Century-Fox until 1974, when Dennis Stanfill suggested to S.R.I. that perhaps DeMeyer might have "burned-out" on the project. DeMeyer believed that this was Stanfill's way to usurp DeMeyer's control. "He feared I was becoming too powerful with the board," said DeMeyer. "Besides, all the drama ended when we got rid of Dick and David. After that, everything became pretty routine." Al Lee replaced DeMeyer.

One of DeMeyer's last projects for S.R.I. took place in Iran, after which he decided he had done enough of cleaning up other people's businesses. He retired, in 1976. The following year he was back, consulting on the U.S. government's proposed Gasoline Rationing Program. As member of the International Executive Service Corps, a group founded by David Rockefeller, DeMeyer undertook a project for a tribal chief in Nigeria.

The trip served as a honeymoon with his fourth wife, Harriet, who goes simply by the name of "Q." The DeMeyers settled in Grass Valley, in northern California, where Q became a real estate agent.

Thinking back to his days on the Fox project, DeMeyer said philosophically, "I am not a religious man, but what I wouldn't give to see Darryl again one last time, just for a good talk."

In December 1987, in the midst of compiling materials for his proposed memoir about his role in redesigning the Lincoln Continental 30 years before, Henry DeMeyer died.

II

When *Cocoon* was released during the summer of 1985, David Brown and Richard Zanuck appeared on "The Today Show" with the affable critic Gene Shalit, a regular luncheon companion of Brown's at the Russian Tea Room.

Henry DeMeyer caught the television interview and thought to himself, "Those two fellows sure have gotten old." DeMeyer also reasoned that it might be time to write and congratulate the producers on their impressive achievements since leaving the studio. "In some strange way," DeMeyer told his wife, "I think I might have done them a big favor."

Lucy Ballentine, Richard Zanuck's secretary, answered DeMeyer from the producers' offices on North Canon Drive in Beverly Hills.

"Mr. Zanuck is in Europe until late September," Ballentine wrote, "but I wanted to acknowledge your nice letter in his absence. I know he will be pleased to hear from you again after all these years and would want me to thank you on his behalf for your good wishes on *Cocoon*."

When Richard Zanuck returned from Europe, he did not write to Henry DeMeyer.

APPENDIX I

BREAKEVEN FOR FEATURE PRODUCTIONS
1964 RELEASES

AS OF DECEMBER 11, 1970
(in thousands)

Picture:	Estimated Film Rentals Required To Breakeven	Ultimate Film Rentals	% of Ultimate To Breakeven
1964 Releases:			
Take Her She's Mine	$ 6,100	$ 5,000	81.9%
Move Over Darling	8,300	8,750	105.4
Man In The Middle	2,800	1,735	61.9
Shock Treatment	2,400	944	39.3
La Bonne Soupe	1,800	1,110	61.6
Third Secret	1,300	615	47.3
What A Way To Go	8,500	9,090	106.9
The Visit	6,100	2,635	43.1
Fate Is The Hunter	4,800	2,210	46.0
Guns At Batasi	1,400	1,845	131.7
Rio Conchos	5,300	4,610	86.9
Goodbye Charlie	7,000	4,555	65.0
TOTAL 1964 RELEASES	$55,800	$43,099	77.2

[Handwritten]
9 Pictures — losers
2 Pictures — just above breakeven
1 Picture — adequate profit

12 Total

TC-F
BREAKEVEN FOR FEATURE PRODUCTIONS
1965 RELEASES

AS OF DECEMBER 11, 1970
(in thousands)

Picture:	Estimated Film Rentals Required To Breakeven	Ultimate Film Rentals	% of Ultimate To Breakeven
1965 Releases:			
The Pleasure Seekers	$ 3,900	$ 3,205	82.1%
Zorba The Greek	3,000	9,400	313.3
Hush, Hush Sweet Charlotte	3,900	4,950	126.9
Dear Brigitte	4,500	2,920	64.8
John Goldfarb, Please Come Home	6,200	3,880	62.5
A High Wind In Jamaica	6,300	2,620	41.5
Up From The Beach	4,200	2,645	62.9
Von Ryan's Express	12,600	13,975	110.9
Morituri	10,500	4,045	38.5
Rapture	2,500	1,310	52.4
Friend Of The Family	1,800	855	47.5
The Reward	4,400	1,615	36.7
The Nanny	1,300	2,175	167.3
Do Not Disturb	7,300	5,275	72.2
	72,400	58,870	81.3%
Sound of Music	29,500	121,500	411.8
Magnificent Men	15,300	29,950	195.7
Agony And The Ecstasy	17,800	8,166	45.8
	62,600	159,616	254.9%
TOTAL 1965 RELEASES	$135,000	$218,486	161.8%

[Handwritten]
11 Pictures — losers
1 Picture — just above breakeven
3 Pictures — good profits
2 Pictures — non recurring exceptions
___
17 Total

TC-F
BREAKEVEN FOR FEATURE PRODUCTIONS
1966 RELEASES

AS OF DECEMBER 11, 1970
(in thousands)

Picture:	Estimated Film Rentals Required To Breakeven	Ultimate Film Rentals	% of Ultimate To Breakeven
1966 Releases:			
Dracula/Zombies	$ 1,500	$ 2,345	156.3%
Our Man Flint	7,700	12,950	168.1
Flight Of the Phoenix	10,800	4,855	44.9
Male Companion	1,400	780	55.7
Rasputin/Reptile	1,200	1,645	137.0
La Fuga	700	230	32.8
Cloportes	1,900	700	36.8
Weekend At Dunkirk	1,700	1,755	103.2
Stagecoach	6,300	6,950	110.3
Modesty Blaise	5,800	4,825	83.1
How To Steal A Million	12,000	10,450	87.0
Batman	3,200	3,900	121.8
Smoky	2,100	1,675	79.7
Fantastic Voyage	9,400	8,880	94.4
Way, Way Out	5,100	3,855	75.5
El Greco	1,300	1,675	128.8
	72,100	67,470	93.5%
Blue Max	14,200	16,850	118.6
The Bible	26,900	25,325	94.1
Sand Pebbles	21,200	20,600	97.1
	62,300	62,775	100.7%
TOTAL 1966 RELEASES	$134,400	$130,245	96.9%

[Handwritten]
11 Pictures — losers
2 Pictures — just above breakeven
6 Pictures — adequate profits

19 Total

TC-F
BREAKEVEN FOR FEATURE PRODUCTIONS
1967 RELEASES

AS OF DECEMBER 11, 1970
(in thousands)

Picture:	Estimated Film Rentals Required To Breakeven	Ultimate Film Rentals	% of Ultimate To Breakeven
1967 Releases:			
Quiller			
Memorandum	$ 2,600	$ 2,575	99.0%
Prehistoric/Devils	1,450	1,265	87.2
1,000,000 Years			
B.C.	2,250	4,425	196.6
In Like Flint	6,975	9,125	130.8
Frankenstein/			
Mummy	1,625	1,590	97.8
Hombre	9,600	9,910	103.2
Two For The Road	8,950	7,200	80.4
Caprice	7,200	4,580	63.6
Guide For The			
Married Man	5,900	7,355	124.6
St. Valentine's Day			
Mass	4,550	4,165	91.5
Fathom	3,875	3,295	85.0
Flim Flam Man	6,400	3,525	55.0
Woman Times			
Seven	2,975	1,100	36.9
Viking Queen	1,625	835	51.3
The Day The Fish			
Came Out	1,350	1,590	117.7
Tony Rome	6,875	6,250	90.9
Valley Of The Dolls	9,700	22,925	236.3
	83,900	91,710	109.3%
Dr. Doolittle	31,275	16,300	52.1%
TOTAL 1967			
RELEASES	$115,175	$108,010	93.7%

[Handwritten]
11 Pictures — losers
1 Picture — just above breakeven
5 Pictures — adequate profits
18 Total

TC-F
BREAKEVEN FOR FEATURE PRODUCTIONS
1968 RELEASES

AS OF DECEMBER 11, 1970
(in thousands)

Picture:	Estimated Film Rentals Required To Breakeven	Ultimate Film Rentals	% of Ultimate To Breakeven
1968 Releases:			
The Incident	$ 2,375	$ 2,075	87.4%
Bedazzled	2,100	2,825	134.5
The Anniversary	1,450	1,352	93.2
5,000,000 Years To Earth	1,200	881	73.4
Planet Of The Apes	12,850	20,825	162.1
Sweet Ride	3,950	2,600	65.8
Vengeance Of She	1,575	850	54.0
Prudence And The Pill	6,425	7,175	111.7
The Detective	8,800	10,275	116.8
Challenge Of Robin Hood	950	675	71.1
Bandolero	10,200	8,800	86.3
Lost Continent	2,025	1,100	54.3
Secret Life American Wife	4,300	3,725	86.6
Deadfall	5,350	2,575	40.6
Pretty Poison	3,600	2,075	57.6
Je T'Aime, Je T'Aime	875	450	51.4
Un Soir, Un Train	1,650	525	31.8
Boston Strangler	8,625	11,125	129.0
Flea In Her Ear	8,450	2,250	26.6%
Lady In Cement	7,150	6,825	95.5
Joanna	3,800	1,900	50.0
	97,700	90,883	93.0
Star	31,350	7,650	24.4
TOTAL 1968 RELEASES	$129,050	$ 98,533	76.4

[Handwritten]
17 Pictures — losers
1 Picture — just above breakeven
4 Pictures — adequate profits
—
22 Total

TC-F
BREAKEVEN FOR FEATURE PRODUCTIONS
1969 RELEASES

AS OF DECEMBER 11, 1970
(in thousands)

Picture:	Estimated Film Rentals Required To Breakeven	Ultimate Film Rentals	% of Ultimate To Breakeven
1969 Releases:			
The Magus	$ 7,000	$ 2,450	35.0%
The Touchables	2,600	825	31.7
The Last Shot You Hear	450	290	64.4
Devil's Bride	1,150	575	50.0
Decline and Fall	3,100	1,475	47.6
Prime of Miss Jean Brodie	5,400	6,650	123.1
One Hundred Rifles	8,225	6,900	83.9
Hard Contract	7,200	3,200	44.4
The Guru	1,675	625	37.3
Che!	9,400	4,100	43.6
The Chairman	9,750	5,425	55.6
Dr. Glas	500	125	25.0
Justine	12,775	2,775	21.7
Staircase	10,675	2,125	19.9
Secret World	2,300	900	39.1
Butch Cassidy & Sundance Kid	13,850	36,825	256.9
A Walk With Love and Death	3,900	825	21.1
The Undefeated	12,425	8,775	70.6
John and Mary	6,300	8,150	129.4
	118,675	93,015	78.4
Hello Dolly	40,800	24,750	60.7
TOTAL 1969 RELEASES	$159,475	$117,765	73.8

[Handwritten]
17 Pictures — losers
3 Pictures — adequate profits
___
20 Total

TC-F
BREAKEVEN FOR FEATURE PRODUCTIONS
1970 RELEASES

AS OF DECEMBER 11, 1970
(in thousands)

Picture:	Estimated Film Rentals Required To Breakeven	Ultimate Film Rentals	% of Ultimate To Breakeven
1970 Releases:			
M*A*S*H	$ 6,550	$ 31,225	476.7%
Kremlin Letter	10,100	3,425	33.9
Only Game In Town	19,300	4,525	23.4
The Sicilian Clan	7,925	9,250	116.7
The Games	7,500	2,825	37.7
Beneath Planet Of The Apes	8,100	13,825	170.7
Myra Breckenridge	8,875	6,200	69.9
Beyond Valley Of The Dolls	4,100	7,000	170.7
Hello-Goodbye	7,225	2,335	32.3
Cover Me Babe (Run Shadow Run)	3,525	1,050	29.8
Move	4,905	5,000	101.9
Great White Hope	16,075	9,325	58.0
	104,180	95,985	92.1%
Patton, Salute To A Rebel	22,525	27,650	122.8
Tora, Tora, Tora	37,150	37,150	100.0
	59,675	64,800	108.6%
TOTAL 1970 RELEASES	$163,855	$160,785	98.1%

[Handwritten]
7 pictures — losers
1 picture — just above breakeven
4 pictures — adequate profits
1 picture — outstanding
1 picture — questionable—Tora

APPENDIX II

[Office instructions for studio's executive secretaries]

FIRST THING IN THE MORNING—Come in around 8:45, RZ will already be in and probably Harry Sokolov and Jim Fisher. Owen McLean, Stan Hough, Charles Bole, and Frank Ferguson will follow. Take RZ's coffee in his cup with a spoon on the saucer and Harry Sokolov's in a cup and saucer first and then take the others theirs as they come in. He will ask for more coffee around 9:15; take the small pot in and fill his and the others. If Harry Sokolov asks for more you will have to take his cup out and pour out the old and bring in fresh. Also, if Owen's should be less than one-half full, bring his out to add Sweeta. Things to do while he is at lunch are listed on the small sheet.

RZ - black Sanka (small pot) saucer with spoon.
HARRY SOKOLOV - black in china cup
JIM FISHER - black in glass
CHARLES BOLE - Sanka in glass
FRANK FERGUSON - black in glass
STAN HOUGH - cream and two sugars in glass
OWEN McLEAN - black with Sweeta
DAVID BROWN - black in glass
JONAS ROSENFIELD - black
ROY METZLER - black
PETE MYERS - no coffee
HENRY KLINGER - cream
DENNIS STANFILL - tea with cream and sugar

Most of the men bring their glasses out with them and Mary Ann brings the rest out. You can do the dishes anytime. Just wash them in the sink with a little Tide; it is easiest to let them soak for awhile since there isn't much room to wash them. Unplug the coffee pots in the afternoon. The guard makes the coffee and takes care of the pots so don't worry about them.

TURN ON THE XEROX

the minute you get in. It takes 15 minutes to warm up and you don't want to be caught with it not on. Be sure to turn it off as you leave at night.

ORDERING SUPPLIES

We keep half and half, cigarettes & matches, coffee, instant and regular, tea, sugar, Sweeta, straws, instant coffee, Rye Krisp, gum, paper coffee cups, and a few other things on hand which we get from the cafe. Keep an eye on them so that we don't run out and when you need things call 2261 and tell whoever answers what you need and that it is for Mr. Zanuck's office and they will get it together and have a Rover bring it to the office. Order *five lbs. Regular Grind* coffee from the cafe, but order five lbs. *Regular Grind Sanka* from Jurgenson's CR 4-8611, charge to Mr. Zanuck, P.O. Box 900 Beverly Hills, and have it delivered to the office. Keep the candy dishes filled and when you are low on candy, call Robinson's and order it. CR 5-5464, ask for candy department. Charge to the same as Sanka only tell the girl you will have our driver pick the order up. Our driver's name is Bill Newton and he will be in and out of the office every hour or so. Here is the usual order, but you can order more or less of any kind when you need it.

Three lbs. of each:

Golden Buttermints	Fruit Bonbons
Court Drops	Chocolate Parfait
Coffee Nips	

ORDERING SUPPLIES

I won't list all the supplies that we keep on hand but you can become familiar with all the stationery items, etc., that are in the cabinet and in the kitchen closet as you use them. Almost everything in that line we get from Stores, ext. 2530. When you need anything, call them and tell them what you want and it is for Mr. Zanuck's office and they will deliver it the next morning. If you need something right away, tell them what it is and then have a Rover pick it up. Some things like Pentel Pens and anything that Stationery doesn't carry you can order through purchasing. Ask for Ethyl.

XEROX

The paper and supplies are kept in the drawer behind you; most of these we get from Stationery also. You will have to know how to put in the paper, change the web, add ink, retrieve papers that get stuck, and I will show you how to do this. You are the only one who will know this. . . .

SCRIPTS

We don't get any T.V. scripts but if some should come in, just send them to Story Files. We keep all the feature scripts up to date, though, and when we get additional pages or revised pages add them to the script and give it to M.A. [Mary Ann McGowan, secretary to R.D.Z.] Every once in awhile M.A. will ask you to go through the script cabinet in her office to make room for new scripts and you will have to ask her what scripts can be sent back to Story Files and what has to be kept.

SCRIPT ENTRY BOOK

Whenever a script or novel is submitted, we list it in the script entry book behind your desk. Follow the form already used listing the title, whether it is a novel, screenplay, or treatment and by whom it was submitted. Add the date and later on whether it was sent to Jim Fisher or returned.

PHONE BOOK

There is no specific time that the phone book has to be revised but you can tell when there are a lot of changes and it begins to look messy or Mary Ann will tell you to do it when it starts bothering her. The master is in the cabinet behind you and you can usually make the changes by blocking out the old numbers with Sno-Pak and typing the new numbers over it. Sometimes you will have to retype pages if there are a lot of names added or dropped. Go over you book and check it against Mary Ann's and Lucy's [Lucy Ballentine, R.D.Z.'s other secretary] to get any new numbers that they may have, verify any you are not sure of, make the changes, and then send the master to script in care of June and ask her to have ten copies run off. Then change all the books when they come back. Tear up all old pages and throw them away.

DISTRIBUTION OF PHONE BOOKS

Yours

Lucy - 2

Mary Ann - 2

RZ - one for office, car, home, Palm Springs house, Newport
house, two for New York office, and one reduced size.

Plus one extra.

MARKING TRADES

Read both the trades each day. Mark the trades in red when he is away
(everything pertaining to [RZ] personally, or to Fox) and put on his
desk so he can glance at them when he returns. Anything he is personally involved in we clip out and save for his scrapbook. The same with
the columns in the papers.

RZ goes to lunch about 12:30 with the men who were in the morning
meeting. Afterward, they go downstairs to his projection room for the
dailies (providing there are any features being shot), Ext. 2407. He
takes only very important calls down there.

APPENDIX III

Zanuck and Brown's Continuation
of *Gone With the Wind*

Following the back-to-back victories of *The Sting* and *Jaws*, Richard Zanuck and David Brown were considered the most successful producers in Hollywood. In 1976, they announced a most audacious upcoming venture, to create a sequel to possibly the most-seen movie of all time, David O. Selznick's 1939 *Gone With the Wind*, which Dick and David intended to call *The Continuation of Gone With the Wind*, shortened later simply to *Tara*.

After the two producers had lost their option on the property (due to a protracted legal dispute between the estate of the novel's author Margaret Mitchell and M-G-M), Brown said that the film had been conceived as a vehicle for Burt Reynolds to play Rhett Butler, although the tall, dark, and handsome leading man had never committed to it, let alone read a script. A leading lady had not come under consideration. In August of 1986, hope for the proposed sequel sprang eternal, and although Zanuck/Brown no longer held the option, the producers were still game to move ahead on *Tara*. David Brown told the press that the casting choices would be Jack Nicholson and Meryl Streep, to play Rhett Butler and Scarlett O'Hara, respectively. In 1987, the New York *Post* ran a readers poll to see what actors would be the public choice to portray the screen lovers. The winners were Jane Seymour, a British beauty familiar to viewers of television mini-series, and Tom Selleck, another TV face although he would score a movie hit late in the year with the comedy *Three Men and a Baby*. Asked at that time whether he harbored any aspiration of filling Clark Gable's shoes, Selleck replied: "I think it's a bad idea. That's not to say I wouldn't do it."

According to David Brown, the sequel to the most famous movie ever made would open with the closing scene from the first picture, reenacted by the new cast. Rhett Butler would announce his imminent departure, declare that he doesn't give a damn for his wife, Scarlett O'Hara Hamilton Kennedy Butler, and she would close the door behind him, believing that she will win him back "tomorrow."

The new film would pick up the morning after, whereupon Scarlett finds her longtime beau Ashley Wilkes a permanently broken man, grief for his just departed wife Melanie too great a burden to bear. Scarlett, hating Ashley's utter uselessness but feeling maternal (and nothing more), dispatches him to the O'Hara family plantation, Tara. There, too, she sends her faithful Mammy, who has endured enough herself, and wants to live out her years in comfortable retirement. Rhett makes a beeline to his old confidante Belle Watling, the Atlanta madam with a heart of gold. As in the past, Belle speaks the voice of common sense. Any notion Rhett has of putting Scarlett O'Hara out of his head is ridiculous, Watling tells him; the man is and always will be poisoned by Scarlett O'Hara.

The paths of the two protagonists cross. Rhett's commodities trading company flourishes, but Scarlett's lumber business flounders, and it is out of kindness that her former husband steps in to lend his acumen. Twice Scarlett succeeds in seducing him, one memorable time in his private railroad car. But, frankly, Rhett doesn't give a damn about a permanent relationship. Out of spite, and the need to remain financially secure, Scarlett marries again, to a man whose physical presence she finds repulsive. He is no less than the governor of Georgia (based on an actual person, said Brown, though it was in fact the governor of Tennessee), a gent who once killed a bear with his own hands. After an impossible domestic life, Scarlett divorces him.

Fate once again unites Scarlett and Rhett, though it is due to sad circumstances, the death of Mammy. Because Rhett had always respected the wise old servant, he attends the funeral at Tara. There, standing in the shadows, is Ashley Wilkes, whom Rhett learns has been living on the plantation these many years. The old fears are rekindled, but then, so are the flames of passion. It's then on-again, off-again for the battling Butlers. On the question of their remarrying, Brown said there had been several lengthy debates (in 1978, Zanuck/ Brown had commissioned James Goldman, playwright of *The Lion in Winter*, to do the screenplay, upon which Anne Edwards, biographer of both Margaret Mitchell and the star of the 1939 movie Vivien Leigh, based a novelization), and the final decision had been, indeed, to bring together Scarlett and Rhett at the end of the picture.

It made for an enchanting luncheon story, but didn't Brown think the very idea of playing with people's indelible mind-sets of long-cherished imaginary characters might prove a suicide mission? "Not at all," he remarked, "I think it would make a very good movie."

[That opportunity presented itself for real in April of 1988, when it was announced by the Margaret Mitchell estate and the William Morris Agency that a sequel to Gone With the Wind *would be written by a 54-year-old Southern author, Alexandra Ripley, to be published in 1990. The movie rights to this novel—which would not adapt the plotline of the earlier Zanuck/Brown/Goldman/Edwards scenario— conceivably would be offered to the highest bidder. Zanuck/Brown were actually knocked out of the running for their 1976 idea by a 1984 federal court ruling that judged that the Mitchell estate, and not M-G-M, which had released the 1939 movie, was in possession of the rights to the sequel. Margaret Mitchell, who died in 1949, had long fought off offers to continue her celebrated novel.]*

ACKNOWLEDGMENTS

The following individuals were responsible for providing much of the material contained in this book. The majority served as primary sources, although several provided significant contributions beyond mere information. In those cases where the interviewee requested anonymity, that desire has been honored.

Renata Adler, Julie Andrews, Robert Altman, Carol Atkinson, Barbara Bladen, Mel Brooks, David Brown, Martin Burden, Sammy Cahn, Kay Carlson, Kathleen Carroll, Michael Crawford, Judith Crist, David Denby, Roger Ebert. Edward Epstein, Robert Evans, Stephen Farber, George Feltenstein, Hugh Fordin, Richard Freedman, Peter and Renee Furst, Frank D. Gilroy, Bruce Goldstein, Morton Gottlieb, Elliott Gould, Peggy Glance, Edward Guthmann, Mike Hall, William Hammerstein, Anne Head, Jerry Herman, Adele Herz, Ron Howard, Donna Jackson, Richard Johnson, Malcolm B. Kahn, Michael Kidd, Joan Klinger, Alfred P. Lowman, Myrna Loy, Norman Mailer, Joseph L. Mankiewicz, Harvey Mann, Irving Mansfield, Walter Matthau, Paul Mazursky, Roddy McDowell, Daniel Melnick, Brian Moore, Barbara and David Morowitz, Ronald Neame, Dusty and Jean Negulesco, Patricia Newcomb, Anthony Newley, Julia Newman, Christopher Plummer, Gladys and Martin Poll, Tyrone Power, Jr., Roger Price, St. Clair Pugh, Marcella Rabwin, Frank Rowley, Harold Rand, Frank Randall, Evelyn Renold, David Robinson, Frank Rowley, Michael Ritchie, Maria Riva, Craig Russell, Gene Saks, Luis Sanjurjo, Mario Sartori, Vernon Scott, Tom Selleck, Aviva Slesin, Liz Smith, John Springer, Howard Squadron, Louis Steinhouse, Larry Steinfeld, Marilyn Stewart, Douglas Stumpf, Cynthia Swartz, Jerry Tallmer, Tom Topor, Maggie Unsworth, Jack Valenti, Nathan Weiss, Edy Williams, Richard Wilbur, Robert Wise, Norman Wong, Richard D. Zanuck, Lili Fini Zanuck, Robert M. Zarem.

Particular credit is due Fred Hift, Bill Kenly, Charles M. Lewis, Patricia Rick, and, most especially, Henry M. DeMeyer.

BIBLIOGRAPHY

In the course of preparing this book, several newspaper articles, short magazine pieces, film reviews, and reference texts were consulted, in addition to the books and lengthier journal articles cited below.

Allvine, Glendon, *The Greatest Fox of Them All*, New York: Lyle Stuart, 1969.

Bach, Steven, *Final Cut*, New York: William Morrow and Company, 1985.

Blume, Mary, "Zanuck—The Last Tycoon," *The International Herald Tribune*, October 25–26, 1969.

Brodsky, Jack, and Nathan Weiss, *The Cleopatra Papers*, New York: Simon & Schuster, 1963.

Brown, David, *Brown's Guide to Growing Gray*, New York: Delacorte Press, 1987.

Brownlow, Kevin, *The Parade's Gone By . . .*, New York: Alfred A. Knopf, 1968.

Calvet, Corinne, *Has Corinne Been a Good Girl?*, New York: St. Martin's Press, 1983.

Canby, Vincent, "Tora-ble, Tora-ble, Tora-ble," *The New York Times*, October 4, 1970.

Champlin, Charles, "Dennis Stanfill: Man in the Middle of Fox Showdown," *The Los Angeles Times*, May 9, 1971.

Considine, Shaun, *Barbra Streisand: The Woman, The Myth, The Music*, New York: Delacorte Press, 1985.

Coward, Noel, (Graham Payne and Sheridan Morley, editors), *The Noel Coward Diaries*, Boston: Little, Brown & Company, 1982.

Dunne, John Gregory, *The Studio*, New York: Farrar, Straus & Giroux, 1968.

Ehrlich, Henry, "Zanuck: Last of the Red-Hot Star-Makers," *Look Magazine*, November 3, 1970.

Farber, Stephen, and Marc Green, *Hollywood Dynasties*, New York: Putnam Books, 1984.

Fordin, Hugh, *Getting to Know Him: A Biography of Oscar Hammerstein*, New York: Random House, 1977.

Friedrich, Otto, *City of Nets*, New York: Harper & Row, 1986.

Green, Stanley *Broadway Musicals Show by Show*, Milwaukee: Hal Leonard Books, 1987.

Griffith, Richard, and Arthur Mayer, *The Movies*, New York: Bonanza Books, 1957.

Haber, Joyce, "Postmortem on the Twentieth Century-Fox Caper," *The Los Angeles Times*, January 10, 1971.

Haber, Joyce, "Zanuck/Brown: An Odd Couple of Executives," *The Los Angeles Times*, July 22, 1973.

Haden-Guest, Anthony, "The Rise, Fall, and Rise of Zanuck-Brown," *New York Magazine*, December 1, 1975.

Hirshberg, Jack, *Hello, Dolly!" Journal*, Twentieth Century-Fox Film Corporation, 1969.

Huston, John, *An Open Book*, New York: Alfred A. Knopf, 1980. Gussow, Mel, *Don't Say Yes Until I Finish Talking: A Biography of Darryl F. Zanuck*, Garden City, New York: Doubleday, 1971 (Epilogue, 1980).

Katz, Ephraim, *The Film Encyclopedia*, New York: Perigee Books, 1979.

Kazan, Elia, *A Life*, New York: Alfred A. Knopf, 1988.

Kluger, Richard, *The Paper: The Life and Death of the New York Herald Tribune*, New York: Alfred A. Knopf, 1986.

Kobal, John, *A History of Movie Musicals: Gotta Sing Gotta Dance*, New York, Exeter Books, 1983

Knight, Arthur, *The Liveliest Art*, New York: Mentor Books, 1957.

Loy, Myrna, and James Kotsilibas-Davis, *Myrna Loy: Being and Becoming*, New York, Alfred A. Knopf, 1987.

McClintinck, David, *Indecent Exposure: A True Story of Hollywood and Wall Street*, New York: William Morrow, 1982.

Morgenstern, Joseph, and Stefan Kanfer, editors, *Film 69/70*, New York: Simon & Schuster, 1970.

Morley, Sheridan, *A Bright Particular Star*, London: Pavilion Books, 1986.

Mosley, Leonard, *Zanuck, The Rise and Fall of Hollywood's Last Tycoon*, Boston: Little, Brown, 1984.

Negulesco, Jean, *Things I Did and Things I Think I Did: A Hollywood Memoir*, New York: Simon & Schuster, 1984.

Parker, Jerry, "Line Forms Here for Portnoy Role," *Newsday*, February 27, 1970.

Robinson, David, *Chaplin: His Life and Art*, London: William Collins Sons and Co., 1985.

Robinson, David, *The History of World Cinema*, New York: Stein and Day, 1973.

Rodgers, Richard, *Musical Stages*, New York: Random House, 1969.

Rotha, Paul (with additional section by Richard Griffith), *The Film Till Now*, London: Spring Books, 1967.

Sadoul, Georges (translated, edited, and updated by Peter Morris), *Dictionary of Film Makers*, Berkeley: University of California Press, 1972.

Schickel, Richard, "Porn and Man at Yale," *Harper's Magazine*, 1970.

Shearer, Lloyd, "Darryl Zanuck in Retirement," *Parade Magazine*, April 27, 1975.

Smilgis, Martha, "In Darryl Zanuck's Last Drama, A Forgotten French Lover Sues for $15 Million," *People Magazine*, July 14, 1980

Taylor, John, *Storming the Magic Kingdom*, New York: Alfred A. Knopf, 1987.

Thistle, Frank, and Robert Buhrman, "Can Dirty Movies Save Dick & Darryl?," *Los Angeles Magazine*, July 1970.

Thomas, Tony, and Aubrey Soloman, *The Films of Twentieth Century-Fox*, Secaucus, New Jersey: Citadel Press, 1979.

Thomson, David, *A Bibliographical Dictionary of Film*, New York: Morrow Quill Paperbacks, 1979.

Truffant, François, *Hitchcock*, New York: Simon and Schuster (Revised Edition), 1984.

Welles, Chris, "Starting Next Week: The End of the Last Tycoon and Coming Attractions in the Fox Proxy Fight," *New York Magazine*, May 8, 1971.

Unsigned, "The Fortunes of Cleopatra," *Newsweek*, March 25, 1963.

Cleopatra Program, National Publishers, Inc., 1963.

"Twentieth Century-Fox Memorabilia" Catalogue, Sotheby-Parke-Bernet, Los Angeles, 1971.

INDEX

351